Homestyle
Family Favorites

Annual Recipes ▪ 2008

Homestyle
Family Favorites
Annual Recipes ▪ 2008

Treasured Dishes for Every Day
and Every Occasion

RODALE

Photographs © Mitch Mandel/Rodale Images

Book design by Christina Gaugler

Food stylists: Melissa Hamilton and Diane Vezza

Prop stylist: Pamela Simpson

Front cover photo: Chicken Potpie, page 112

ISBN-13 978–1–59486–714–9

ISBN-10 1–59486–714–3

2 4 6 8 10 9 7 5 3 1   hardcover

We inspire and enable people to improve their lives and the world around them
For more of our products visit **rodalestore.com** or call 800-848-4735

CONTENTS

INTRODUCTION

"It isn't so much what is on the table that matters, as what's on the chairs."

—W. S. GILBERT

This quote from famous lyricist W. S. Gilbert is certainly a fitting introduction for a cookbook that encourages sitting down at the table as often as possible for enjoyable meals with family and friends. Indeed, meals shared with those closest to you—meals filled with laughter and great conversation—are certainly the best meals. But we do beg to differ a bit with Mr. Gilbert. In addition to wanting the best company at our table, we do care just as much about the quality of the food that's served.

That's why in this taste-tempting annual, you'll find more than 250 delicious recipes that have been specially selected because they suit homestyle cooking. But just what does "homestyle" mean these days? As always, it's the food we grew up with served in the place we call home. "Homestyle cooking" means preparing food in your own kitchen that's pleasing and satisfying, that uses the freshest ingredients from market and garden, and that makes people say "yum" and ask for second helpings. It's cooking that harkens back to a time when meals really were family affairs, a time when people, old and young, loved sitting at the table to share the day's experiences...no cell phones, no BlackBerrys, no TV in sight.

Dishes for Every Day and Every Occasion

As you look through this book, you'll find recipes that suit the way you live and entertain, whether it's cooking dinner every night for four, preparing a fun weekend lunch for just yourself, having the neighbors over for a backyard barbecue, or throwing a more elegant party meal meant to impress. There are quick recipes like Chicken Cacciatore on Polenta (page 99) and Sweet-and-Sour Pork (page 151) that you can make in under 30 minutes when you're superbusy, as well as recipes like Root Vegetable Soup (page 54) and Braised

Beef Brisket (page 138) that need longer cooking to achieve maximum flavor. There are time-tested classics like Baked Turkey Tetrazzini (page 123), Spaghetti with Meatballs (page 214), and Molasses Baked Beans (263), as well as contemporary twists on old favorites, like Cajun Potato Salad (page 78) and Mexicali Meat Loaf (page 137). And, of course, there's fancier fare like Smoked Salmon with Creamy Dill Linguine (page 220) and Grilled Garlic-Lime Game Hens (page 115). You'll find starters and snacks, soups and salads, meat, fish, and poultry entrées, filling pastas, meatless main dishes, satisfying side dishes, and tantalizing desserts. In addition, this book is filled with loads of cooking tips and tricks, make-ahead and leftover suggestions, and ideas for delicious accompaniments. You'll never be at a loss for what to cook, whatever the occasion.

Read the Recipes First

To make sure there are no unexpected glitches, we suggest that you read through the recipes you intend to use a day or so ahead. This will help you feel more confident, organized, and prepared when you're trying recipes for the first time. You'll also know what ingredients, utensils, and pans are needed; what the marinating, soaking, and cooking times are; and how many servings a recipe makes. You should also look at the ingredient lists to see if any "pre-prep" is required. For example, some recipes may call for toasted nuts, fresh bread crumbs, precooked rice, or hard-boiled eggs, and you'll want to have them on hand before beginning.

To give you a better idea of how long a recipe actually takes from start to finish, we've provided "Hands-On Time" and "Total Time." Hands-On Time is the time you spend chopping, stirring, pulsing the food processor, and so on. Total Time includes Hands-On Time plus the time you're, say, doing your nails while the pasta water comes to a boil or the cake bakes. Since marinating and soaking times can vary considerably, from a few hours to overnight, we've indicated when these are required (in parentheses next to the Total Time) but have not included them in that total number.

Because we prefer to believe that family-style cooking really is "hands on," the majority of the recipes in this book call for fresh ingredients that you prep yourself, whether it's dicing the potatoes, chopping the celery, or slicing a fresh pineapple. However, we know that many home cooks aren't actually home for much of the day and that getting a meal on the table for a hungry family after work can be a hectic affair. Luckily, nearly every supermarket is now brimming with convenience products designed to make family meals faster and easier for time-challenged cooks. You'll find prewashed greens, prechopped onions and garlic, precrumbled cheeses of all types, shredded cabbage, broccoli and cauliflower florets, freshly sliced and diced fruits, and so much more. And while these products can be pricey, it's often a toss-up between your precious time and a few dollars more. We've included some recipes that call for these pre-prepped ingredients, but you can certainly use them in any recipe when time is short.

Cooking for Maximum Satisfaction

If you're a fan of Julia Child, you know she never skimped on the butter, red meat, or wine. As far as "health food" was concerned, her consistent message was: "Ignore it." Her mantra: "Indulge—in moderation. Eat food of all kinds in normal portions." For this book, we've taken a cue from Julia and not skimped. We've included butter when it makes a dish taste better and full-fat cheeses, milk, and mayo for better texture and flavor. We want to make sure our classic family favorites still taste the way Grandma used to make them, before reduced-fat products became ubiquitous. At the same time, we're totally aware that many Americans are a tad overfed. Therefore, we've watched our portions in these dishes, and we leave it up to you as a smart cook to do what's best for your family. If you prefer to use reduced-fat dairy products instead of full-fat, or olive oil instead of butter, or a sugar substitute instead of sugar, go right ahead.

Expanding Your Repertoire

Like most home cooks, you probably make 12 recipes 80 percent of the time. With this book, however, we hope you'll be inspired to expand your culinary horizons. Not only will you get personal pleasure from experimenting with dishes you may never have prepared before, your hungry recipients will be thrilled with the delicious new choices you offer. Even if classics like Quick Roast Chicken (page 89), Stuffed Baked Potatoes (page 308), Garlicky Green Beans (page 286), and Old-Fashioned Strawberry Shortcake (page 342) are what your family has always enjoyed, we encourage you to also try more adventurous dishes like Braised Provençal Lamb Shanks (page 155), Curried Brussels Sprouts (page 291), Millet Pilaf (page 274), and Pumpkin Panna Cotta (page 348). So get that apron on and start cooking. With this Homestyle Family Favorites collection, you've got a year's worth of surefire, sure-to-please dishes at your fingertips. Enjoy!

Super Starters

"The appetite is sharpened by the first bites."

—Dr. José Rizal

Mushroom-Stuffed Mushrooms

Hands-On Time: 30 minutes ■ Total Time: 40 minutes

These delicious mushrooms, stuffed with the mushroom stems and parsley-flavored bread crumbs, make an elegant pass-around appetizer or first course for a sit-down dinner. A sprinkling of Parmesan before broiling takes them over the top.

20	medium white mushrooms	1	teaspoon olive oil
1	small onion, finely chopped	½	cup soft bread crumbs
¼	cup chicken broth	2	tablespoons chopped fresh parsley
2	cloves garlic, minced	2	teaspoons grated Parmesan cheese

1. Preheat the broiler.

2. Separate the stem from each mushroom cap. Coarsely chop the stems and set aside. Place the mushroom caps, round side up, on a large baking sheet. Broil 4" from the heat for 4 minutes, or until the mushrooms are wrinkled and exude moisture. Remove from the oven and set aside to cool.

3. In a large nonstick skillet, combine the onion, broth, garlic, oil, and chopped mushroom stems. Cook, stirring frequently, over medium-high heat for 10 minutes, or until the onion is translucent (do not brown). Remove from the heat. Add the bread crumbs and parsley. Stir well to combine.

4. Pack the onion mixture into the mushroom caps. Set the mushrooms, stuffed side up, on the baking sheet. Sprinkle with the cheese. Broil 4" from the heat for 5 minutes, or until golden brown. Remove from the baking sheet and allow to cool slightly before serving.

Makes 20 stuffed mushrooms

Make-Ahead

Savory stuffed mushrooms are a popular low-cost appetizer that can be made up to 3 months ahead and frozen. To freeze, stuff the mushrooms (but don't sprinkle with the Parmesan cheese) and place them on a tray. Freeze for several hours, or until solid. Transfer to a freezer-quality plastic bag and return them to the freezer. Don't thaw the mushrooms before broiling. Just sprinkle with the Parmesan and add an extra 3 minutes to the broiling time to heat them through.

Greek Spinach Pie

Hands-On Time: 30 minutes ■ Total Time: 1 hour 30 minutes (plus optional chilling)

Phyllo dough is a low-fat parchmentlike Greek pastry that's used for appetizers, desserts, and main dishes. Look for it near the desserts in your supermarket's frozen-food case. Classic recipes brush quite a lot of melted butter on the phyllo to keep the layers separate and to promote crispness. We've achieved the same results more easily and conveniently with butter-flavored cooking spray.

2 packages (10 ounces each) frozen chopped spinach	$\frac{1}{2}$ cup chopped onion
3 egg whites	1 tablespoon dried dill
2 eggs	$\frac{1}{8}$ teaspoon salt
2 cups cottage cheese	1 package (16 ounces) frozen phyllo dough, thawed
$\frac{3}{4}$ cup grated Romano cheese	2 tablespoons butter, melted

1. Cook the spinach according to the package directions. Drain well in a colander, pressing out all of the liquid.

2. In a medium bowl, beat together the egg whites and eggs. Stir in the spinach, cottage cheese, Romano, onion, dill, and salt. Set the mixture aside.

3. Coat a 15" × 10" baking pan with butter-flavored cooking spray. Place 1 sheet of the phyllo dough in the pan. (Cover the remaining sheets of phyllo with a damp cloth to keep them from drying out.) Coat the sheet of dough in the pan with cooking spray. Repeat layering and spraying until half the sheets are layered in the pan.

4. Spoon the spinach mixture over the phyllo in the pan. Top with the remaining sheets of phyllo, coating each sheet with cooking spray. Cover and refrigerate for up to 24 hours, if desired.

5. Preheat the oven to 375°F.

6. Cut the spinach pie into 48 rectangles before baking. Drizzle with the melted butter. Bake for 35 minutes, or until brown. Cool on a wire rack for 15 minutes before serving.

Makes 48 pieces

Heavenly Stuffed Eggs

Hands-On Time: 20 minutes ■ Total Time: 25 minutes

These deviled eggs are a delicious change of pace—the savory filling is made from garlic-scented potatoes and just one hard-boiled yolk for the whole batch. They're a heavenly addition to picnics, barbecues, and party buffets. The fact that they're low-cholesterol is a bonus.

5 hard-boiled eggs

1 baking potato, cooked, peeled, and cubed

2 cloves garlic, minced

3 tablespoons chicken broth

2 tablespoons fresh lemon juice

1 tablespoon white wine vinegar

1 teaspoon extra-virgin olive oil

¼ teaspoon ground black pepper

2 tablespoons snipped chives or minced scallion greens

1. Peel the eggs and cut them in half lengthwise. Lift out the yolks. Set aside 2 yolk halves for use in the filling. Discard the remaining yolks or reserve them for another use.

2. Shave a thin slice off the bottom of each white so it will stand upright. Arrange the whites, hollow side up, on a large plate.

3. In a medium bowl, combine the potato, garlic, and the 2 yolk halves. Mash with a potato masher or the back of a fork until well-blended. Stir in 2 tablespoons of the broth, 1 tablespoon of the lemon juice, and 1 teaspoon of the vinegar until well-blended.

4. Add the oil and the remaining 1 tablespoon broth, 1 tablespoon lemon juice, and 2 teaspoons vinegar. Beat with a spoon until smooth and fluffy. Fold in the pepper and 1 tablespoon of the chives.

5. Using a teaspoon or a pastry bag fitted with a large star tip, fill the egg whites with the potato mixture. Sprinkle the tops with the remaining 1 tablespoon chives.

Makes 10 eggs

Leftovers

Leftover deviled eggs make delicious egg salad sandwiches that are low in fat and high in protein. For each sandwich, lightly toast 2 thin slices whole wheat bread. In a small bowl, coarsely mash 4 deviled eggs with the back of a fork. Stir in 1 to 1½ tablespoons light mayonnaise. Spread over 1 slice of the toast. Top with a lettuce leaf and the remaining toast. Cut in half diagonally.

Crispy Egg Rolls

Hands-On Time: 40 minutes ▪ Total Time: 55 minutes

Baking these crispy appetizers makes them much less messy to prepare than traditional deep-fried egg rolls. Serve them with hot mustard and sweet-and-sour sauce.

½ pound ground pork loin

1 tablespoon reduced-sodium soy sauce

1 teaspoon cornstarch

1 teaspoon dry sherry or water

8 ounces bean sprouts

2 cups finely shredded cabbage

1 carrot, shredded

1 bunch scallions, white and light green parts, finely chopped (½ cup)

½ cup finely chopped celery

2 tablespoons all-purpose flour

16 egg roll wrappers

1. Coat a large skillet with cooking spray. Add the pork, soy sauce, cornstarch, and sherry. Cook over medium heat, stirring, until the pork is broken up and no longer pink. With a slotted spoon, transfer to a large bowl.

2. Using the same skillet, cook the bean sprouts, cabbage, carrot, scallions, and celery over medium heat until just softened. Drain and add to the pork mixture. Stir in the flour and mix well.

3. Preheat the oven to 375°F. Coat a baking sheet with cooking spray.

4. Spoon about ¼ cup of the pork mixture diagonally across the center of an egg roll wrapper. Fold one point of the wrapper over the filling and tuck the point under the filling. Fold in the sides of the wrapper and roll up the egg roll. When the roll reaches the remaining point, dampen the point of the wrapper with water and press firmly to seal. Place on the baking sheet.

5. Repeat with the remaining wrappers and filling. Coat the egg rolls generously with cooking spray.

6. Bake for 8 minutes, then turn the egg rolls and bake for 4 to 5 minutes longer, or until light brown and crisp.

Makes 16 egg rolls

Kitchen Tip

Gently peel apart the egg roll wrappers to separate, if necessary (the wrappers may not be perfectly square). Work with one wrapper at a time, keeping the remaining wrappers covered with plastic wrap so they don't dry out.

Make-Ahead

Freeze the baked egg rolls in foil for spur-of-the-moment entertaining. To reheat, bake the egg rolls in the foil at 350°F for 25 to 30 minutes.

Miniature Black Bean Burritos

Hands-On Time: 20 minutes ■ Total Time: 20 minutes

These bite-size burritos get their flavor from onions, garlic, and plenty of spices. They're a great addition to a Mexican-themed appetizer party.

⅔ cup minced onion	⅛ teaspoon crushed red pepper flakes
2 cloves garlic, minced	4 flour tortillas (6" in diameter)
2 tablespoons chicken broth	¼ cup salsa
2 cups cooked black beans	¼ cup fat-free sour cream
¼ teaspoon ground cumin	¼ cup chopped fresh cilantro
⅛ teaspoon ground coriander	

1. In a large nonstick skillet, combine the onion, garlic, and broth. Cook, stirring, over medium heat for 3 minutes. Add the beans, cumin, coriander, and red pepper flakes. Cook, stirring, for 1 minute. Remove from the heat and mash the beans.

2. Place the tortillas on a paper towel. Microwave on high power for 30 seconds, or until warm. Spread each tortilla with the bean mixture. Roll up, then cut each roll into 4 pieces. Top with dollops of salsa and sour cream. Sprinkle with the cilantro.

Makes 8 servings

Shortcut

The obvious shortcut for this recipe is to use canned black beans.
Be sure to rinse and drain them first.

Variation

Use any other type of bean you like: Cannellini, kidney,
or pinto beans work well, and chickpeas are good, too.

Cocktail Meatballs Florentine

Hands-On Time: 15 minutes ■ Total Time: 45 minutes

Spinach and cheese are what make these versatile and delicious meatballs "Florentine." Serve the meatballs with salsa or warmed marinara sauce for dipping.

8 cloves garlic, unpeeled	2 teaspoons dried oregano
1 teaspoon olive oil	½ teaspoon ground black pepper
4 shallots	½ teaspoon dried dill
1 cup fresh spinach leaves	¼ teaspoon ground nutmeg
½ cup ricotta cheese	¾ pound lean ground beef
1 egg white	⅓ cup fresh whole wheat bread crumbs

1. Preheat the oven to 400°F.

2. Combine the garlic and oil in a custard cup, cover with foil, and bake for 15 minutes, or until soft when tested with the tip of a knife. Do not allow the garlic to brown. Let cool slightly, then slip off the skins and trim off the hard stem ends. Leave the oven on.

3. In a food processor, purée the garlic, shallots, spinach, ricotta, and egg white. Add the oregano, pepper, dill, and nutmeg. Process briefly to combine.

4. In a large bowl, combine the beef and bread crumbs. Add the spinach mixture and mix well.

5. Shape into 32 meatballs. Coat a large nonstick skillet with cooking spray. Cook the meatballs, in batches if necessary, until browned on all sides, about 15 minutes.

Makes 32 meatballs

Make-Ahead

You can freeze the meatballs either cooked or uncooked, but the uncooked meatballs have a longer freezer life (4 months) than the cooked ones do (2 months). The uncooked meatballs will also be moister. To keep cooked or uncooked meatballs from freezing into a solid mass, freeze them individually on a cookie sheet first, then place them in a freezer-quality plastic bag. To use, thaw overnight in the refrigerator, then bake as above; if they're precooked, heat at 350°F until warmed through.

Chicken Nuggets with Spicy Orange Salsa

Hands-On Time: 25 minutes ■ Total Time: 50 minutes

Making these nuggets ahead and freezing them gives you easy party fare at the drop of a hat. They also make a popular main course for children's birthday parties (just don't serve the kids the jalapeño salsa!).

Nuggets

¼ cup honey

¼ cup Dijon mustard

1 tablespoon curry powder

1 tablespoon fresh lemon juice

1 pound boneless, skinless chicken breasts, cut into 1" cubes

Salsa

2 navel oranges

1 small jalapeño pepper, seeded and minced (wear plastic gloves when handling)

2 tablespoons brown sugar

2 tablespoons chopped fresh cilantro

1 tablespoon extra-virgin olive oil

1. *To make the nuggets:* Preheat the oven to 350°F.

2. In a small saucepan, combine the honey, mustard, curry powder, and lemon juice. Mix well. Bring to a boil over medium-high heat, then pour into a medium bowl. Add the chicken and toss well to coat.

3. Coat a large baking sheet with cooking spray. Arrange the chicken on the baking sheet in a single layer. Bake for 25 minutes, or until the chicken is no longer pink in the center. (Check by inserting the tip of a sharp knife into a cube.)

4. *To make the salsa:* While the chicken cooks, peel 1 orange and chop it. Place the pieces in a medium bowl. Juice the other orange and add the juice to the bowl. Add the jalapeño pepper, sugar, cilantro, and oil. Stir well to combine. Let stand at room temperature for 20 minutes, stirring occasionally. Serve with the nuggets.

Makes 8 servings

Make-Ahead

To freeze the baked nuggets, place them on a tray and freeze for several hours, or until solid. Transfer to a freezer-quality plastic bag. Pack the salsa in a freezer-quality plastic container. To use, thaw both overnight in the refrigerator. Place the nuggets on a large baking sheet, cover with foil to keep them from drying out, and reheat at 350°F for 10 minutes, or until hot.

Chicken Drummettes with Blue Cheese Dip

Hands-On Time: 20 minutes ■ Total Time: 50 minutes (plus marinating)

You can buy frozen chicken drummettes (chicken wings with the tips removed) in bulk at your local warehouse store. If you like, make this recipe ahead of time and freeze the cooked drummettes for up to 3 months (see Make-Ahead, below).

Drummettes

1 pound (24) frozen chicken drummettes, thawed

¼ cup hot pepper sauce

3 tablespoons cider vinegar

1 teaspoon olive oil

Blue Cheese Dip

1 cup ricotta cheese

½ cup plain yogurt

1 clove garlic, minced

2 tablespoons crumbled blue cheese

¼ teaspoon paprika

1. *To make the chicken drummettes:* Remove as much skin as possible from the chicken. In a large, shallow, nonmetal baking dish, combine the chicken, hot pepper sauce, vinegar, and oil. Toss to combine. Cover and refrigerate for 8 hours, or overnight, turning occasionally.

2. Preheat the oven to 350°F. Line a large baking pan with foil. Transfer the chicken to the pan. Discard any marinade that doesn't cling to the chicken. Bake for 30 minutes, or until the chicken is no longer pink and juices run clear. (Check by inserting the tip of a sharp knife into the thickest part of a drummette.)

3. *To make the blue cheese dip:* While the chicken bakes, in a blender or food processor, combine the ricotta, yogurt, garlic, and 1 tablespoon of the blue cheese. Process until smooth. Spoon into a serving bowl. Stir in the remaining 1 tablespoon blue cheese. Sprinkle with the paprika. Cover and refrigerate for 20 minutes, or until the flavors blend.

Makes 24 drummettes

Make-Ahead

To freeze, place the cooled cooked drummettes on a tray and freeze for several hours, or until solid. Transfer to a freezer-quality plastic bag. Pack the dip in a freezer-quality plastic container. To use, thaw both overnight in the refrigerator. Place the drummettes on a large baking sheet and reheat at 350°F for 15 minutes, or until hot. Process the dip briefly in a blender or food processor until creamy.

Chinese Chicken Wings
with Hot Apricot Glaze

Hands-On Time: 10 minutes ■ Total Time: 40 minutes (plus marinating)

Sizzling spicy wings are made-to-order for a casual get-together. They practically cook themselves while you join the party.

¼ cup vegetable oil or olive oil

¼ cup soy sauce

1 tablespoon grated fresh ginger

3 pounds (12) chicken wings

⅓ cup all-fruit apricot spread

2 teaspoons Asian chile-garlic sauce

1. In a large zip-top bag, combine the oil, soy sauce, and ginger. Massage the bag to mix. Add the wings. Close and massage the bag to coat the wings evenly. Refrigerate for 30 minutes.

2. Meanwhile, in a small bowl, combine the apricot spread and chile-garlic sauce. Set aside.

3. Preheat the oven to 425°F. Line a large baking pan with foil. Coat with cooking spray.

4. Place the wings in the pan. Discard the marinade. Bake for 25 minutes, or until browned and sizzling. Drizzle on the apricot sauce. Turn the wings to coat. Bake for 5 minutes, or until the chicken is no longer pink and juices run clear.

Makes 6 servings (2 wings per serving)

Kitchen Tip

The fastest way to peel ginger is to use the back of a teaspoon to scrape off the skin. It fits nicely into the little indentations in the ginger.

Black Bean–Chipotle Dip
with White Tortilla Chips

Hands-On Time: 10 minutes ▪ Total Time: 10 minutes

This recipe is spicy yet mellow. The flavors of the black beans and chipotles (smoked jalapeños) meld beautifully. If chipotle salsa isn't available, substitute ½ cup mild tomato salsa mixed with 1 tablespoon canned chipotles in adobo sauce (you can freeze the extra canned chipotles and sauce in a zip-top bag).

1 can (16 ounces) refried black beans

½ cup jarred chipotle salsa

1 container (1 pound) prepared guacamole

1 cup sour cream

½ cup preshredded Mexican four-cheese blend

1 bunch scallions, white and light green parts, sliced (½ cup)

Bite-size white tortilla chips

1. In a large serving dish, combine the beans and salsa. Stir to mix.

2. Spread on the guacamole and then the sour cream. Sprinkle with the cheese and scallions. Serve with the tortilla chips.

Makes about 4 cups

Make-Ahead

The dip can be prepared up to 2 days before serving. Cover with plastic wrap and refrigerate.

Bruschetta Toppings

Bruschetta makes a wonderful appetizer, and most of the toppings we suggest can be prepared ahead of time. To make bruschetta, slice a loaf of long narrow bread (such as a baguette) into ½"- to ¾"-thick slices and toast them under the broiler, on the grill, or in a 400°F oven. While the toast is warm, rub it with a cut garlic clove and brush, drizzle, or spray one side with olive oil cooking spray. Then top the oil-coated side with one of the following toppings. Each recipe makes enough to top 1 sliced baguette, or about 16 pieces total.

Mozzarella, Arugula, and Tomato. Place 1 thin slice fresh mozzarella cheese (16 slices total; about ½ pound) onto each hot toast. Add 1 arugula leaf (16 leaves total; about ⅓ cup packed) to each, and top with 1 thin slice plum tomato (about 4 tomatoes total). Sprinkle with a pinch of salt and a pinch of ground black pepper.

Tomato-Basil. Cut 6 to 8 plum tomatoes in half lengthwise. Cut out the cores and gently squeeze out the seeds. Finely chop the tomatoes and mix with ½ cup shredded fresh basil, 1 to 2 tablespoons olive oil, ½ teaspoon salt, and ¼ teaspoon ground black pepper. Divide the mixture among the hot toasts.

Pesto, Tomato, and Provolone. Preheat the oven to 400°F. Spread each toast with 1 teaspoon pesto (about ⅓ cup total). Top each with 1 slice plum tomato (about 4 tomatoes total) and 1 small, thin slice provolone cheese (16 slices total; about ½ pound). Arrange on a baking sheet and bake in the top of the oven for 2 to 4 minutes, or until the cheese melts.

Tomato-Anchovy. Preheat the oven to 400°F. Place 1 slice plum tomato (about 4 tomatoes total) on each toast, and top with 1 anchovy fillet (or half, if you are not a big fan). Sprinkle each toast with ½ teaspoon grated Parmesan cheese. Arrange on a baking sheet and bake in the top of the oven for 2 to 4 minutes, or until the cheese melts and turns golden.

Broccoli Rabe and Parmesan. Drop 1 or 2 bunches broccoli rabe into a large pot of lightly salted boiling water over high heat. Cook for 2 to 3 minutes, or just until tender (it will shrink considerably). Drain well. While the broccoli rabe is cooling, preheat the oven to 400°F. Coarsely chop the broccoli rabe when cool enough to handle. Heat 2 to 3 tablespoons olive oil in a large skillet over medium heat. Add ½ to 1 teaspoon minced garlic and cook, stirring constantly, for 20 to 30 seconds. Add the broccoli rabe and ½ teaspoon salt. Cook for 3 to 5 minutes. Sprinkle each piece of toast with ½ teaspoon grated Parmesan cheese and arrange on a baking sheet. Bake in the top of the oven for 2 to 4 minutes, or until the cheese is golden. Divide the reserved broccoli rabe topping among the toasts.

Mushrooms and Parmesan. Preheat the oven to 400°F. Thickly slice about 8 large white or brown (cremini) mushrooms. (Divide mushrooms among toasts.) Coat a large skillet with olive oil and add the mushroom slices close together. Brown one side over medium-high heat, then stir and cook for 1 minute longer. Sprinkle with ½ teaspoon dried oregano and ¼ cup dry white wine and cook for 1 minute longer. Arrange 1 mushroom slice on each toast. Sprinkle each toast with ½ teaspoon grated Parmesan cheese. Arrange on a baking sheet and bake for 2 to 4 minutes, or until the cheese is golden.

Caramelized Onion. In a large nonstick skillet, heat 2 tablespoons butter over medium-high heat. Add 2 cups chopped onion, 1 tablespoon sugar, and ½ teaspoon dried thyme. Cook, stirring often, for about 10 minutes. If dry, add 2 tablespoons water and continue cooking for about 5 minutes longer, or until the onions caramelize and turn medium brown. Stir in 1 tablespoon balsamic vinegar or sherry vinegar. Mound 1 tablespoon topping on each toast and serve warm.

Mediterranean Olive. In a food processor, combine ¾ cup pitted kalamata olives, 3 tablespoons olive oil, 2 tablespoons capers, 4 flat anchovy fillets, 1 tablespoon fresh lemon juice, 1 tablespoon Dijon mustard, and ¼ teaspoon ground black pepper. Process to a coarse purée. Divide the mixture among the hot toasts.

Grilled Zucchini with Pesto. Preheat a grill or grill pan to medium heat. Cut 2 small zucchini crosswise into rounds about ¼" thick. Brush the zucchini with olive oil and grill until softened and charred on both sides. Spread ½ teaspoon prepared pesto over each toast and top with 1 zucchini round and ½ teaspoon grated Parmesan cheese.

White Bean and Lentil Spread

Hands-On Time: 20 minutes ■ Total Time: 1 hour 20 minutes

Beans taste anything but basic in this simple spread featuring lentils, curry spices, and aromatic vegetables.

¼ cup dry sherry or chicken broth

1 small onion, minced

2 cloves garlic, minced

2 cups cooked lentils

1 cup cooked navy beans or other white beans

1 egg

¼ cup chopped parsley

1 teaspoon curry powder

½ teaspoon dried basil

½ teaspoon ground paprika

½ teaspoon salt

¼ teaspoon ground nutmeg

1 cup soft rye bread crumbs

¼ cup grated Parmesan cheese

1. Preheat the oven to 350°F. Coat a 9" × 5" loaf pan with cooking spray.

2. In a small saucepan, bring the sherry to a boil over medium-high heat. Add the onion and garlic. Cook, stirring, for 3 minutes. Remove from the heat.

3. In a medium bowl, mash the lentils, navy beans, and egg. Stir in the onion mixture, parsley, curry powder, basil, paprika, salt, and nutmeg. Add the bread crumbs and Parmesan, and mix well. Spoon the mixture into a round casserole, smoothing the top with a rubber spatula.

4. Bake for 40 minutes, or until slightly browned. Cool for 20 minutes before serving from the casserole.

Makes 2⅔ cups

Crab and Artichoke Dip

Hands-On Time: 35 minutes ▪ Total Time: 1 hour 10 minutes

This is an elegant appetizer for special occasions. If you're entertaining guests who are concerned about calories, substitute reduced-fat yogurt and light mayonnaise. If you want to halve the recipe, bake it in an 8" round cake pan for about 25 minutes.

1 large green bell pepper, chopped

2 cans (14 ounces each) artichoke hearts, drained and finely chopped

1 cup mayonnaise

1 cup plain yogurt

⅔ cup grated Parmesan cheese

1 bunch scallions, white and light green parts, thinly sliced (½ cup)

½ cup bottled roasted red bell peppers, drained and chopped

1 tablespoon plus 2 teaspoons fresh lemon juice

1 tablespoon plus 1 teaspoon Worcestershire sauce

1 tablespoon seeded and finely chopped pickled jalapeño pepper (wear plastic gloves when handling)

¼ teaspoon celery seeds

1 pound lump crabmeat, picked over and flaked

¼ cup sliced almonds (optional)

1. Coat a small skillet with cooking spray. Add the green bell pepper and cook, stirring, over medium heat for 3 minutes, or until softened. Remove from the heat and set aside to cool to room temperature.

2. Preheat the oven to 375°F. Coat an 8" × 8" baking pan with cooking spray.

3. In a large bowl, combine the reserved bell pepper, artichoke hearts, mayonnaise, yogurt, Parmesan, scallions, red peppers, lemon juice, Worcestershire, jalapeño pepper, and celery seeds. Gently stir in the crabmeat. Spoon into the prepared baking pan. Sprinkle with the almonds, if using.

4. Bake for 30 to 35 minutes, or until golden and bubbly.

Makes about 5½ cups

Make-Ahead

This robust dip can be prepared in advance to cut down on last-minute fuss at party time. Assemble the ingredients and spoon them into the baking dish. Cover the dish and refrigerate for up to 4 hours. Bake the dip for 40 to 45 minutes before serving.

Variations

If you can't get fresh crab, substitute 2 cans (6 ounces each) crabmeat, drained and flaked, or 12 ounces surimi (imitation crabmeat), chopped.

Baba Ghannouj with Pita Wedges

Hands-On Time: 20 minutes ■ Total Time: 1 hour 20 minutes

Middle Eastern cooks use this rich-tasting eggplant and garlic spread as a dip, in sandwiches, and even as a baste for grilled foods. It's great for parties; serve it with pita wedges or crudités for dipping.

1 medium eggplant

1 teaspoon olive oil

½ cup minced onion

3 large cloves garlic, minced

¼ cup fresh lemon juice

3 tablespoons peanut butter

1 tablespoon minced fresh parsley

½ teaspoon ground black pepper

4 pitas (6" diameter)

1. Preheat the oven to 400°F. Pierce the eggplant in several places with a fork and place on a baking sheet. Bake for 1 hour, or until the eggplant is very soft and has collapsed. Cool, then scoop out the flesh into a blender or food processor. Discard the skin.

2. In a small nonstick skillet, heat the oil over medium-high heat. Add the onion and garlic, and cook, stirring occasionally, for 3 minutes, or until the onions are soft. Transfer to the blender or food processor. Add the lemon juice and peanut butter. Process until smooth. Transfer to a serving bowl and stir in the parsley and pepper.

3. Cut each pita into 6 wedges and toast, if desired. Serve with the baba ghannouj.

Makes 6 servings

Kitchen Tip

For an even tastier dish, grill the whole eggplant over low coals on
a charcoal grill or over low heat on a gas grill. The skin will blacken
and can be peeled off after the eggplant cooks and cools.

Chicken-Olive Crostini

Hands-On Time: 10 minutes ▪ Total Time: 10 minutes

Select your favorite prepared olive spread for this nosh, which is impressive served on an appetizer plate with Bacon-Cheddar Pinwheels (page 20). Jarred kalamata olive spread, tapenade, olive pâté, or bruschetta olive topping are all zesty options.

1 rotisserie chicken breast or 1 pound roasted chicken breast

3 scallions, cut into 1" pieces

1 sprig fresh rosemary (about 1 teaspoon leaves)

½ cup mayonnaise

½ teaspoon ground black pepper

2 tablespoons prepared olive spread

1 box (3 ounces) mini toasts or 36 slices plain cocktail bread

1. Remove and discard the bones and skin from the chicken breast, if necessary. Tear the chicken into chunks. Set aside.

2. In a food processor, combine the scallions and rosemary. Pulse about 12 times, or until minced. Add the mayonnaise, pepper, olive spread, and chicken. Pulse about 24 times, or until the chicken is minced and the ingredients are well mixed. Serve with the toasts.

Makes 36 crostini

Make-Ahead

The chicken-olive spread can be prepared up to 3 days in advance. Refrigerate it in a tightly covered container. Let stand at room temperature for 15 minutes before using.

Bacon-Cheddar Pinwheels

Hands-On Time: 25 minutes ■ Total Time: 45 minutes

These tasty pinwheels couldn't be simpler to put together and are delicious with Chicken-Olive Crostini (page 19).

2 tubes (8 ounces each) refrigerated crescent-roll dough

¾ cup shredded sharp Cheddar cheese

1 cup (4 ounces) crumbled cooked bacon

½ cup finely chopped onion

1 teaspoon dried thyme

1. Preheat the oven to 375°F.

2. Separate the dough into 8 rectangles. Using your fingertips, push together the perforations in each rectangle to seal them up.

3. Scatter on the Cheddar, bacon, onion, and thyme. Roll up each rectangle, starting at the short end. Cut each roll crosswise into 4 slices. Place the slices, cut side down, on a baking sheet and flatten slightly. Bake for 15 to 20 minutes, or until puffed and golden.

Makes 32 pinwheels

Variations

Fill the crescent-roll dough with herbed cream cheese, crab, or another filling, then slice it crosswise before baking.

Zesty Mexican Dip

Hands-On Time: 15 minutes ■ Total Time: 25 minutes

We make this hot-from-the-oven dip with ground turkey breast, but you can use whatever ground turkey you prefer. Often ground turkey is a mix of dark and light meat.

½ pound ground turkey breast

1 large onion, chopped

2 cans (16 ounces each) fat-free refried beans

1 can (4 ounces) diced green chile peppers, drained

2 cups shredded mozzarella cheese

1 cup shredded Cheddar cheese

1 can (10 ounces) diced tomatoes and green chile peppers

1 cup sour cream

1. Preheat the oven to 400°F. Coat a 13" × 9" baking pan with cooking spray. Set aside.

2. Coat a medium skillet with cooking spray. Add the turkey and onion. Cook over medium heat, stirring occasionally, for about 5 minutes, or until the turkey is no longer pink. Add the refried beans and stir to combine.

3. Spread the turkey mixture evenly in the prepared baking pan. Top with the diced peppers. Sprinkle with 1 cup of the mozzarella and ½ cup of the Cheddar. Cover with the mixed tomatoes and peppers.

4. Bake for 20 minutes. Sprinkle with the remaining 1 cup mozzarella and ½ cup Cheddar. Bake for 5 minutes longer, or until heated through.

5. Cool slightly, then spoon the sour cream on top.

Makes about 3 cups

Nutri-Note

If you're keeping a close watch on your sodium intake, you can eliminate about 135 milligrams per serving by using only 1 cup mozzarella and replacing the canned chile peppers with ¼ cup chopped fresh jalapeño or serrano peppers and the canned mixed tomatoes and peppers with 1 cup chopped fresh ripe tomatoes.

Crispy Snack Mix

Hands-On Time: 10 minutes ■ Total Time: 55 minutes

Ingredients in many packaged snack mixes are tossed with seasonings and lots of butter or oil. For this lighter version, egg whites replace the fat to produce a crispier snack.

2 egg whites, lightly beaten

1 tablespoon plus 1½ teaspoons Worcestershire sauce

1 teaspoon garlic powder

2 cups crispy corn or rice cereal squares

1½ cups bite-size whole wheat cereal biscuits

½ cup unsalted peanuts

1 cup pretzels

1 cup raisins (optional)

1. Preheat the oven to 300°F. Lightly coat a large, shallow baking pan with cooking spray.

2. In a small bowl, use a fork to beat together the egg whites, Worcestershire, and garlic powder.

3. In a large bowl, combine the cereal squares, cereal biscuits, and peanuts. Drizzle with the egg-white mixture and stir to coat well. Stir in the pretzels.

4. Spread the mixture in the prepared pan and bake for 40 to 45 minutes, stirring every 15 minutes. Add the raisins, if using, and toss gently. Let cool before serving.

Makes about 5 cups

Variations

You can use any nuts you like in this recipe. Almonds are good, as are hazelnuts. For the kids, add chocolate bits instead of raisins after the mixture has cooled, or use both.

Pita Party Pizzas

Hands-On Time: 10 minutes ■ Total Time: 20 minutes

Pita rounds make perfect instant pizza crusts. The feta cheese, spinach, and olives give these pizzas Greek flair.

2 whole wheat pitas (6" diameter)

1 package (10 ounces) frozen chopped spinach, thawed and squeezed dry

½ cup shredded mozzarella cheese

¼ cup crumbled feta cheese

¼ cup sliced black olives

1 tomato, diced

¼ cup thinly sliced red onion

1. Preheat the oven to 400°F.

2. Prick the pitas several times with a fork. Spread the spinach over the pitas. Sprinkle each with the mozzarella, feta, olives, tomato, and onion. Place the pitas on a baking sheet and bake for 10 minutes.

3. To serve, cut each pizza into 8 slices.

Makes 16 slices

Ingredients Note

There are many types of feta cheese sold in the supermarket, ranging from mild to very salty. We prefer salty Greek feta for this recipe.

Fresh Tomato and Black Bean Salsa

Hands-On Time: 15 minutes ■ Total Time: 30 minutes

Here's a versatile, substantial salsa to serve with Tex-Mex dishes or to offer as a snack with tortilla chips. You can leave out the jalapeño peppers for milder salsa, or make it hotter by using a serrano chile.

1¼ cups coarsely chopped tomatoes

1 cup canned black beans, rinsed and drained

¼ cup loosely packed chopped fresh cilantro

¼ cup chopped scallions

1 small jalapeño pepper, minced (wear plastic gloves when handling)

2 tablespoons red wine vinegar

1 small clove garlic, minced

¼ teaspoon dried oregano

¼ teaspoon salt

1. In a glass bowl, mix the tomatoes, beans, cilantro, scallions, jalapeño pepper, vinegar, garlic, oregano, and salt.

2. Cover and refrigerate for at least 15 minutes to allow the flavors to blend.

Makes 3 cups

Make-Ahead

The salsa can be made a day ahead and kept in a well-covered container in the refrigerator. Don't keep it too long or it loses its freshness. You can also make extra batches of salsa, pack it into 1-cup containers, and freeze it for up to 3 months.

A Selection of Fresh Salsas

Highly seasoned salsas characterize much of the Mexican food that is served in America. Salsas make great appetizers served with chips, pita wedges, or crudités and can also be used as a topping for grilled chicken, turkey, pork, fish, or baked potatoes. The word *salsa* simply means "sauce," and while traditional versions are based on red tomatoes (or green tomatillos, in salsa verde), many American cooks have expanded salsas to include ingredients such as fresh fruits, corn, and beans. To get the best flavor and texture, let the salsa stand at room temperature for an hour or two before serving. Longer than that, and the acidic ingredients will soften the salsa and ruin its fresh textures.

Here are a few homemade salsas you might want to try.

Spicy Fresh Tomato Salsa. In a medium bowl, combine 4 large seeded and chopped summer tomatoes, $\frac{2}{3}$ cup finely chopped sweet onion (or 4 finely chopped scallions), $\frac{1}{3}$ cup finely chopped fresh cilantro, 1 to 2 seeded and finely chopped fresh jalapeño chile peppers (leave the seeds in for more heat, and wear plastic gloves when handling), 2 teaspoons fresh lime juice, and 1 teaspoon salt. Toss, let sit for 1 hour at room temperature, and serve. Makes about $3\frac{1}{4}$ cups.

Fragrant Corn Salsa. In a medium bowl, combine the kernels cut from 2 ears cooked corn (or $2\frac{1}{2}$ cups frozen and thawed corn), $\frac{1}{2}$ finely chopped red bell pepper, 1 tablespoon chopped fresh cilantro, 1 teaspoon finely chopped jalapeño pepper (wear plastic gloves when handling), 1 teaspoon ground cumin, $\frac{1}{2}$ teaspoon salt, and $\frac{1}{4}$ teaspoon ground black pepper. Makes $2\frac{1}{2}$ cups.

Salsa Verde (Basic Green Salsa). Remove and discard the papery husks from 8 large tomatillos and place the tomatillos in a saucepan. Cover with water and heat to boiling. Reduce the heat to medium-low and simmer until tender, about 5 minutes. Using a slotted spoon, transfer the tomatillos to a food processor. Set the cooking liquid aside. Add $\frac{1}{3}$ cup chopped onion, 1 minced garlic clove, $\frac{1}{2}$ teaspoon salt, and $\frac{1}{8}$ teaspoon red pepper flakes (or more to taste) to the tomatillos. Process just until combined. With the machine running, add just enough of the reserved cooking liquid to make the mixture saucy. Makes about $2\frac{1}{4}$ cups.

Fennel-Orange Salsa. In a medium bowl, combine 1 trimmed and finely chopped fennel bulb, 1 small chopped scallion, 4 sectioned and chopped seedless oranges, 1 tablespoon chopped fresh basil, 2 teaspoons fresh lemon juice, $\frac{1}{4}$ teaspoon each salt and ground black pepper, a pinch each red pepper flakes and sugar, and 1 peeled, pitted, and chopped avocado. Makes 3 cups.

Island Breeze. In a medium bowl, combine 1 can (8 ounces) unsweetened pineapple chunks (with juice), 1 papaya (seeded and diced), 1 teaspoon minced jalapeño pepper (wear plastic gloves when handling), and the juice of 1 lime. Mix well. Add chopped fresh cilantro and salt to taste. Makes 3 cups.

Chili Tortilla Strips

Hands-On Time: 15 minutes ■ Total Time: 35 minutes

This snack couldn't be simpler. Strips of flour tortillas are dusted with a spicy mix, then baked until golden and crisp. The thinner the tortilla, the crispier the tortilla strip.

1   teaspoon chili powder

1   teaspoon garlic powder

½   teaspoon salt

¼   teaspoon ground cumin

¼   teaspoon ground black pepper

8   flour tortillas (6" diameter)

4   teaspoons olive oil

1. Preheat the oven to 400°F. Coat a large baking sheet with cooking spray.

2. In a small bowl, combine the chili powder, garlic powder, salt, cumin, and pepper. Mix well.

3. Brush both sides of the tortillas with the oil. Sprinkle with the spice mixture.

4. With kitchen scissors, cut each tortilla in half, then cut each half into 6 strips. Arrange the strips in a single layer on the prepared baking sheet. Bake in two batches, if necessary, to avoid crowding. Bake for 10 minutes, or until golden brown and crisp.

Makes 8 servings

Ingredients Note

For the best taste, make your own chili powder and keep a supply on hand for using in this recipe, as well as in White Bean and Turkey Chili with Cilantro Yogurt (page 127), Beef and Black Bean Chili (page 147), and Vegetable Chili (page 236). You'll need mild to hot dried chile peppers of your choice (look for them dried in gourmet food markets), ground cumin, ground paprika, and dried oregano, if you like. Grind the dried chiles in a spice grinder until fine. To make the mix, use about half as much cumin and paprika as ground chiles, and add oregano to taste, if using; stir together until well combined. Your homemade chili powder can be stored in an airtight glass container indefinitely.

Satisfying Soups

"Good soup draws the chair to it."

—GHANIAN PROVERB

Quick Gazpacho

Hands-On Time: 10 minutes ■ Total Time: 10 minutes (plus chilling)

By combining good-quality canned tomatoes and a few selected fresh ingredients, this refreshing soup truly rivals the made-from-scratch fresh tomato standard.

1   red bell pepper, quartered

⅓   English cucumber (15 ounces)

2   cans (14.5 ounces each) diced tomatoes, with juice

½   cup tomato salsa

1   bunch scallions, white and light green parts, sliced (½ cup)

1   teaspoon ground black pepper

1   cup ice water

In a food processor, combine the bell pepper, cucumber, tomatoes (with juice), salsa, scallions, and black pepper. Pulse until coarsely chopped. Transfer to serving bowl and stir in the water. Refrigerate for 1 hour before serving.

Makes 4 to 6 servings

Make-Ahead

This soup can be made up to 2 days ahead and stored in a covered container in the refrigerator.

Kitchen Tip

Store unopened canned tomatoes along with the salsa in the refrigerator
to eliminate the chilling time for the soup.

Backyard Garden Tomato Soup

Hands-On Time: 25 minutes ■ Total Time: 45 minutes

Homegrown tomatoes capture the essence of summer in this ripe-red soup. Use the bounty of your own garden or visit a nearby farmers' market for the freshest ingredients. If you hanker after that just-from-the-garden flavor during the winter, canned or boxed tomatoes give better flavor than the not-so-great fresh tomatoes you'll find in the supermarket.

1 tablespoon olive oil	4 cups diced plum tomatoes
1½ cups diced onion	2 cups water
1 red bell pepper, diced	¼ cup minced fresh basil
2 cloves garlic, minced	2 tablespoons minced fresh mint

1. In a large saucepan, heat the oil over medium heat. Add the onion, pepper, and garlic. Cook, stirring, for 1 minute. Cover, reduce the heat to low, and cook for 5 minutes longer.

2. Add the tomatoes, water, basil, and mint. Bring to a boil over medium heat, then reduce the heat and simmer for 15 minutes, or until the vegetables are just softened.

Makes 4 servings

Ingredients Note

Mint and tomatoes make a beautiful pair. The sweetness of mint counteracts the natural acidity of tomatoes and eliminates the need for added sugar.

Shortcut

To mince basil quickly, roll 8 or 10 leaves together into a little "cigar." Thinly slice, then mince the slices.

Homemade Stocks

Making your own stock not only helps you save money but also puts you in control of the sodium and fat content of your soups. In these recipes, we have not added salt or black pepper. You can do this to your taste after straining.

Thrift experts encourage saving any leftover bones or scraps from meat and fish to make great stock. Many butchers also give away beef or lamb bones and other great stock ingredients. Look for free fish heads or fish bones at your fish market. Or save your own shrimp shells for flavorful stock; use them in addition to or in place of the fish bones.

Cook stock in an uncovered Dutch oven or stockpot to allow some of the water to evaporate and the flavors to concentrate.

Each of the following recipes will provide you with about 12 cups of stock. You can save time by cooking a double batch and freezing the extra (see Kitchen Tip on the opposite page).

VEGETABLE STOCK

14 cups water

4 stalks celery (with leaves), chopped

4 carrots, chopped

1 cup chopped green cabbage

1 cup mushrooms

1 onion, chopped

12 cloves garlic

10 sprigs fresh parsley

2 bay leaves

1. In a Dutch oven or stockpot, combine the water, celery, carrots, cabbage, mushrooms, onion, garlic, parsley, and bay leaves. Bring to a boil over medium-high heat. Reduce the heat to medium and cook for 1 hour, or until the stock is golden brown.

2. Strain the stock through a colander, pressing the vegetables lightly to extract their flavors. Discard the solids.

Makes 12 cups

CHICKEN STOCK

14 cups water

4 pounds chicken pieces (thighs, drumsticks, backs, and necks)

2 large carrots, quartered

2 small onions, roughly chopped (don't bother to peel)

6 cloves garlic

2 bay leaves

1. In a Dutch oven or stockpot, combine the water, chicken, carrots, onions, garlic, and bay leaves. Bring to a boil over medium-high heat. Skim the foam from the top and reduce the heat to low. Cook for 2 hours, or until the stock has a rich chicken flavor.

2. Strain the stock through a colander, pressing the ingredients to extract their flavors. Save the chicken for another use and discard the other solids. Refrigerate the stock overnight. Defat by skimming off and discarding any solidified fat before using.

Makes 12 cups

FISH STOCK

- 14 cups water
- 2 pounds fish heads or fish bones
- 2 large carrots, quartered
- 2 small onions, roughly chopped (don't bother to peel)
- 6 cloves garlic
- 2 bay leaves

1. In a Dutch oven or stockpot, combine the water, fish heads, carrots, onions, garlic, and bay leaves. Bring to a boil over medium-high heat. Skim the foam from the top and reduce the heat to low. Cook for 2 hours, or until the stock has a rich fish flavor.

2. Strain the stock through a colander, pressing the ingredients to extract their flavors. Discard the solids. Refrigerate the stock overnight. Defat by skimming off and discarding any solidified fat before using.

Makes 12 cups

BEEF STOCK

- 14 cups water
- 3 to 4 pounds meaty beef bones (such as shank or shin, tail, or short ribs), or 2 pounds chuck meat
- 2 large carrots, quartered
- 2 small onions, roughly chopped (don't bother to peel)
- 2 stalks celery, cut into chunks
- 6 cloves garlic
- 10 sprigs fresh parsley
- 2 bay leaves

1. In a Dutch oven or stockpot, combine the water, beef bones, carrots, onions, celery, garlic, parsley, and bay leaves. Bring to a boil over medium-high heat. Skim the foam from the top and reduce the heat to low. Cook for 2 hours, or until the stock has a rich beef flavor.

2. Strain the stock through a colander, pressing the ingredients to extract their flavors. Discard the solids. Refrigerate the stock overnight. Defat by skimming off and discarding any solidified fat before using.

Makes 12 cups

Kitchen Tip

Freeze stock flat: Pour cooled defatted stock into heavy-duty zip-top freezer bags, leaving a small amount of empty space for expansion. Press out the excess air, seal the bag, and wipe off any moisture on the outside of the bag. Lay the bags on a sheet of wax paper on the freezer floor or on a baking sheet so that they freeze flat. Then stand the bags on edge for space-efficient storage. Stock stored this way also defrosts faster than stock stored in plastic tubs.

Italian Minestrone

Hands-On Time: 30 minutes ■ Total Time: 1 hour 20 minutes

This hearty soup is quite light on calories (just 160 per serving), especially when you consider that it's virtually a meal in itself. The combination of beans and pasta makes it especially filling, and the beans have an added benefit: They've been shown to actually help lower cholesterol.

½ cup coarsely chopped carrots

½ cup coarsely chopped celery

½ cup coarsely chopped onion

2 tablespoons water

1 tablespoon olive oil

5 cups beef or chicken broth

1 can (14.5 ounces) diced Italian tomatoes, with juice

1½ cups cooked red kidney beans

1 cup packed chopped escarole

¼ cup orzo

½ cup French-cut green beans

½ cup frozen peas

½ cup thinly sliced zucchini

Ground black pepper

½ cup chopped fresh parsley

2 strips (½" × 2") lemon zest

1 clove garlic, chopped

Salt

1. In a 3-quart saucepan or Dutch oven, combine the carrots, celery, onion, water, and oil. Cover and cook over low heat for about 15 minutes, or until the vegetables are softened but not browned.

2. Add the broth, tomatoes (with juice), kidney beans, escarole, and orzo. Bring to a boil, stirring occasionally, then reduce the heat to medium-low. Simmer, uncovered, for about 25 minutes, or until the vegetables and pasta are tender.

3. Add the green beans, peas, and zucchini. Simmer, partially covered, for 8 to 10 minutes, or until the vegetables are softened. Add black pepper to taste.

4. In a food processor or by hand, finely chop the parsley, lemon zest, and garlic together. Stir into the soup for the last 5 minutes of cooking. Add salt to taste. Serve hot.

Makes 6 servings

Variations

Use other vegetables, such as Swiss chard, Savoy cabbage, lima beans, and yellow squash, and add rice instead of orzo.

Provençal Vegetable Soup

Hands-On Time: 20 minutes ■ Total Time: 2 hours 55 minutes (plus overnight soaking)

Adding the basil-infused oil and the Parmesan at the end of the cooking time gives remarkable richness to this French-inspired soup, often called *pistou* in France.

½ pound kidney beans, rinsed and soaked overnight in water to cover

4 large carrots, diced

2 medium potatoes, diced

2 leeks, thinly sliced

½ pound green beans, cut into ½" pieces

3 cloves garlic, crushed

⅛ teaspoon ground black pepper

2 tablespoons finely chopped basil

½ cup olive oil

1 cup very thin egg noodles

¼ cup tomato purée or 1 fresh tomato, peeled and finely diced

½ cup soft bread crumbs

¼ cup grated Parmesan cheese plus additional for sprinkling

1. In an 8-quart soup pot, bring the beans and soaking water to a boil. Cook for about 1 hour, or until the beans are tender.

2. Add the carrots, potatoes, leeks, green beans, garlic, and pepper. Add enough water to fill the pot. Bring to a boil, then simmer for about 15 minutes, or until the vegetables are cooked but still crisp.

3. Meanwhile, in a small bowl, soak the basil in the oil. Set aside to allow the flavors to blend.

4. Return the soup to a boil and add the noodles and tomato purée. Cook, uncovered, at a slow boil for about 15 minutes, or until the noodles are tender.

5. After the noodles have cooked for 5 minutes, stir in the bread crumbs, ¼ cup of the Parmesan, and the oil mixture. Serve the soup hot and pass a bowl of Parmesan at the table, for sprinkling.

Makes 6 servings

Make-Ahead

You can prepare the soup through step 2 and the basil oil a day in advance. When you're ready to complete and serve the soup, bring it to a boil before adding the noodles.

Yellow Pepper Soup

Hands-On Time: 35 minutes ■ Total Time: 1 hour 5 minutes

This sunflower-bright soup can be made in big batches at the end of the summer, when yellow bell peppers are a bargain at farm stands. Store it in the freezer for sips of sunshine all winter long.

2 teaspoons butter

2 medium yellow bell peppers, coarsely chopped

1 medium leek, chopped

1 small onion, chopped

1 stalk celery, chopped

⅛ teaspoon salt

⅛ teaspoon ground black pepper

2 cups chicken broth

1. In a medium saucepan, melt the butter over medium heat. Add the peppers, leek, onion, celery, salt, and pepper. Cook, stirring, for 10 minutes, or until the vegetables are crisp-tender.

2. Add the broth and bring to a boil. Reduce the heat to low, cover, and simmer for 20 minutes. Remove the saucepan from the heat and let stand for 5 minutes to cool slightly.

3. Transfer the soup to a blender or food processor. Blend until smooth. Return the mixture to the saucepan and heat through.

Makes 4 servings

Variation

For a "smokier" soup, grill the peppers in advance, put them in a paper bag,
and let them stand for about 10 minutes. Then remove and discard the charred skin.
Chop the peppers and add them to the soup when you add the broth.

Herbed Broccoli-Cauliflower Soup

Hands-On Time: 40 minutes ■ Total Time: 55 minutes

"Yummy" describes this homey herbed soup. It goes especially well with garlic bread or Parmesan cheese toasts and a tossed garden salad.

1½ teaspoons butter

1 large onion, chopped

1 large stalk celery, chopped

3¼ cups diced potatoes

3 cups chicken broth

1 tablespoon Dijon mustard

1 teaspoon dry mustard

1 teaspoon dried tarragon

¾ teaspoon dried marjoram

½ teaspoon curry powder

3 cups mixed frozen or fresh broccoli and cauliflower florets

1 cup milk

Salt (optional)

Ground black pepper

1. In a large, heavy saucepan or Dutch oven, melt the butter over medium heat. Add the onion and celery. Cook, stirring, for 5 minutes, or until the onion is softened.

2. Add the potatoes, broth, Dijon mustard, dry mustard, tarragon, marjoram, and curry powder. Bring to a boil.

3. Reduce the heat and simmer for 12 to 15 minutes, or until the potatoes are softened.

4. Transfer 2 cups of the soup to a blender. Blend until smooth.

5. Return the puréed soup to the pot and add the broccoli and cauliflower and milk. Bring to a boil over medium-high heat. Cook, stirring frequently, for 5 to 8 minutes, or until the florets are crisp-tender. Season with salt, if using, and pepper to taste.

Makes 4 servings

Leftovers

Turn leftover Herbed Broccoli-Cauliflower Soup into Creamy Penne with Vegetables: Spoon 2 cups of the soup into a saucepan and heat to simmering. In a small bowl, whisk together 2 tablespoons milk, 1½ tablespoons cornstarch, and ½ teaspoon salt. Add to the saucepan and cook, stirring frequently, until the mixture thickens. Add ¼ cup shredded mozzarella and ¼ cup ricotta cheese. Stir until the cheese melts, then toss with 3 cups hot cooked penne or other pasta.

Butternut Squash Bisque

Hands-On Time: 35 minutes ▪ Total Time: 50 minutes

This simple soup is a fast and delicious way to incorporate high beta-carotene butternut squash into your meals.

1 large butternut squash	½ teaspoon ground cumin
2¼ cups chicken broth	¼ to ½ teaspoon ground red pepper
1 teaspoon extra-virgin olive oil	Salt
2 cups chopped onion	Ground black pepper
1 cup chopped red bell pepper	¼ cup plain yogurt
2 teaspoons minced garlic	

1. Pierce the squash several times with a sharp knife. Place it on a paper towel in the microwave. Microwave on high power for 5 minutes. Halve the squash lengthwise and remove and discard the seeds. Microwave for 5 minutes longer.

2. Meanwhile, in a large saucepan over medium-high heat, combine ¼ cup of the broth and the oil. Bring to a boil. Add the onion, bell pepper, and garlic. Cook, stirring often, for 5 minutes.

3. Scoop the squash from its shell and cut into chunks. Add the squash, cumin, ground red pepper, and the remaining 2 cups broth to the saucepan. Cover and bring to a boil. Reduce the heat and simmer for 15 minutes.

4. Working in batches, transfer the soup to a blender or food processor, and blend until smooth. Return the puréed soup to the saucepan and heat through. Add salt and black pepper to taste. Serve with a dollop of the yogurt.

Makes 4 servings

Ingredients Note

To save time, you can buy a bag of already peeled and cubed butternut squash in the produce section of most large supermarkets (you will need about 4 cups). You can still microwave it until soft; just keep an eye on the timing. Or, in a pinch, you can use frozen cubed squash. If you go the frozen route, just thaw it and put it into the broth mixture.

Variations

Use acorn or Hubbard squash instead of butternut, if you prefer, and top with crème fraiche instead of yogurt.

French Onion Soup

Hands-On Time: 45 minutes ■ Total Time: 1 hour 35 minutes

Traditionally, this onion-packed soup is topped with bread and Swiss cheese. This version features Gruyère on top of the bread.

2 tablespoons olive oil

8 large sweet onions, thinly sliced and separated into rings

2 tablespoons all-purpose flour

¼ teaspoon ground black pepper

4 cups beef or vegetable broth

2 cups water

Mild or hot pepper sauce

4 slices French bread, lightly toasted

½ cup shredded Gruyère cheese

Parsley sprigs, for garnish

1. In a large saucepan, heat the oil over medium-high heat. Add the onions and cook, stirring frequently, for 5 minutes, or until translucent. Reduce the heat to medium-low, cover, and cook for 10 minutes longer, or until the onions are very soft.

2. Uncover the saucepan and increase the heat to medium. Cook, stirring frequently, for 30 minutes, or until the onions are golden and almost caramel colored.

3. Sprinkle the flour and black pepper over the onions and stir to combine. Pour in the broth and water, and stir well to smooth out the lumps. Bring to a boil. Reduce the heat to low, cover, and simmer for 30 minutes, stirring occasionally. Stir in the pepper sauce to taste.

4. Meanwhile, preheat the oven to 425°F.

5. Ladle the soup into 4 ovenproof soup bowls. Top each serving with the bread and Gruyère. Bake for 5 minutes, or until the cheese is melted and bubbly. Garnish each serving with a parsley sprig.

Makes 4 servings

Make-Ahead

Slice the onions in advance and freeze them in an airtight container for up to 3 months.

Ingredients Note

You can choose any type of sweet onion you like. Try Vidalia (from Georgia), Walla Walla (from Washington), or Maui (from Hawaii).

Hot and Hearty Seafood Chowder

Hands-On Time: 35 minutes ■ Total Time: 1 hour

This warming New England soup should hit the spot on really cold evenings. Serve it with a tossed salad and cornbread for a complete meal.

12 shucked chowder clams

5 cups chicken broth

2 large baking potatoes, peeled and diced

1 large onion, diced

1 stalk celery, diced

1 tablespoon minced fresh parsley

1 bay leaf

½ teaspoon dried oregano

¼ teaspoon dried tarragon

¼ teaspoon ground black pepper

½ pound cod, cut into 1" pieces

1 cup milk

¼ teaspoon ground white pepper

1. In a large, heavy saucepan or Dutch oven, bring the clams and 2 cups of the broth to a boil over medium-high heat. Reduce the heat to medium and simmer for 3 minutes. Remove the clams with a slotted spoon and set aside.

2. Add the potatoes, onion, celery, parsley, bay leaf, oregano, tarragon, black pepper, and the remaining 3 cups broth to the pot. Bring to a boil. Reduce the heat and simmer for 15 minutes, or until the vegetables are softened. Remove and discard the bay leaf.

3. Ladle half of the vegetables and 1 cup of the liquid into a food processor or blender. Process until smooth. Return to the pot. Add the cod and simmer for 5 minutes, or until the cod is cooked through.

4. Finely chop the clams and add to the pot. Stir in the milk and heat briefly. Sprinkle with the white pepper and serve.

Makes 4 servings

Ingredients Note

If you buy clams in the shell, be sure the shells are tightly closed. If a shell is slightly open, tap it lightly. If it doesn't snap shut, the clam is dead and should be discarded. You can store live clams in an open container covered with a moist cloth for up to 2 days in the refrigerator before shucking.

Quick Oyster Stew

Hands-On Time: 25 minutes ■ Total Time: 20 minutes

If you have extra time, you can shuck your own oysters for this chowder. Otherwise, purchase already-shucked oysters, which are sold in their liquor in the seafood sections of larger supermarkets. Save the liquor to use in the recipe, or use bottled clam juice.

1 tablespoon butter	1½ cups chicken broth
1 onion, minced	½ cup oyster liquor or bottled clam juice
1 stalk celery, minced	½ cup corn
1 clove garlic, minced	1½ cups small oysters, drained
½ teaspoon dried thyme	1½ cups milk
1 baking potato, diced	¼ cup minced fresh parsley

1. In a large, heavy saucepan, heat the butter over medium heat. Add the onion and celery. Cook, stirring frequently, for 5 minutes, or until softened.

2. Add the garlic and thyme, and stir for 30 seconds. Add the potato, broth, and oyster liquor. Cover and bring to a boil. Reduce the heat and simmer for 15 minutes.

3. Stir in the corn and oysters. Simmer over low heat for 5 minutes, or until the oysters are just cooked through and their edges have begun to curl. Add the milk and parsley, and heat briefly.

Makes 4 servings

Nutri-Note

Oysters are a good source of important minerals, including iron and zinc. They also contain a fair share of copper, which helps regulate cholesterol metabolism.

Potato, Leek, and Parsley Chowder

Hands-On Time: 35 minutes ■ Total Time: 1 hour 15 minutes

This economical chowder gets its creamy texture from puréed potatoes rather than cream or butter. We recommend yellow potatoes (often on sale in fall) because of their buttery flavor, but red potatoes work equally well.

4 cups chicken broth

2 cups chopped yellow or red potatoes

1 cup sliced leeks

1 medium onion, finely chopped

1 cup buttermilk

⅓ cup chopped fresh parsley

½ teaspoon ground black pepper

¼ teaspoon salt

1 tablespoon chopped fresh chives

1. In a large, heavy saucepan or Dutch oven, combine the broth, potatoes, leeks, and onion. Bring to a boil over medium-high heat. Cover and cook, stirring occasionally, for 35 minutes, or until the potatoes are very soft when pierced with a sharp knife.

2. Let the soup cool slightly. Transfer to a blender or food processor, in batches if necessary, and blend until smooth. Return the puréed soup to the pot.

3. Add the buttermilk, parsley, pepper, and salt, and stir to combine. Bring to a simmer and cook until warmed through, about 5 minutes. Serve sprinkled with the chives.

Makes 4 servings

Kitchen Tip

How do you clean a leek? It's easy. Slice off the root end, then slit the leek from top to bottom. Holding the cut side under running water, fan the layers and allow any sand to rinse out. Then slice each half into thin half circles.

Hold the Salt! Seasoning Tips for Homemade Soups

Seasoning mixes from the store are not only three times more expensive than homemade, but they're also salted with a heavy hand, making them too high in sodium for everyday use. Skilled cooks learn how to season homemade soups with combinations of fresh or dried herbs and spices, augmented with small amounts of salt when needed. A pinch or a dash of any of these seasoning mixes can turn a simple stock into a wonderful soup.

Seasoning mixes keep for about 6 months in a dark cupboard at room temperature, or store them for up to 1 year in the freezer in small sealed containers. You can easily make larger quantities of any of these.

Cajun. Combine 2 teaspoons paprika, 1 teaspoon garlic powder, 1 teaspoon ground black pepper, ¾ teaspoon onion powder, ¾ teaspoon ground red pepper, ¾ teaspoon dried thyme, and ¾ teaspoon dried oregano. Use in bean and vegetable soups.

French. Combine 1 teaspoon dried tarragon, 1 teaspoon dried parsley, ½ teaspoon garlic powder, ½ teaspoon ground black pepper, and ¼ teaspoon salt. Use in creamy vegetable soups.

Indian. Combine 1 tablespoon mild curry powder, ½ teaspoon ground cinnamon, ½ teaspoon ground cumin, ½ teaspoon ground coriander, ¼ teaspoon turmeric, and ¼ teaspoon ground red pepper. Use in winter squash or other vegetable soups.

Mediterranean. Combine 1 tablespoon dried basil, 2 teaspoons dried oregano, 1 teaspoon dried marjoram, ½ teaspoon ground black pepper, and 1 teaspoon garlic powder. Use in tomato-based soups.

Middle Eastern. Combine 1 tablespoon paprika, ½ teaspoon turmeric, ½ teaspoon ground black pepper, ¼ teaspoon ground red pepper, and ¼ teaspoon salt. Use in chicken, bean, and grain-based soups.

Southwestern. Combine 1 tablespoon paprika, 2 teaspoons ground coriander, 2 teaspoons ground cumin, 2 teaspoons dried oregano, 1 teaspoon chili powder, 1 teaspoon garlic powder, and ½ to 1 teaspoon ground red pepper. Use in chicken, beef, or vegetable soups.

Super-Healthy Chicken Soup

Hands-On Time: 50 minutes ■ Total Time: 1 hour 30 minutes

The hot water vapor that you inhale when you eat chicken soup does much to help clear your sinuses when you have a cold. The added splash of hot pepper sauce gives this soup an extra punch of sinus-clearing benefits, and the tomato and sweet potato offer vitamin C and beta-carotene.

4 whole bone-in chicken legs

4 cups chicken broth

2 cups water

5 cloves garlic, minced

2 tablespoons finely chopped fresh ginger

¼ teaspoon ground black pepper

3 carrots, sliced

1 large leek, white part and some of the green, cut into ½" slices

1 large sweet potato (12 ounces), peeled and cut into large chunks

6 cups packed torn spinach

1 large tomato, cut into ½" chunks

¼ to 1 teaspoon hot pepper sauce

1. Cut the chicken legs into thighs and drumsticks. Remove and discard the skin and any visible fat.

2. Place the chicken in a large, heavy saucepan or Dutch oven. Add the broth, water, garlic, ginger, and black pepper. Bring to a boil over high heat. Skim off any foam that rises to the surface. Reduce the heat to low, cover, and simmer for 15 minutes, skimming the surface occasionally.

3. Stir in the carrots, leek, and sweet potato. Cover and simmer for 20 minutes, or until the vegetables are softened and the chicken is cooked through.

4. Add the spinach and tomato. Cook for 5 minutes, or until the spinach is wilted and the tomato is heated through. Add the hot pepper sauce to taste.

Makes 4 servings

Make-Ahead

This soup can be made ahead and frozen for up to 3 months.

Kitchen Tip

The fastest way to remove the skin from bone-in chicken legs is to use two paper towels. Hold the leg in one hand with a paper towel, and then pull off the skin using another paper towel to get a good grip. This way, the skin pulls right off and your hands don't slip.

Chinese Chicken Soup

Hands-On Time: 30 minutes ■ Total Time: 1 hour 10 minutes

Serve this clear soup over cooked rice, Chinese-style, for a warming one-dish meal. The tofu boosts the protein profile while keeping the saturated fat low.

8 ounces boneless, skinless chicken breast, cut into 1" cubes

1 tablespoon reduced-sodium soy sauce

½ teaspoon sugar

½ teaspoon ground black pepper

1 cup chopped onion

1 cup sliced zucchini or yellow summer squash

½ cup sliced carrots

1 teaspoon sesame oil

6 cups chicken broth

8 ounces firm tofu, cut into ½" cubes

½ cup minced fresh cilantro

⅓ cup chopped scallions

1 teaspoon fresh lime juice

1. In a shallow dish, combine the chicken, soy sauce, sugar, and pepper. Toss to coat. Let stand for 10 minutes, stirring occasionally.

2. In a large, heavy saucepan or Dutch oven, combine the onion, zucchini, carrots, and oil. Cook, stirring, over medium-high heat for 5 minutes, or until the onions are softened but not browned. Add the broth and bring to a boil. Reduce the heat to medium. Cover and cook, stirring occasionally, for 20 minutes.

3. Add the chicken and marinade. Cook for 5 to 7 minutes, or until the chicken is no longer pink in the center. (Check by inserting the tip of a sharp knife into a cube.) Add the tofu, cilantro, and scallions. Cook for 1 minute, or until the tofu is heated through. Add the lime juice. Stir well to combine and serve.

Makes 6 servings

Kitchen Tip

Get full value from any bunch of herbs you purchase. After using the amount you need for a recipe, chop and freeze the remaining leaves in a small freezer-quality plastic bag. Cilantro and other herbs will remain green and flavorful. Use the herbs while still frozen in your next recipe.

Curried Yellow Split-Pea Soup

Hands-On Time: 45 minutes ■ Total Time: 3 hours

This thick and hearty soup will warm you to the bone on a cold fall or winter's night. If you like, use green split peas or lentils and add some chopped cooked chicken during the last few minutes of cooking. The soup benefits from being made ahead.

1 large carrot, finely chopped

1 cup chopped onion

½ cup chopped celery

1 clove garlic, minced

2 teaspoons olive oil

1 tablespoon plus 8 cups water

1 tablespoon curry powder

1 cup dried yellow split peas

½ cup fresh or frozen green peas

½ cup diced red bell pepper

Pinch of ground black pepper

Salt

½ cup plain yogurt

¼ cup chopped dill sprigs

1. In a 3- or 4-quart saucepan, combine the carrot, onion, celery, garlic, oil, and 1 tablespoon of the water. Cook the vegetables over low heat, stirring frequently, for about 10 minutes, or until softened but not browned. Add the curry powder and cook for 1 minute longer.

2. Add the remaining 8 cups water and the split peas. Bring to a boil, reduce the heat to medium-low, and cook, uncovered, for about 2 hours, or until the split peas are tender and the soup has thickened. (Add additional liquid if the soup gets too thick.)

3. Add the peas, bell pepper, black pepper, and salt to taste. Cook, uncovered, for about 5 minutes, or until the vegetables are softened.

4. Meanwhile, in a small bowl, combine the yogurt and dill.

5. Ladle the soup into shallow bowls and dollop each with a spoonful of the yogurt mixture.

Makes 8 servings

Black Bean Soup

Bean soups—from sustaining Yankee bean to savory Italian minestrone—find favor all over the world. The note of cumin in this one gives it Indian overtones.

2 cans (19 ounces each) black beans, rinsed and drained (2 cups)

1¾ cups chicken broth

1 cup water

1 teaspoon ground cumin

¼ teaspoon dried oregano

¼ teaspoon ground black pepper

Large pinch of ground red pepper

1 teaspoon olive oil

½ large red bell pepper, slivered, plus extra for garnish

½ large green bell pepper, slivered, plus extra for garnish

½ teaspoon freshly grated lemon zest

1. In a large, heavy saucepan, combine the beans, broth, water, cumin, oregano, black pepper, and ground red pepper. Cover and bring to a boil over high heat. Reduce the heat to low and simmer, stirring once or twice, for 15 minutes, or until the flavors are blended.

2. Meanwhile, in a small nonstick skillet, heat the oil over medium-high heat. Add the bell peppers, reduce the heat to medium, and cook, stirring frequently, for 4 to 6 minutes, or until softened.

3. Ladle half the soup into a food processor or blender, in batches if necessary, and process until smooth. Return the puréed soup to the saucepan. Add the lemon zest.

4. Ladle the soup into bowls and garnish each serving with some of the bell peppers.

Makes 4 servings

Ingredients Note

If you'd like to make this soup with dried black beans instead of canned, place 1 pound of beans in a large pot with cold water to cover, and refrigerate overnight. Drain the beans, cover with fresh water, and simmer for 1¼ hours, or until tender, skimming the foam as they cook. You'll have enough for this recipe, plus leftovers for other dishes.

White Bean Soup with Basil and Tomatoes

Hands-On Time: 30 minutes ■ Total Time: 45 minutes

A surprisingly light yet satisfying soup, this is best in the summer when fresh basil and tomatoes are at their peak.

½ teaspoon olive oil

¼ cup chopped onion

1 clove garlic, minced

2 cups chicken broth

2 cups water

1 can (15 ounces) navy or cannellini beans, rinsed and drained

1 large potato, peeled and diced

1 teaspoon chopped fresh oregano

Salt

Ground black pepper

¼ cup finely diced tomatoes

2 tablespoons chopped fresh basil

1. In a large, heavy saucepan, heat the oil over medium heat. Add the onion and garlic. Cook, stirring, for 1 minute.

2. Add the broth, water, beans, potato, and oregano. Cover and bring to a boil. Reduce the heat to medium-low and simmer for 15 minutes, or until the potato is softened.

3. Transfer about three-quarters of the soup to a blender or food processor, and blend until smooth. Return the puréed soup to the saucepan and heat through. Add salt and pepper to taste. Stir in the tomatoes and basil just before serving.

Makes 4 servings

Variation

In the winter, substitute chopped sun-dried tomatoes (which should be soaked in hot water for 10 minutes, or until soft, before using) for the fresh tomatoes and fresh parsley for the basil.

Hearty Red Cabbage Soup

Hands-On Time: 45 minutes ■ Total Time: 1 hour 5 minutes

Cabbage is one of the cancer-preventing cruciferous vegetables. Soup is an excellent way to get this super vegetable into your diet. This soup is nice and hearty—just the thing for cold-weather lunches.

1 tablespoon olive oil	½ cup tomato purée
1 large onion, thinly sliced	1 teaspoon ground black pepper
4 cloves garlic, chopped	½ teaspoon dried thyme
1 pound red cabbage, thinly sliced	1 bay leaf
4 stalks celery, thinly sliced	1½ cups cooked great Northern beans
¼ cup red wine vinegar	Salt
1 tablespoon caraway seeds	¼ cup sour cream
6 cups chicken broth	1 bunch scallions, white and light green parts, thinly sliced (½ cup)

1. In a large saucepan, heat the oil over medium heat. Add the onion and garlic. Stir, cover the pan, and cook for 10 minutes, stirring frequently.

2. Add the cabbage, celery, vinegar, and caraway seeds. Cover and cook for 10 minutes, stirring frequently.

3. Add the broth, tomato purée, pepper, thyme, and bay leaf. Cover and simmer for 20 minutes. Remove the bay leaf. Stir in the beans and heat through. Add salt to taste. Add a dollop of sour cream and a sprinkling of scallions to each serving.

Makes 6 servings

Make-Ahead

This soup keeps well and can be stored in the refrigerator for up to 5 days.

Root Vegetable Soup

Hands-On Time: 50 minutes ■ Total Time: 2 hours

This vitamin-rich soup is a meal unto itself and makes a great dinner for a fall or winter evening. Not only is it healthy, it's easy: Once the soup is simmering, you barely have to watch it. Serve it with a watercress or arugula salad dressed lightly with lemon juice and extra-virgin olive oil. For dessert, have Apple-Oatmeal Crumble (page 327).

1 tablespoon olive oil

6 cloves garlic, minced

2 large onions, chopped

½ teaspoon dried marjoram

½ teaspoon dried sage

¼ teaspoon salt

½ teaspoon ground black pepper

1 pound lean, well-trimmed beef round, cut into 1" cubes

3 cups beef broth

3 cups water

1 can (28 ounces) whole tomatoes, drained and broken up

4 small turnips, peeled and cut into ½" chunks

3 medium beets, peeled and cut into ½" chunks

3 large carrots, cut into ½" chunks

2 medium parsnips, peeled and cut into ½" chunks

1. In a large saucepan, heat the oil over medium heat. Add the garlic and onions. Cook, stirring, for 5 minutes, or until softened. Stir in the marjoram, sage, salt, and pepper. Add the beef and cook, stirring, for 5 minutes, or until browned.

2. Add the broth, water, and tomatoes. Bring to a boil over high heat. Reduce the heat to low, cover, and simmer, stirring occasionally, for 45 minutes, or until the beef is very tender.

3. Add the turnips, beets, carrots, and parsnips. Return to a simmer, cover, and cook, stirring occasionally, for 25 minutes longer, or until the vegetables are softened.

Makes 6 servings

Make-Ahead

This soup can be made ahead and frozen for up to 3 months.

Ingredients Note

You can use half dry white wine and half water rather than 3 cups of water, if you like.

Sensational
Salads

*"You can put everything, and the more things
the better, into salad, as into conversation;
but everything depends upon the mixing."*

—Charles Dudley Warner

Chicken and Corn Salad

Hands-On Time: 15 minutes ■ Total Time: 15 minutes

Bright bell peppers and juicy, sweet corn mingle with wholesome black beans and crunchy scallions to create a delicious splash of color, texture, and taste in this summery chicken salad.

3 tablespoons extra-virgin olive oil

3 tablespoons red wine vinegar

1 teaspoon ground cumin

¼ teaspoon salt

2 cups cubed cooked chicken

2 cans (16 ounces each) whole kernel corn, drained

1 can (16 ounces) black beans, rinsed and drained

1 red bell pepper, chopped

2 scallions, sliced

2 tablespoons chopped fresh cilantro

In a large bowl, whisk together the oil, vinegar, cumin, and salt. Add the chicken, corn, beans, pepper, scallions, and cilantro. Toss to coat well.

Makes 4 servings

Accompaniments

Precede the salad with Quick Gazpacho (page 30), and follow it with Marbled Brownies (page 338).

Autumn Chicken Salad

Hands-On Time: 25 minutes ■ Total Time: 25 minutes (plus chilling)

You'll love the sweetness of a ripe red pear atop bright, crisp lettuce. Chopped toasted walnuts lend extra crunch.

½ cup sour cream

¼ cup mayonnaise

1 tablespoon chopped fresh thyme or 1 teaspoon dried

1 tablespoon fresh lemon juice

½ teaspoon freshly grated lemon zest

½ teaspoon salt

4 cups cubed cooked chicken

2 stalks celery, chopped

1 red pear, cut into ½" cubes

1 head Boston or Bibb lettuce

¼ cup chopped toasted walnuts

1. In a large bowl, combine the sour cream, mayonnaise, thyme, lemon juice, lemon zest, and salt. Add the chicken, celery, and pear. Toss to coat well. Cover and refrigerate for at least 1 hour.

2. Evenly divide the lettuce among 4 plates. Top with the chicken salad and sprinkle with the walnuts.

Makes 4 servings

Ingredients Note

Use Bosc or red Bartlett pears in this recipe. Since a pear's flesh discolors rapidly once it is cut, wait until just before you're ready to add the pear to the dressing to cut it. The lemon juice in the dressing will keep it looking fresh.

Turkey and Sweet Potato Salad

Hands-On Time: 45 minutes ■ Total Time: 1 hour 10 minutes

When Thanksgiving is a distant memory, cook some fresh turkey and sweet potatoes for this delectable warm salad. It's tossed with an orange-curry-chutney dressing that's like nothing you've ever eaten on "Turkey Day."

¾ cup plain yogurt

1 pound sweet potatoes, peeled and cut into 1" chunks

½ cup chicken broth

¼ cup water

3 tablespoons frozen orange juice concentrate, thawed

2 teaspoons curry powder

¾ pound boneless, skinless turkey breast, cut into ½" cubes

2 stalks celery, sliced diagonally

3 scallions, sliced diagonally

3 tablespoons raisins

¼ cup mango chutney

⅛ teaspoon hot pepper sauce

⅛ teaspoon salt

3 tablespoons chopped toasted pecans

1. Line a small strainer with cheesecloth or paper towels and suspend it over a small bowl. Spoon the yogurt into the strainer and let it drain for 15 minutes. Discard the whey that has drained off and dry the bowl, then turn the drained yogurt into the bowl. Set aside.

2. While the yogurt is draining, place the sweet potatoes in a medium saucepan and add cold water to cover. Cover the pan and bring to a boil over high heat. Reduce the heat to medium and simmer for 9 to 11 minutes, or until the sweet potatoes are fork-tender but not mushy. Drain in a colander and cool briefly under gently running cold water.

3. In a medium skillet, combine the broth, water, 1 tablespoon of the orange juice concentrate, and 1 teaspoon of the curry powder. Cover and bring to a boil over high heat.

4. Stir the turkey into the broth mixture and reduce the heat to medium. Cover and cook for 4 to 5 minutes, stirring frequently, or until the turkey is cooked through. Drain the turkey in a colander, reserving 3 tablespoons of the cooking liquid.

5. Place the sweet potatoes in a large salad bowl and add the turkey, celery, scallions, and raisins.

6. To the yogurt, add the chutney, hot pepper sauce, salt, the reserved turkey cooking liquid, the remaining 2 tablespoons orange juice concentrate, and the remaining 1 teaspoon curry powder. Stir to blend.

7. Pour the dressing over the salad and toss gently to coat. Sprinkle with the pecans and serve.

Makes 4 servings

Thai Beef Salad

Hands-On Time: 40 minutes ■ Total Time: 50 minutes

There is a category of delicious Thai salads called, appropriately enough, *yum*. These salads consist of greens topped with meat, poultry, fish, or shellfish. *Yum gong,* for instance, comes with curry-flavored shrimp, while *yum pla muok* is made with spiced squid and pickled garlic. This recipe is based on *yum nuer,* a salad topped with slices of spicy grilled beef. Fresh herbs characterize of all these salads; here, fresh cilantro and mint are in the dressing.

¾ pound lean, trimmed boneless beef sirloin or top round steak

2 cloves garlic, 1 halved and 1 minced

¼ teaspoon ground black pepper

¼ cup rice wine vinegar

2 teaspoons olive oil

1 teaspoon sesame oil

1 teaspoon sugar

½ teaspoon grated fresh ginger

¼ teaspoon salt

¼ teaspoon crushed red pepper flakes

2 scallions, thinly sliced

¾ pound green-leaf lettuce, torn into bite-size pieces

1 cup thinly sliced kirby or English cucumbers

1 cup loosely packed fresh cilantro leaves, chopped

1 cup loosely packed fresh mint leaves, chopped

1 small ripe mango or papaya, peeled and cubed

2 medium carrots, julienned

1 tablespoon chopped unsalted dry-roasted peanuts

1. Coat the broiler-pan rack with cooking spray. Preheat the broiler.

2. Rub the meat on both sides with the halved garlic clove, then sprinkle with the black pepper. Place it on the prepared broiler-pan rack. Broil 4" to 6" from the heat, turning once, for 5 minutes per side, or until a thermometer inserted in the center registers 145°F (medium-rare). Transfer the steak to a plate and let stand for 5 minutes.

3. Meanwhile, make the dressing. In a large bowl, whisk together the vinegar, olive oil, sesame oil, sugar, ginger, salt, red pepper flakes, and minced garlic.

4. Transfer the steak to a cutting board and pour any juices remaining on the steak plate into a medium bowl. Add 1 tablespoon of the dressing and the scallions to the juices, and stir to combine.

5. Carve the steak into ¼"-thick slices. Add the steak to the bowl with the scallions and toss to coat.

6. Add the lettuce, cucumbers, cilantro, and mint to the dressing in the large bowl and toss to coat. Arrange the lettuce mixture on 4 plates. Mound the steak mixture on top, then top with the mango and carrots. Sprinkle with the peanuts.

Makes 4 servings

Cobb Salad with Parmesan Dressing

Hands-On Time: 40 minutes ▪ Total Time: 40 minutes

Cobb salad, made famous at Hollywood's Brown Derby restaurant, is the ultimate in composed salads. This version is both sweet and smoky, satisfying all your tastebuds.

Dressing

½ cup buttermilk

¼ cup sour cream

¼ cup packed fresh basil leaves, cut into thin strips

2 tablespoons grated Parmesan cheese

1 tablespoon balsamic vinegar

½ teaspoon coarsely cracked black pepper

Salad

2 cups mixed salad greens, such as romaine and chicory

3 cups smoked chicken, cut into strips

⅓ cup crumbled feta cheese

2 red and/or yellow bell peppers, chopped

1 small red onion, chopped

4 hard-boiled egg whites, finely chopped

4 slices pork or turkey bacon, cooked, drained, and crumbled

1. *To make the dressing:* In a small bowl, whisk together the buttermilk, sour cream, basil, Parmesan, vinegar, and black pepper.

2. *To make the salad:* Divide the greens among 4 salad plates. Top with the chicken, mounding it in the center of the greens. Arrange small mounds of feta, bell peppers, onion, egg whites, and bacon around the chicken. Serve with the Parmesan dressing.

Makes 4 servings

Variations

Add cubes of avocado to this salad, if you like. You can also replace the Parmesan in the dressing with blue cheese.

Salad Dressings for Every Occasion

Salad dressings are extraordinarily versatile and only as good as what you put into them. So it is important to start with good-quality ingredients, such as extra-virgin olive oil and high-quality wine vinegar. Aside from their classic use on salads, dressings also make great marinades and sauces. Basic vinaigrettes can be stored at room temperature; creamier dressings should be refrigerated. Whisk before using.

Basic Vinaigrette and Variations

For each recipe below, follow the Basic Vinaigrette recipe, altering ingredients as necessary to make the flavor variations. Each recipe makes about ¾ cup.

Basic Vinaigrette. In a small bowl or jar with a tight-fitting lid, combine 3 tablespoons red wine vinegar, ½ minced garlic clove or 1 small finely chopped shallot, ½ teaspoon Dijon mustard, and ½ teaspoon salt. Whisk or shake until the salt dissolves. Add about ½ cup extra-virgin olive oil, at first drop by drop, to the bowl. Then, as the ingredients begin to blend, add the oil in a steady trickle. If using a jar, add about ¼ teaspoon of the oil, shake vigorously, then add the remaining oil and shake until blended. Add ½ teaspoon ground black pepper to either the vinaigrette or the salad itself.

Creamy Herb Vinaigrette. Replace the red wine vinegar with ¼ cup white wine vinegar or apple cider vinegar. After adding the oil, add ¼ cup heavy cream and 1 to 2 tablespoons chopped fresh herbs, such as thyme or tarragon.

Citrus Vinaigrette. Add 1 teaspoon grated lemon and/or lime zest along with the mustard. Replace the vinegar with ¼ cup fresh lemon and/or lime juice.

Greek Vinaigrette. Replace the red wine vinegar with fresh lemon juice. Add ¼ cup finely crumbled feta cheese and 3 tablespoons each chopped fresh mint and chopped kalamata olives.

Other Vinaigrettes

Basic Low-Fat Vinaigrette. Whisk together ¼ cup chicken broth or apple juice, ¼ cup red wine vinegar, 2 tablespoons extra-virgin olive oil, 1 teaspoon Dijon mustard, ½ teaspoon honey, and ½ teaspoon salt. Makes about ⅔ cup.

Balsamic Vinaigrette. Whisk together ½ cup extra-virgin olive oil, ¼ cup balsamic vinegar, 1 tablespoon fresh lemon juice, 1 minced garlic clove, ½ teaspoon salt, ¼ teaspoon ground black pepper, and a pinch of ground red pepper. Makes ¾ cup.

Hot-Pepper Peanut Vinaigrette. Whisk together 3 tablespoons rice wine vinegar, 2 tablespoons peanut butter, 2 tablespoons vegetable oil, 2 finely chopped scallions, ¼ minced garlic clove, 1 teaspoon finely chopped fresh ginger, 1 teaspoon soy sauce, ½ teaspoon hot pepper sauce, a pinch of ground coriander, and a pinch of ground cumin. Makes about ⅔ cup.

Creamier Dressings

Honey-Mustard Dressing. Whisk together ½ cup extra-virgin olive oil, ¼ cup cider vinegar, 2 tablespoons spicy brown mustard, 1 tablespoon apple juice, 1 tablespoon honey, ¼ teaspoon salt, and ⅛ teaspoon ground black pepper. Makes 1 cup.

Easy Ranch Dressing. Whisk together ¼ cup mayonnaise, 3 tablespoons buttermilk, 2 minced garlic cloves, 1 teaspoon cider vinegar, 1 teaspoon seasoned salt (or salt-free seasoning blend), ½ teaspoon onion powder, and ¼ teaspoon ground black pepper. Makes about ½ cup.

Tarragon Ranch Dressing. Whisk together 1 cup buttermilk, 1 tablespoon fresh lemon juice, 2 minced garlic cloves, 1 tablespoon chopped fresh tarragon or 2 teaspoons dried tarragon, and a pinch each of salt, ground black pepper, and sugar.

Real Russian Dressing. Whisk together ¼ cup mayonnaise, ¼ cup sour cream, 3 tablespoons fresh lemon juice, and 2 tablespoons ketchup. Fold in 2 tablespoons red or black caviar. For Quick Russian Dressing, omit the caviar. Makes about 1 cup.

Italian Tomato Dressing. Whisk together ⅓ cup extra-virgin olive oil, 3 tablespoons tomato purée, 2 tablespoons red wine vinegar, 1 tablespoon chopped fresh herbs (basil works well), ½ minced garlic clove, ½ teaspoon salt, and ¼ teaspoon ground black pepper. Makes about ¾ cup.

Orange-Basil Yogurt Dressing. Whisk together ½ cup plain yogurt, the grated zest and juice of ½ orange, 1 minced garlic clove, ½ teaspoon chopped fresh parsley, ½ teaspoon salt, ¼ teaspoon dried basil, and ¼ teaspoon ground black pepper. Makes about ¾ cup.

Cool-and-Spicy Cucumber Dressing. Peel and shred enough cucumber to make ½ cup. Squeeze out all excess moisture. Combine with 1 cup plain yogurt or sour cream, 1 teaspoon Dijon mustard, 1 minced garlic clove, and a pinch each of salt and ground black pepper.

Eggless Caesar Dressing. Mix together 1 crushed garlic clove, 2 finely chopped anchovy fillets, and 1 tablespoon Dijon mustard. Add 1 tablespoon red wine vinegar, 2 teaspoons Worcestershire sauce, and 1½ teaspoons fresh lemon juice. In a slow, steady stream, whisk in ½ cup extra-virgin olive oil. Stir in 1 tablespoon grated Parmesan cheese, ¼ teaspoon ground black pepper, and ¼ teaspoon salt. Makes about ¾ cup.

Fresh Fruit Dressing. In a blender or food processor, combine ½ cup chopped fruit (strawberries, pears, peaches, or other fruit), ¼ cup lemon yogurt, 1 tablespoon fresh lime juice, 1 teaspoon honey, and 1 teaspoon Dijon mustard. Purée until smooth. Use to drizzle on fruit salads or green salads. Makes about ¾ cup.

Three-Bean Salad with Mustard Dressing

Hands-On Time: 15 minutes ■ Total Time: 25 minutes (plus standing)

You'll love the fresh flavors of this tangy salad. Beans are high in hunger-appeasing complex carbohydrates, so they help fill you up even though they're not that high in calories. One study found that beans can help suppress your appetite for hours because they're digested very slowly.

Salad

2 cups halved green beans	1 cup cooked or canned kidney beans
1 cup cooked or canned chickpeas	1 large tomato, seeded and diced

Mustard Dressing

2 tablespoons Dijon mustard	1 teaspoon honey
2 tablespoons extra-virgin olive oil	¼ teaspoon ground black pepper
2 tablespoons water	¼ cup snipped fresh chives
1 tablespoon chopped fresh basil or 1½ teaspoons dried	

1. *To make the salad:* In a vegetable steamer, cook the green beans for 5 minutes, or until crisp-tender. Place the green beans in a large bowl. Add the chickpeas, kidney beans, and tomato. Mix well.

2. *To make the mustard dressing:* In a blender, combine the mustard, oil, water, basil, honey, and pepper. Blend for 1 minute. Pour the dressing over the salad, sprinkle with the chives, and toss well. Let stand for 20 minutes before serving.

Makes 8 servings

Variations

Serve the salad in lettuce cups. For variety, use colorful greens such as radicchio, ornamental kale, or Boston lettuce. Garnish with fresh basil. You can also use other beans. Try fresh limas or wax beans in place of the green beans. Replace the chickpeas or kidney beans with fava, pinto, cranberry beans, black, or anasazi beans.

White Bean Salad with Tomatoes and Herbs

Hands-On Time: 25 minutes ■ Total Time: 25 minutes

Here's a great summer salad entrée—full of crisp vegetables, marinated beans, and ripe tomato chunks. It also makes a good side salad for grilled chicken or fish.

2 cans (15 ounces each) navy or cannellini beans, rinsed and drained

2 cups seeded and diced tomatoes

½ cup chopped celery

⅓ cup shredded carrots

⅓ cup chopped scallions

¼ cup chopped fresh parsley

1 tablespoon minced shallots

¼ cup white wine vinegar

2 tablespoons extra-virgin olive oil

1 tablespoon honey or sugar

1 to 2 teaspoons Dijon mustard

1 teaspoon minced fresh rosemary

1 teaspoon minced fresh thyme

Salt (optional)

Ground black pepper

4 cups shredded leaf lettuce

1. In a large bowl, toss together the beans, tomatoes, celery, carrots, scallions, parsley, and shallots.

2. In a small bowl, whisk together the vinegar, oil, honey, mustard, rosemary, thyme, and salt (if using) and pepper to taste. Pour over the salad mixture and toss gently. Serve on a bed of lettuce.

Makes 4 servings

Leftovers

Turn leftover White Bean Salad into Mediterranean Tomato-Bean Torta, a hearty summer sandwich that is very popular in Provence. Start with a 6" round of hearty peasant bread, halved crosswise. Scoop the soft interior from the bottom half, leaving a 1"-thick shell. Mound 2 to 3 cups of leftover salad into the bread shell, then replace the top. Wrap the sandwich in plastic and let stand at room temperature for up to 30 minutes before slicing into thick wedges.

Caribbean Seafood and Black Bean Salad

Hands-On Time: 20 minutes ■ Total Time: 20 minutes (plus chilling)

This festive seafood salad will enliven any special family occasion. At a more formal dinner, serve it as a plated appetizer on a bed of lettuce leaves. It also makes waves as part of an appetizer buffet, accompanied by soft pita wedges.

3 tablespoons olive oil

½ pound peeled and deveined medium or large shrimp, cut into chunks

½ pound bay scallops

1 tablespoon minced garlic

1 can (15 ounces) black beans, rinsed and drained

1 cup drained jarred tropical fruit in light syrup

¼ cup chopped fresh cilantro

3 tablespoons frozen limeade concentrate

1 teaspoon hot pepper sauce

½ teaspoon salt

Lettuce leaves (optional)

1. Heat the oil in a medium skillet over medium-high heat. Add the shrimp, scallops, and garlic. Cook, stirring, for 2 minutes, or until the shrimp and scallops are opaque in the center. Transfer to a bowl.

2. Add the beans, fruit, cilantro, lime juice concentrate, hot pepper sauce, and salt to the bowl. Stir. Cover and refrigerate for at least 1 hour or up to 24 hours. Serve on a bed of lettuce, if desired.

Makes 8 to 10 servings

Spinach Salad with Strawberry Mayonnaise

Hands-On Time: 10 minutes ■ Total Time: 10 minutes

This recipe gives commercial mayo a flavor boost by blending in fresh strawberries. The salad itself is a snap to toss together, requiring only spinach, onion, berries, and canned oranges. Serve it as a light lunch with goat cheese and warm sourdough bread or dinner rolls.

1 red onion, thinly sliced crosswise

8 cups packed baby spinach leaves

20 large strawberries, halved

1 can (11 ounces) mandarin oranges, drained

½ cup mayonnaise

¼ cup crushed strawberries

1. Separate the onion slices into individual rings.

2. In a large bowl, combine the onion, spinach, strawberries, and oranges. Toss well.

3. In a small bowl, mix the mayonnaise and crushed strawberries. Spoon over the salad and toss again.

Makes 8 servings

Variations

Serve the strawberry mayonnaise as a dip with vegetables or fruit. Try carrot sticks, blanched broccoli spears, lightly cooked asparagus, whole strawberries, banana slices, and pineapple chunks. For a bolder taste, add a little minced garlic to the mayonnaise.

Calico Slaw with Poppy Seed Dressing

Hands-On Time: 20 minutes ■ Total Time: 20 minutes

Poppy seed dressing is usually associated with fruit salads, but this citrusy-sweet version is also tasty on a colorful toss of cabbage, peppers, snow peas, and carrots.

⅓ cup mayonnaise

1 tablespoon frozen orange juice concentrate, thawed

2 teaspoons fresh lemon juice

1 teaspoon toasted poppy seeds

½ teaspoon honey

¼ teaspoon ground black pepper

1½ cups finely shredded green cabbage

1½ cups finely shredded red cabbage

½ cup thinly sliced red bell pepper

½ cup julienned snow peas

¼ cup coarsely grated carrots

1. In a salad bowl, combine the mayonnaise, orange juice concentrate, lemon juice, poppy seeds, honey, and black pepper. Whisk until well blended.

2. Add the green and red cabbage, bell pepper, snow peas, and carrots. Toss until the vegetables are well coated with the dressing.

Makes 4 servings

Kitchen Tip

To easily shred the cabbage, cut the head of cabbage in half through its core.
Remove the wedge-shaped core section from each cabbage half. Halve each half
again, then lay each quarter flat on a board and shred it crosswise.

Orange-Scented Cucumber Salad

Hands-On Time: 15 minutes ■ Total Time: 15 minutes (plus chilling)

This refreshing side salad is virtually fat-free and incredibly low in calories. What's more, the addition of oranges gives you fully one-third of your daily requirement of vitamin C.

1 cucumber	2 teaspoons orange juice
1 navel orange	1 teaspoon lemon juice
2 tablespoons plain yogurt	1 tablespoon thinly sliced mint leaves
2 teaspoons honey	4 lettuce leaves

1. If desired, peel the cucumber. Cut it in half lengthwise, then thinly slice on the diagonal.

2. Use a vegetable peeler to remove a few thin strips of zest from the orange. Remove only the colored part, not the underlying bitter white pith. Very finely slice the zest into shreds. Measure out 2 teaspoons.

3. Peel the orange, remove the membranes, divide into sections, and dice the sections.

4. In a medium bowl, whisk together the yogurt, honey, orange juice, and lemon juice. Mix in the mint leaves, cucumbers, diced orange, and orange zest.

5. Chill for 20 minutes. To serve, place a lettuce leaf on each of 4 salad plates. Divide the salad among the leaves.

Makes 4 servings

Variations

Add very thinly sliced sweet onions, chopped scallions,
or snipped chives. If desired, use two oranges.

Kitchen Tip

When choosing an orange, opt for one that feels heavy for
its size—it will have plenty of juice inside.

Marinated Cucumbers and Tomatoes

Hands-On Time: 15 minutes ▪ Total Time: 15 minutes (plus standing)

Serve this simple yet flavorful salad at the peak of summer when tomatoes are at their best. It's a great accompaniment to a grilled steak or pork loin main dish.

2 large cucumbers, peeled, seeded, and thinly sliced

2 large tomatoes, sliced

2 tablespoons balsamic vinegar

1 tablespoon minced fresh mint

1 teaspoon minced garlic

½ teaspoon ground black pepper

¼ teaspoon salt

1. Arrange the cucumbers and tomatoes on a large serving platter.

2. In a small bowl, combine the vinegar, mint, and garlic. Sprinkle over the cucumbers and tomatoes. Cover with plastic wrap, and let stand at room temperature for 30 minutes.

3. Sprinkle with the pepper and salt just before serving.

Makes 4 servings

Ingredients Note

Today, there are so many different varieties of tomatoes available that you can choose what's best in the market for this salad. Farmers' markets often sell heirloom tomatoes, notable for their wide range of colors (including white and black) and unusual names (Marvel Striped, White Wonder, and Black Krim, for example). You can also find all manner of tiny tomatoes, including yellow pear tomatoes, grape tomatoes, and currant tomatoes, in most supermarkets.

Creative Croutons

Homemade croutons are easy and economical to make and are vastly superior to the rock-hard, stucco-textured prepackaged versions. Croutons add substance and crunchiness to salads and can be made ahead of time. Rather than frying the croutons in oil, we prefer baking them with a light coating of cooking spray. Use olive oil spray rather than vegetable spray for best flavor. Choose a firm-textured whole grain bread or cornbread. Day-old bread actually works better than fresh, as it's slightly hard and holds its shape during cooking. Let the croutons cool to room temperature before tossing into a salad. You can also store them in an airtight container for a few days.

- **Garlic-Herb Croutons.** Preheat the oven to 300°F. Cube 4 slices of bread and spread on a baking sheet. Coat lightly with cooking spray. Toss and coat lightly again with cooking spray. Sprinkle with 1 teaspoon minced garlic, $\frac{1}{4}$ teaspoon dried oregano, and $\frac{1}{8}$ teaspoon salt. Bake for 20 minutes, or until crisp.

- **Italian Pepper Croutons.** Preheat the oven to 300°F. Cube 4 slices of bread and spread on a baking sheet. Coat lightly with cooking spray. Toss and coat lightly again with cooking spray. Sprinkle with 1 teaspoon dried basil, $\frac{1}{2}$ teaspoon dried oregano, $\frac{1}{2}$ teaspoon ground black pepper, and $\frac{1}{8}$ teaspoon salt. Bake for 20 minutes, or until crisp.

- **Parmesan Croutons.** Preheat the oven to 300°F. Cube 4 slices of bread and spread on a baking sheet. Coat lightly with cooking spray. Toss and coat lightly again with cooking spray. Sprinkle with $\frac{1}{4}$ cup grated Parmesan cheese, 1 teaspoon olive oil, and $\frac{1}{8}$ teaspoon salt. Bake for 20 minutes, or until crisp.

Sicilian Cauliflower-Olive Salad

Hands-On Time: 10 minutes ■ Total Time: 20 minutes

This change-of-pace, quick-to-prepare salad, inspired by the rustic cooking of Sicily, is a natural served with Rigatoni Alfredo (page 230).

1 cup water	1 tablespoon red or white wine vinegar
16 ounces fresh or frozen cauliflower florets	¼ teaspoon red pepper flakes
¼ cup extra-virgin olive oil	3 tablespoons jarred green olive salad

1. Bring the water to a boil in a covered saucepan. Add the cauliflower. Cover and cook for about 5 minutes, or until crisp-tender. Drain and rinse under cold running water. Cut the florets into thick slices.

2. Meanwhile, in a serving bowl, whisk the oil, vinegar, and pepper flakes. Add the olive salad and the cauliflower. Toss to combine.

Makes 4 to 6 servings

Ingredients Note

When you have the time, make your own olive salad using any green or black olives you like and adding some roasted peppers (page 302) and tiny white pickled onions.

Make-Ahead

This salad can be made up to 6 hours ahead and allowed to sit, covered, at room temperature so the cauliflower absorbs the flavors.

Easy Macaroni Salad

Hands-On Time: 15 minutes ■ Total Time: 35 minutes

Planning a picnic or barbecue? This salad is perfect to prepare a day ahead of time. By using sour cream and mayonnaise for the dressing, you get super creaminess and a nice tang.

8 ounces elbow macaroni	2 hard-boiled eggs, coarsely chopped
4 stalks celery, sliced	½ cup mayonnaise
3 scallions, sliced	½ cup sour cream
½ cup frozen peas, thawed	3 tablespoons cider vinegar
1 jar (7 ounces) roasted red peppers, drained and finely chopped	½ teaspoon salt
	½ teaspoon white pepper

1. Bring a large pot of water to a boil. Cook the macaroni according to package directions until al dente. Rinse under cold water and drain.

2. Meanwhile, in a large bowl, combine the celery, scallions, peas, roasted peppers, eggs, mayonnaise, sour cream, vinegar, salt, and pepper.

3. Add the macaroni and toss to coat well. Serve immediately or refrigerate for up to 24 hours.

Makes 8 servings

Ingredients Note

When you have the time, make your own roasted peppers (see page 302).

Variation

Although it's called macaroni salad, this salad would taste just as good made with any pasta shape. Go with tricolor pasta for a festive touch.

Picnic Potato Salad

Hands-On Time: 25 minutes ▪ Total Time: 45 minutes

Potato salad is an all-American favorite, and this one is a classic. Combining the potatoes with the dressing while they're still warm allows them to absorb more flavor from the dressing.

1½ pounds red potatoes, cut into 1" cubes

1 cup thinly sliced celery

2 scallions, minced

¼ cup thinly sliced red onion

1 hard-boiled egg, chopped (optional)

1 Roma tomato, diced

2 tablespoons minced fresh dill

½ cup mayonnaise

1 tablespoon coarse mustard

1 tablespoon fresh lemon juice

1 tablespoon extra-virgin olive oil

1 tablespoon apple-cider vinegar

1 teaspoon honey

1 teaspoon minced fresh parsley

1 teaspoon reduced-sodium soy sauce (optional)

¼ teaspoon ground black pepper

⅛ to ¼ teaspoon celery seed

1. Bring a large pot of water to a boil over medium-high heat. Add the potatoes. Cook for 10 minutes, or until the potatoes are softened but not mushy. Drain in a colander.

2. In a large bowl, combine the potatoes, celery, scallions, onion, egg, tomato, and dill. Toss well.

3. In a small bowl, whisk together the mayonnaise, mustard, lemon juice, oil, vinegar, honey, parsley, soy sauce, pepper, and celery seed.

4. Pour over the potato mixture and toss well. Serve warm or chilled.

Makes 6 servings

Ingredients Note

The best spuds for salads are boiling potatoes. They have waxy flesh that contains less starch than baking potatoes, so they're less likely to fall apart when boiled. Although this recipe calls for red potatoes, you may also use brown ones.

Creamy Potato Salad with Corn and Peas

Hands-On Time: 15 minutes ■ Total Time: 35 minutes (plus chilling)

Dress up plain potato salad for pennies with an assortment of vegetables from the freezer. You can use low-fat sour cream and light or fat-free mayonnaise, if you prefer.

5 cups cubed potatoes	½ teaspoon ground black pepper
¾ cup sour cream	½ cup frozen whole kernel corn, thawed
¼ cup mayonnaise	½ cup frozen peas, thawed
¼ cup minced fresh parsley	¼ cup frozen chopped red bell peppers, thawed
2 tablespoons minced fresh basil	

1. Bring a large pot of water to a boil over medium-high heat. Add the potatoes. Cook for 10 minutes, or until the potatoes are softened but not mushy. Drain in a colander.

2. In a large bowl, combine the sour cream, mayonnaise, parsley, basil, and black pepper. Mix well.

3. Add the corn, peas, red peppers, and potatoes. Toss well to coat. Cover and refrigerate for 20 minutes, or until chilled.

Makes 4 servings

Ingredients Note

Ounce for ounce, potato skins are the most nutritious part of the potato, providing most of the iron, calcium, and fiber. If you prefer to peel your potatoes for this salad, save the skins for a fun snack that's hard to resist. Scrub the potatoes well, then peel them slightly thicker than normal, trying to get large pieces. Place the potato peels in a bowl and coat with cooking spray. Sprinkle with ground black pepper, grated Parmesan cheese, and a pinch of salt, and toss well to coat. Coat a large baking sheet with cooking spray. Spread the peels on the baking sheet. Bake at 400°F for 10 minutes, or until crisp and golden brown. Eat right away or refrigerate in a plastic container. To crisp, place on a baking sheet in a 400°F oven for 5 to 8 minutes.

Cajun Potato Salad

Your family will never complain about boring spuds salad again after a taste of this quick and easy Louisiana specialty. Offer it with fried chicken, grilled catfish, or Blackened Snapper (page 193).

½ cup mayonnaise

1½ teaspoons Cajun seasoning mix

1 can (16 ounces) sweet potatoes or yams, rinsed, drained, and patted dry

1 can (14 ounces) white potatoes, rinsed, drained, and patted dry

⅓ cup chopped red, yellow, and/or green bell pepper

⅓ cup chopped celery

⅓ cup chopped fresh parsley

1 bunch scallions, white and light green parts, sliced (½ cup)

In a large bowl, combine the mayonnaise and seasoning mix. Stir to mix well. Add the sweet potatoes, white potatoes, pepper, celery, parsley, and scallions. Stir to coat thoroughly with the dressing. Cover and refrigerate for at least 1 hour or up to several hours to chill.

Makes 4 to 6 servings

Shortcut

Store the canned sweet potatoes or yams and the white potatoes in the refrigerator to eliminate the chilling time for the salad.

Ingredients Note

Cajun seasoning mixes are available in most supermarkets. They typically contain salt, ground red pepper, paprika, black and white pepper, and onion and garlic powder.

Summery Pasta Salad

Hands-On Time: 25 minutes ■ Total Time: 50 minutes

Loaded with vegetables and beans, this hearty salad works as a meal in itself. Follow it with a summery dessert of blueberry or strawberry shortcake (see pages 340 and 342).

8 ounces rotelle pasta

3 tablespoons extra-virgin olive oil

2 tablespoons fresh lime juice

2 teaspoons Dijon mustard

1 clove garlic, minced

1 teaspoon ground cumin

½ teaspoon salt

½ teaspoon ground black pepper

1 can (15 ounces) red kidney beans, rinsed and drained

1 cup shredded sharp Cheddar cheese

1 cup frozen corn, thawed

1 small green bell pepper, chopped

3 plum tomatoes, diced

3 scallions, thinly sliced

¼ cup sliced kalamata olives

1. Bring a large pot of water to a boil. Cook the rotelle according to package directions. Drain and rinse under cold water.

2. Meanwhile, in a serving bowl, combine the oil, lime juice, mustard, garlic, cumin, salt, and black pepper.

3. Add the beans, Cheddar, corn, bell pepper, tomatoes, scallions, olives, and rotelle. Toss to coat well.

Makes 8 servings

Make-Ahead

This salad can be made up to a day in advance and refrigerated in a covered container. The flavors improve after standing.

Variations

Feel free to vary the pasta shape, the variety of beans, and the vegetables, depending on what you have on hand.

Asian Noodle Salad

Hands-On Time: 25 minutes ▮ Total Time: 50 minutes (plus standing)

Flat egg noodles are great for this slightly spicy Asian salad, but you can also use other types of noodles (see Ingredients Note, below). You can make it heartier by adding cooked seafood or chicken.

8 ounces egg noodles

¼ cup chopped fresh cilantro

3 tablespoons reduced-sodium soy sauce

2 tablespoons fresh lemon juice or lime juice

2 tablespoons sugar

1 tablespoon minced garlic

1 teaspoon minced fresh ginger

1 teaspoon sesame oil

1 teaspoon peanut butter

⅛ teaspoon red pepper flakes

1 cup peeled, seeded, and sliced cucumbers

1 cup sliced snow peas

½ cup diced red bell pepper

⅛ teaspoon salt

⅛ teaspoon ground black pepper

1. Bring a large pot of water to a boil. Cook the noodles according to package directions until al dente. Drain well.

2. In a large bowl, combine the cilantro, soy sauce, lemon juice, sugar, garlic, ginger, oil, peanut butter, and red pepper flakes. Stir well. Add the cucumbers, snow peas, bell pepper, and noodles, and toss well. Let stand, covered, at room temperature for 1 hour, stirring occasionally.

3. Add the salt and pepper, toss again, and serve.

Makes 4 servings

Ingredients Note

Asian egg noodles can be purchased dried in Asian markets or large supermarkets.
You could also use cellophane noodles, ramen, or soba noodles.

Tortellini and Broccoli Salad

Hands-On Time: 20 minutes ■ Total Time: 40 minutes

Tortellini makes a wonderful cold salad when tossed with fresh vegetables and a robust vinaigrette. Serve it at your next family picnic.

1 package (16 ounces) cheese- or meat-filled tortellini

3 cups broccoli florets

¼ cup extra-virgin olive oil

2 tablespoons red wine vinegar

1 tablespoon stone-ground mustard

2 cloves garlic, minced

2 teaspoons dried basil

2 teaspoons honey

½ teaspoon salt

½ pint cherry tomatoes, halved

¾ cup shredded Romano cheese

1 small red onion, chopped

4 scallions, sliced

1. Bring a large pot of water to a boil. Cook the tortellini according to package directions until al dente. Add the broccoli during the last 3 minutes of cooking. Rinse under cold water and drain.

2. Meanwhile, in a large bowl, whisk together the oil, vinegar, mustard, garlic, basil, honey, and salt. Add the tomatoes, cheese, onion, and scallions.

3. Add the drained tortellini and broccoli to the bowl. Toss to coat well.

4. Serve immediately or refrigerate for up to 24 hours.

Makes 6 servings

Variation

Choose any type of tortellini that appeals to you. In gourmet markets, you can find tortellini stuffed with three cheeses, with cheese and spinach, with pumpkin, with mushrooms, and more.

Accompaniments

Offer the salad with a crusty Italian bread and good extra-virgin olive oil for dipping. End the meal with Tiramisu Cheesecake (page 320).

A Leafy Greens Glossary

Rich in beta-carotene and other healthful compounds, leafy greens can help protect against cancer, circulatory diseases, and many problems linked to aging. As to which greens are the best, here's a simple, if imperfect, rule: The harder they are to pronounce and the more they cost, the better they taste.

GREEN	APPEARANCE	TASTE
Arugula (roquette)	Long, medium-green, sometimes scalloped leaves	Aggressive peppery taste
Beet	Reddish stems with tender leaves	Mild cabbage flavor
Belgian endive	Tight, elongated head with blanched white to pale yellow-green leaves	Slightly bitter flavor
Chard	Narrow, fan-shaped loose green leaves, with white or red veins and stems	Tastes slightly of mustard
Chicory	Bushy, frizzy head made of thick, crisp, narrow leaves with curly, frilly edges	Ranges from slightly bitter when young to extremely bitter when old
Collard	Large, smooth, silvery green leaves	Tastes like a cross between spinach and watercress
Dandelion	Jagged, medium-green leaves	Young leaves have a pleasant, slightly bitter flavor; older leaves are more pungent
Escarole	Broad, curly-edged, dark green leaves with pale, yellowish heart	Bitter flavor
Kale	Very curly, dark green, coarse leaves with frilly edges	Fresh, grassy flavor
Lettuce, butterhead	Small, round, loosely formed head of soft leaves	Buttery, slightly sweet flavor
Lettuce, loose leaf	Curly, loose, coarse leaves	Mild flavor
Lettuce, oak leaf	Narrow leaves with rounded edges in an oak-leaf pattern; in red and green	Extremely mild flavor with just a hint of sweetness
Lettuce, red leaf	Red-tinged, large, loose leaves	Delicate flavor
Lettuce, romaine	Elongated head with large, medium to dark green leaves that branch out from a white base	Mild, sweet, nutty flavor
Mizuma (mizuna)	Light green, lacy leaves	Mildly bitter, with a slight mustard taste
Radicchio	Red, cabbagelike leaves	Sweetly bitter flavor
Sorrel	Bright green, tongue-shaped leaves	Sour flavor
Spinach	Dark green, tender leaves	Mild but musky flavor
Watercress	Dark green, dime-size glossy leaves	Spicy, peppery flavor

Festive Fruit Salad

Hands-On Time: 25 minutes ▪ Total Time: 25 minutes (plus standing)

This fruit salad is extra refreshing, with a honey-lime dressing and the ripest summer fruits. To enjoy it at other times of the year, simply substitute seasonal fruits.

Honey-Lime Dressing

1 cup plain yogurt

½ cup red raspberries

¼ cup fresh lime juice

2 to 4 tablespoons honey or other sweetener

1 teaspoon vanilla extract

Fruit Salad

2 peaches or nectarines, sliced

1 cup green or red grapes

1 cup honeydew chunks

1 cup pineapple chunks

1 cup red raspberries

1 cup blackberries

Mint leaves, for garnish

1. *To make the honey-lime dressing:* Place the yogurt, raspberries, lime juice, honey, and vanilla extract in a blender. Process until smooth.

2. *To make the fruit salad:* In a large bowl, combine the peaches, grapes, honeydew, pineapple, raspberries, and blackberries. Add the dressing and toss well. Allow to sit for 30 minutes, covered, at room temperature.

3. Garnish with mint leaves just before serving.

Makes 6 servings

Accompaniments

Serve this salad as a light lunch with nut bread and reduced-fat cottage cheese.

Variations

Substitute other fruits that look good in the supermarket. Try strawberries, kiwifruit, cantaloupe, watermelon, papaya, or apricots. In the winter, use apples and pears, and top with a sprinkling of pomegranate seeds.

Sunny Waldorf Salad

Hands-On Time: 20 minutes ■ Total Time: 20 minutes

This Waldorf salad is a contemporary variation on the traditional salad created in the 1890s by Oscar Tschirky, the dining room manager at the Waldorf Hotel in New York City. The original version contained only apples, celery, and a good mayonnaise. Chopped walnuts were added later. Our recipe uses an orange-yogurt dressing instead of mayo and adds oranges, raisins, and cashews.

¾ cup plain yogurt

½ cup orange juice

1½ tablespoons honey

½ teaspoon ground cinnamon

3 apples, cut into ½" chunks

1 large orange, separated into segments

1 stalk celery, chopped

½ cup golden raisins

3 tablespoons coarsely chopped cashews

In a large bowl, combine the yogurt, orange juice, honey, and cinnamon. Add the apples, orange, celery, raisins, and cashews. Toss well to coat.

Makes 6 servings

Variations

Make a main course salad by adding cubed cooked chicken or turkey. You can also add dried cranberries or blueberries or chopped apricots or dates. If you're a fan of blue cheese, sprinkle some on top or add it to the dressing.

Plain & Fancy
Poultry

"Poultry is for the cook what canvas
is for the painter . . ."

—JEAN-ANTHELME BRILLAT-SAVARIN

Roast Chicken with Vegetables

Hands-On Time: 30 minutes ■ Total Time: 2 hours

Roasting vegetables with a whole chicken gives them a lovely caramelized glaze. Be sure to serve the pan juices with this dish—they're brimming with rich flavors.

3 cloves garlic, minced

$\frac{1}{2}$ teaspoon salt

$\frac{1}{2}$ teaspoon ground black pepper

1 broiler-fryer chicken ($3\frac{1}{2}$ pounds)

1 pound small red potatoes, quartered

2 carrots, cut diagonally into $1\frac{1}{2}$" pieces

1 onion, cut into wedges

$\frac{1}{4}$ cup olive oil

3 tablespoons orange juice concentrate, thawed

3 tablespoons red wine vinegar

2 teaspoons fennel seeds, crushed

$\frac{1}{2}$ cup frozen peas

1. Preheat the oven to 375°F.

2. In a small bowl, combine the garlic, salt, and pepper.

3. Rinse the chicken and pat it dry with paper towels. Remove and discard any excess fat from inside the chicken. Place the chicken, breast side up, on a rack in a shallow roasting pan. Using your fingers, gently loosen the skin from the breast meat and spread the garlic mixture under the skin. Press down on the skin to spread the mixture evenly.

4. In a large bowl, combine the potatoes, carrots, onion, oil, orange juice concentrate, vinegar, and fennel seeds. Arrange the vegetable mixture around the chicken in the pan. Roast the chicken, basting occasionally, for 40 minutes. Cover with foil and roast, basting occasionally, for 30 minutes longer. Add the peas to the pan and roast for an additional 10 minutes, or until the chicken is no longer pink in the center and the juices run clear.

5. Remove the chicken to a serving platter. Using a slotted spoon, remove the vegetables to the platter with the chicken. Let stand for 10 minutes. Skim off and discard the fat from the pan drippings. Serve the pan juices alongside the chicken and vegetables.

Makes 6 servings

Accompaniments

Begin this meal with a light salad of mixed greens, and end it
with a plate full of homemade cookies.

Quick Roast Chicken

A halved broiler-fryer cooks more quickly than a whole bird, and it tastes even better than a plain roast chicken, if you treat it to this under-the-skin seasoning rub of lemon and herbs.

1 large lemon	$\frac{1}{2}$ teaspoon dried rosemary
2 cloves garlic, minced	$\frac{1}{2}$ teaspoon ground black pepper
2 teaspoons olive oil	$\frac{1}{4}$ teaspoon salt
1 teaspoon dried thyme	1 broiler-fryer chicken ($3\frac{1}{2}$ pounds), halved

1. Preheat the oven to 475°F. Set a broiler-pan rack or wire cooling rack in a jelly-roll pan and coat the rack with cooking spray.

2. Grate $2\frac{1}{2}$ teaspoons of zest from the lemon. Squeeze 2 tablespoons of juice from the lemon into a cup. Add the lemon zest, garlic, oil, thyme, rosemary, pepper, and salt. Mix well.

3. Rinse the chicken and pat it dry. Using your fingers, gently loosen the skin from the breast and thigh meat and spread half of the herb mixture under the skin. Press down on the skin to spread the mixture evenly. Spread the other half of the herb mixture over both sides of the chicken. Place the chicken halves, cut sides down, on the prepared rack.

4. Roast the chicken for 30 to 35 minutes, or until the skin is crisp and browned and the juices run clear. Transfer the chicken to a platter and let stand for 5 minutes for easier carving.

Makes 6 servings

Ingredients Note

Save money and split a whole chicken yourself. All you need is a good sharp pair of poultry shears. With the chicken breast side up, start at the tail end and use the shears to cut through the rib bones along one side of the breastbone. Then cut along both sides of the backbone to separate the two halves of the chicken. Discard the backbone or save it to make stock.

8 Simple Sauces for Poultry

On a busy night, nothing's easier than broiled, grilled, or poached chicken breasts or turkey cutlets. Wake up your next poultry dinner with these easy and delicious sauces. Each minirecipe makes 4 servings, enough to generously sauce 4 boneless, skinless chicken breasts or turkey cutlets, cooked your favorite way.

1. Caribbean Salsa. Combine 1 finely chopped mango or papaya, ½ cup finely chopped pineapple, 2 tablespoons chopped fresh mint, 2 tablespoons chopped onion, ¼ teaspoon salt, and ¼ teaspoon ground red pepper. Let the sauce rest for 1 hour before serving to develop flavors.

2. Cherry. In a small saucepan, combine ⅓ cup apple jelly, 3 tablespoons orange juice, 2 tablespoons cider vinegar or balsamic vinegar, 2 teaspoons fresh thyme, and ½ teaspoon black pepper. Cook over low heat for about 8 minutes, or until blended. Stir in 1 cup pitted dark cherries and cook until heated through. Serve hot.

3. Lemon Goat Cheese. In a small skillet, brown 1 tablespoon butter. Stir in 1 tablespoon all-purpose flour. Cook for 1 minute. Whisk in 1½ cups chicken broth and cook, stirring constantly, until the sauce boils. Stir in 4 to 6 ounces mild goat cheese (such as Montrachet) and ½ teaspoon grated lemon zest.

4. Mushroom. In a medium nonstick skillet, heat 1 teaspoon olive oil over medium heat. Add 1½ cups sliced mushrooms and ¼ cup finely chopped onion. Cook until the vegetables are softened. Stir in 2 tablespoons balsamic vinegar and 1 tablespoon crushed fresh rosemary or thyme. Cover and cook for 2 minutes. Uncover and boil until the sauce is reduced by half. Season with ¼ teaspoon salt and a pinch of ground black pepper.

5. Peperonata. In a medium nonstick skillet, heat 1 teaspoon olive oil over medium heat. Add ¼ cup diced cooked ham and ¼ cup chopped onion. Cook until the onion is softened. Add ½ cup red and/or green bell pepper strips, ¼ teaspoon dried thyme, and ½ cup chicken broth. Cover and cook until the peppers are softened. Serve with chopped parsley.

6. Santa Fe. In a dry, medium nonstick skillet, toast ¾ teaspoon dried oregano, ½ teaspoon chili powder, and ¼ teaspoon ground cinnamon just until fragrant. Stir in ½ cup rinsed and drained canned black beans and 1 diced tomato. Heat to boiling. Stir in ¼ cup chopped fresh cilantro. Serve with lime wedges and sour cream.

7. Sesame. In a small saucepan, heat ½ teaspoon peanut oil and ½ teaspoon sesame oil. Add 1 minced garlic clove and cook over medium heat for 2 minutes. Add ¾ cup chicken broth, ½ teaspoon grated fresh ginger, ½ teaspoon soy sauce, and ⅛ teaspoon crushed red pepper flakes. Bring to a boil. In a small cup, stir together 2 tablespoons water and 1 teaspoon cornstarch until smooth. Whisk the cornstarch mixture into the sauce and cook, stirring constantly, until thickened and boiling. Serve with toasted sesame seeds.

8. Tomatillo Salsa. Roast 12 ounces fresh peeled tomatillos under the broiler, turning frequently, until softened and blackened on all sides. Transfer to a food processor or blender. Meanwhile, in a medium nonstick skillet, heat 3 teaspoons olive oil. Add 1 medium chopped onion and 2 chopped garlic cloves. Cook until softened. Transfer to the food processor or blender. Add 1 small minced jalapeño chile pepper and 1 tablespoon fresh lime juice. Pulse until the ingredients form a coarse purée.

Lemon-Rosemary Chicken Breasts

Hands-On Time: 15 minutes ■ Total Time: 45 minutes

Here's a quick dinner that you can put together even when there's no time to shop. You can keep all the ingredients on hand, including the fresh rosemary (see Kitchen Tip, below). Of course, you could also use dried rosemary instead of fresh. If you're substituting the dried herb, crumble it between your fingers to release its fragrance.

2 large lemons

2 tablespoons light brown sugar

1½ teaspoons coarsely chopped fresh rosemary leaves or ½ teaspoon dried

¼ teaspoon salt

¼ teaspoon ground black pepper

4 bone-in, skinless chicken breast halves (2 pounds)

1 teaspoon cornstarch

1 tablespoon cold water

Fresh rosemary sprigs for garnish (optional)

1. Preheat the oven to 400°F. Coat a 13" x 9" baking pan with cooking spray.

2. Grate 2 teaspoons of zest from 1 lemon, then halve the lemon and squeeze 3 tablespoons of juice from it into a shallow, medium bowl. Cut the other lemon into thin slices, discarding the ends.

3. Add the lemon zest, sugar, rosemary, salt, and pepper to the bowl of lemon juice, and whisk to blend. One at time, dip the chicken breasts into the lemon mixture, turning to coat both sides.

4. Arrange the chicken, skin side up, in the prepared pan and place some of the lemon slices on top of each piece. (If any of the lemon mixture remains in the bowl, spoon it over the chicken.) Bake, basting twice with the pan juices, for 25 to 30 minutes, or until the chicken is no longer pink in the center and the juices run clear.

5. Transfer the chicken to 4 serving plates. Pour the pan juices into a small saucepan. Dissolve the cornstarch in the water and stir it into the saucepan. Bring to a boil over medium heat, stirring constantly, until thickened. Spoon the pan juices over the chicken. Garnish with rosemary sprigs, if desired.

Makes 4 servings

Kitchen Tip

Wrap fresh rosemary in a paper towel, place it in a small plastic bag, and store it in the crisper drawer of the refrigerator. It will keep for up to 10 days.

Accompaniments

Garlicky Green Beans (page 286) or yellow wax beans (or a mix of the two) and crisp rolls make this meal complete.

Chicken with Creamy Mustard Sauce

Hands-On Time: 20 minutes ■ Total Time: 20 minutes

This simple dish is elegant enough for your fussiest guest. Chicken cutlets bathed in a thyme-mustard cream sauce make an impressive main dish that comes together in about 20 minutes.

3 tablespoons butter

4 thin, boneless, skinless chicken breasts (1 pound)

2 large shallots, sliced

½ teaspoon dried thyme

1 tablespoon all-purpose flour

¾ cup chicken broth

1 tablespoon Dijon mustard

¼ cup half-and-half or heavy cream

1. In a large skillet, heat 2 tablespoons of the butter over medium-high heat. Add the chicken and cook, turning occasionally, for 5 minutes, or until browned and no longer pink in the center. Remove to a serving platter and keep warm.

2. In the same skillet, heat the remaining 1 tablespoon butter over medium-high heat. Add the shallots and thyme. Cook, stirring occasionally, for about 4 minutes, or until the shallots are softened. Sprinkle the flour over the shallots and cook, stirring constantly, for 1 minute longer.

3. Stir in the broth and mustard. Bring to a boil and continue boiling, stirring frequently, for 1 minute, or until the sauce is slightly thickened. Stir in the cream and heat through.

4. Spoon the sauce over the chicken and serve.

Makes 4 servings

Kitchen Tip

If you can't get thin chicken breasts, pound thicker breasts between two sheets of plastic wrap using the back of a heavy frying pan.

Accompaniments

Serve the chicken with Millet Pilaf (page 274) and Minted Sugar Snap Peas (page 300) for a lovely presentation.

Basil Chicken with Potatoes

Potatoes cooked in the same pan with a whole chicken come out crisp, savory—and high in fat, having soaked up the greasy drippings from the meat. But when you're cooking skinless chicken breasts, that's not a problem. Here the chicken, potatoes, and tomatoes are kept moist with a basil-garlic rub that's made with just 2 teaspoons of healthy olive oil. To speed preparation of this meal, the potatoes are parboiled for 5 minutes before they go into the oven.

1½ cups firmly packed basil leaves

¼ cup chicken broth

2 cloves garlic, peeled

2 teaspoons olive oil

½ teaspoon dried thyme

½ teaspoon ground black pepper

½ teaspoon salt

4 bone-in, skinless chicken breast halves (2 pounds)

1 pound small red potatoes, cut into wedges

6 plum tomatoes, cut into wedges

8 green or black olives, pitted and halved

1. Coat a 13" x 9" baking pan with cooking spray.

2. In a food processor, combine the basil, broth, garlic, oil, thyme, pepper, and salt, and process until puréed. Place the chicken in the prepared pan and use ¼ cup of the basil mixture to rub both sides of each breast. Set aside.

3. Preheat the oven to 425°F.

4. Place the potatoes in a medium saucepan and cover with cold water. Cover the pan and bring to a boil over high heat, then reduce the heat to medium and simmer for 5 minutes. Drain the potatoes.

5. Arrange the potatoes and tomatoes around the chicken and spoon the remaining basil mixture over the vegetables. Sprinkle the olives over the chicken and vegetables.

6. Bake for 25 minutes, or until the chicken is no longer pink in the center and the juices run clear and the potatoes are softened.

Makes 4 servings

Accompaniments

Start with a salad of Bibb or Boston lettuce. Use a little sesame oil in the vinaigrette and sprinkle the greens with toasted sesame seeds.

Chicken Kebabs

Hands-On Time: 40 minutes ■ Total Time: 40 minutes (plus marinating)

Kebabs are always great fun. Here each guest gets two colorful skewers.

3 tablespoons olive oil

3 tablespoons balsamic vinegar

2 tablespoons maple syrup

1 tablespoon stone-ground Dijon mustard

2 cloves garlic, minced

¼ teaspoon ground black pepper

¼ teaspoon salt

1 pound boneless, skinless chicken breasts, cut into 1" pieces

2 red and/or green bell peppers, cut into 1" pieces

1 large onion, cut into 1" pieces

1. In a 13" × 9" baking dish, combine the oil, vinegar, maple syrup, mustard, garlic, black pepper, and salt. Thread the chicken, bell peppers, and onion alternately onto 8 metal skewers. Lay the skewers in the baking dish and baste with the marinade. Cover and refrigerate for up to 3 hours, turning occasionally.

2. Coat a grill rack or broiler pan with cooking spray and heat to medium-high.

3. Grill the skewers, turning occasionally, for 12 to 14 minutes, or until the chicken is no longer pink in the center and the vegetables are softened.

Makes 4 servings

Make-Ahead

If you like lots of grilled veggies with your chicken, start early. Make extra marinade and grill extra onions and bell peppers earlier in the day. The vegetables are delicious at room temperature with a touch more balsamic added just before serving.

Greek-Style Lemon-Garlic Chicken

Hands-On Time: 15 minutes ■ Total Time: 1 hour

As the lemon slices roast, the natural sugars caramelize, providing a tantalizing accompaniment to the herbed chicken. This recipe is designed to provide chicken for two meals—that's why you'll be buying 7 pounds! Three of the breasts are used to make Chicken Cacciatore on Polenta on page 99.

10 bone-in chicken breast halves (7 pounds)

½ cup olive oil

1 lemon, thinly sliced

8 cloves garlic, halved

8 bay leaves

1 teaspoon dried oregano

1 teaspoon ground black pepper

½ teaspoon salt

1. Preheat the oven to 400°F.

2. Place the chicken in a large baking pan. Add the oil, lemon, garlic, bay leaves, oregano, pepper, and salt. Toss to coat all the chicken pieces. Overlap the chicken breasts slightly, if necessary. Tuck the garlic and bay leaves underneath the chicken. Place the lemon slices over the chicken.

3. Bake for about 45 minutes, or until the chicken is no longer pink in the center and the juices run clear. Set aside 3 breast halves to cool completely. When cool, place them in a zip-top bag and refrigerate for up to 3 days. Use these chicken breasts to make Chicken Cacciatore on Polenta (page 99).

4. Meanwhile, place the remaining chicken on a platter. Remove and discard the bay leaves. Skim off and discard any fat in the baking pan. Smash the garlic and leave it in the pan, along with the lemon slices. Place the pan over medium heat and cook for 2 minutes, scraping with a spatula to remove all the browned bits. Pour the heated pan juices, lemon, and garlic over the chicken before serving.

Makes 4 to 6 servings

Accompaniments

Serve this dish with Buttermilk Mashed Potatoes (page 305). You could also precede the chicken with Orange-Scented Cucumber Salad (page 70).

Chicken Cacciatore on Polenta

Hands-On Time: 20 minutes ■ Total Time: 25 minutes

This Italian chicken stew is also wonderful served with country-style bread or spooned over cooked pasta.

¼ cup olive oil

1 onion, sliced

1 red bell pepper, sliced

3 ounces mushrooms, sliced

3 Greek-Style Lemon-Garlic Chicken breasts (see page 97), boned, skinned, and cut or torn into chunks

2 cans (14.5 ounces each) diced basil-garlic-oregano-seasoned tomatoes, with juice

½ teaspoon ground black pepper

½ teaspoon salt

1 tube (16 ounces) refrigerated basil-garlic polenta, cut into ½"-thick slices

1. In a large skillet, heat the oil over medium heat. Add the onion, bell pepper, and mushrooms. Stir to combine. Cover and cook, stirring occasionally, for about 4 minutes, or until the mushrooms are browned.

2. Add the chicken and tomatoes (with juice) to the skillet. Add the black pepper and salt. Bring the mixture to a brisk simmer, reduce the heat, and simmer gently for 10 minutes.

3. Meanwhile, place the polenta in a single layer on a microwaveable plate. Cover with wax paper. Microwave on high power for 2 minutes, or until heated. Spoon the stew over the polenta.

Makes 4 to 6 servings

Ingredients Note

Cacciatore means "hunter style," and rustic mushrooms are a signature ingredient of this dish. Instead of using white button mushrooms, try cremini, which have a more intense flavor. You could also use shiitake or more expensive chanterelles.

Chicken Fajitas

Hands-On Time: 30 minutes ■ Total Time: 40 minutes (plus marinating)

With a little advance preparation, fajitas are a quick and easy dinner dish the whole family will enjoy. They're also another tasty way to work low-fat, high-protein chicken breast into your menus.

2½ tablespoons fresh lime juice

2 cloves garlic, minced

2 teaspoons olive oil

½ teaspoon red pepper flakes

¾ pound boneless, skinless chicken breasts, cut into ½" strips

4 large flour tortillas

½ cup mashed avocado

½ teaspoon minced jalapeño pepper or other chile pepper (wear plastic gloves when handling)

1 cup refrigerated or jarred salsa

1 cup low-fat or fat-free plain yogurt

¼ cup minced fresh cilantro

1. In a cup, combine 2 tablespoons of the lime juice with the garlic, oil, and red pepper flakes.

2. Place the chicken in a large bowl. Add the garlic mixture, toss to coat, and refrigerate, covered, for at least 2 hours or up to 24 hours.

3. About 10 minutes before serving, preheat the oven to 350°F. Wrap the tortillas in foil and place them in the oven to warm while the chicken is cooking.

4. In a small bowl, combine the avocado and jalapeño pepper with the remaining ½ tablespoon lime juice. Set aside.

5. Coat a large nonstick skillet or grill rack with cooking spray. Heat over medium-high heat until very hot. Add the chicken strips, a few at a time, and cook, turning once, for 5 to 7 minutes, or until browned.

6. To serve, allow guests to make their own fajitas as follows: Place some chicken on a tortilla and top with a spoonful each of the avocado mixture, salsa, and yogurt. Sprinkle with some of the cilantro. Roll up to enclose the filling. Top with more salsa, yogurt, and cilantro.

Makes 4 servings

Accompaniments

Serve the fajitas with Mexican Red Rice and Beans (page 258) and
Calico Slaw with Poppy Seed Dressing (page 69).

Chicken Curry in a Hurry

Hands-On Time: 25 minutes ■ Total Time: 35 minutes

If curry is new to your cooking repertoire, this dish is for you. Tomatoes, onion, and bell pepper blend with sweet raisins and pungent curry powder to create a mild yet flavorful sauce. Serve over couscous or rice.

2 tablespoons olive oil

1 pound boneless, skinless chicken breast halves, cut into 1" pieces

1 onion, cut into wedges

1 red bell pepper, chopped

1½ teaspoons curry powder

¼ teaspoon ground allspice

1 can (14.5 ounces) diced tomatoes, with juice

¼ cup raisins

1. In a large nonstick skillet, heat 1 tablespoon of the oil over medium-high heat. Add the chicken and cook, stirring occasionally, for 5 minutes, or until browned. Remove to a plate and keep warm.

2. In the same skillet, heat the remaining 1 tablespoon oil over medium-high heat. Add the onion, pepper, curry powder, and allspice. Cook, stirring occasionally, for 5 minutes, or until the vegetables are softened.

3. Stir in the tomatoes (with juice), raisins, and chicken. Bring to a boil. Reduce the heat to low, cover, and simmer for 5 minutes, or until the chicken is no longer pink in the center.

Makes 4 servings

Ingredients Note

The blend of spices in curry powder can vary widely, but it is generally a mix of turmeric, cardamom, coriander, cumin, fenugreek, ground cinnamon, and ground white, black, and/or red pepper. Homemade definitely beats the commercial blends sold in supermarkets. To make your own, in a small dry skillet, heat 2 teaspoons peppercorns and 4 teaspoons each cumin seeds, coriander seeds, and cardamom seeds, until lightly toasted. Transfer to a spice grinder and grind to a fine powder. Stir in 2 tablespoons turmeric and ¾ teaspoon each ground cinnamon and fenugreek. This makes about ½ cup and can be stored indefinitely in an airtight container.

Chicken Lo Mein

Hands-On Time: 35 minutes ■ Total Time: 40 minutes

The flavors of Asia are abundant in this colorful dish. Serve the chicken with a spinach and mandarin orange salad with ginger vinaigrette to complete the meal. For a fun finish, offer fortune cookies for dessert.

8 ounces lo mein noodles or thin spaghetti

2 tablespoons sesame oil

1 pound boneless, skinless chicken breasts, cut into thin strips

1 onion, chopped

1 large red bell pepper, chopped

2 large cloves garlic, minced

1 cup snow peas

½ cup chicken broth

3 tablespoons rice wine vinegar

3 tablespoons soy sauce

1 tablespoon freshly grated ginger

1. Bring a large pot of water to a boil. Cook the noodles according to package directions until al dente.

2. Meanwhile, in a large nonstick skillet, heat 1 tablespoon of the oil over medium-high heat. Add the chicken and cook, stirring occasionally, for about 6 minutes, or until browned and no longer pink in the center. Remove to a plate and keep warm.

3. In the same skillet, heat the remaining 1 tablespoon oil over medium-high heat. Add the onion, pepper, garlic, and snow peas. Cook, stirring occasionally, for about 8 minutes, or until crisp-tender. Stir in the broth, vinegar, soy sauce, and ginger. Cook for 2 minutes. Add the chicken and noodles, stir well, and heat through.

Makes 4 servings

Ingredients Note

Rice wine vinegar, made from fermented rice, is sold in supermarkets, but it doesn't hold a candle to the higher-quality product sold in Asian markets. If you don't have a local Asian market, you can also shop for it online.

Mediterranean Chicken Thighs

Hands-On Time: 30 minutes ■ Total Time: 1 hour

This French-inspired dish is good dinner party fare because it can easily be doubled or tripled.
Serve it with steamed asparagus and cooked pasta tossed with a splash of extra-virgin olive
oil and chopped fresh basil or parsley.

1	teaspoon olive oil	⅛	teaspoon dried rosemary
1½	cups sliced onion	⅛	teaspoon dried thyme
1	tablespoon minced garlic		Pinch of red pepper flakes
1	green bell pepper, thinly sliced	1¼	pounds boneless, skinless chicken thighs
1	yellow bell pepper, thinly sliced	2	teaspoons red wine vinegar
10	whole Niçoise olives or 5 pitted black olives, chopped	⅛	teaspoon ground black pepper
¼	teaspoon fennel seeds		

1. Preheat the oven to 425°F.

2. In a large, nonstick skillet, heat the oil over medium heat. Add the onion and garlic. Cook, stirring frequently, for 4 to 5 minutes, or until the onion is translucent.

3. Add the bell peppers. Cook, stirring frequently, for 5 to 6 minutes, or until softened. Add the olives, fennel, rosemary, thyme, and red pepper flakes. Cook, stirring, for 1 minute longer.

4. Place the chicken in a shallow baking dish and arrange in a single layer. Drizzle with the vinegar and sprinkle with the black pepper. Spoon the vegetable mixture over the chicken.

5. Bake for 25 to 30 minutes, or until the chicken is no longer pink in the center and the juices run clear.

Makes 4 servings

Shortcut

See page 46 for the fastest way to skin chicken thighs. (Buying them with the skin
on and removing the skin yourself is cheaper than buying them skinless.)

Variations

Use chicken cutlets instead of thighs. They may cook a little faster than the thighs,
so check for doneness after 15 minutes. If yellow peppers are not available,
use all green or a mixture of red and green.

Chicken Problem Solvers

Here are a few quick tips to keep your chicken delicious every time.

- **To keep chicken pieces from drying out in the refrigerator:** Soak a large, thick kitchen towel in ice water, wring it well, and use it to line a large, rimmed baking sheet. Arrange the chicken pieces in a single layer on top of the wet towel and cover loosely with wax paper. The chicken will remain moist in the refrigerator for up to 12 hours.

- **To evenly cook boneless, skinless breasts:** Position the breasts in a hot pan so that the thin, tapered ends are toward the pan edges, where foods tend to cook more slowly. It also helps to remove the small tenderloin, which cooks up in just a few minutes. Or use the dull side of a chef's knife to pound each breast to an even thickness.

- **To evenly cook mixed chicken pieces:** Legs and wings will cook faster than breasts and thighs, so add the legs and wings halfway through the cooking time. If the legs and wings cook through before the breasts and thighs, pull them from the heat and cover with foil while the other pieces finish cooking.

- **To get a crisp, golden skin on roasted chicken:** Rub the bird all over with mayonnaise before roasting, or baste periodically with melted butter.

- **To keep breast meat moist on a roasted chicken:** Set the chicken in the roasting pan, breast side down.

- **To lift a hot, roasted chicken onto a carving board:** Insert a long-handled wooden spoon into the hollow of the carcass, lift, and transfer.

- **To salvage a dry, overcooked chicken:** Chop the chicken into small pieces and use to prepare a chicken salad. Or slice the chicken into thin pieces on the diagonal and serve with a quick sauce (see page 90), chutney, or gravy.

- **To save a stew that has overcooked pieces of bone-in chicken:** Shred the meat off the bone and add it back to the stew just before serving.

Creamy Blue Cheese Chicken

Hands-On Time: 10 minutes ■ Total Time: 1 hour 5 minutes

This delicious dish requires almost no prep because you're buying bagged carrots, prepared Alfredo sauce, and precrumbled blue cheese. It's perfect for those nights when you don't have a lot of energy for cooking.

1 bag (1 pound) baby carrots

1 container (10 ounces) refrigerated Alfredo sauce

1 cup milk

1 cup orzo

2 to 2½ pounds boneless, skinless chicken thighs

1 bunch scallions, white and light green parts, sliced (½ cup)

1 teaspoon ground black pepper

½ teaspoon poultry seasoning

¼ cup dried bread crumbs

¾ cup precrumbled blue cheese

1. Preheat the oven to 375°F. Coat a 13" × 9" glass or ceramic baking dish with cooking spray.

2. Place the carrots in an 8" × 8" microwaveable baking dish. Add enough water to come ¼" up the sides of the dish. Cover with plastic wrap, leaving a small corner vent. Microwave on high power for 4 minutes, or until partially cooked. Drain and set aside.

3. Meanwhile, in a bowl, whisk the Alfredo sauce and milk until smooth. Pour half of the mixture into the prepared dish. Sprinkle the uncooked orzo evenly over the sauce. Top with the chicken, scallions, pepper, poultry seasoning, and the carrots.

4. Pour the remaining sauce evenly over the top. Sprinkle on the bread crumbs and then the cheese. Cover with foil and bake for 40 minutes. Remove the foil and bake for 10 minutes longer, or until the chicken is no longer pink in the center and the juices run clear.

Makes 4 to 6 servings

Make-Ahead

You can assemble the ingredients in the baking dish, cover with foil,
and refrigerate for a day before baking.

Accompaniments

Cleaned and trimmed sugar snap peas would add color and crunch to this meal.
Serve them on the side, either raw or stir-fried for 1 minute in a hot skillet lightly
coated with oil. Season with a squeeze of fresh lemon juice and salt to taste.

Crumbly Baked Chicken

Hands-On Time: 25 minutes ▪ Total Time: 1 hour 5 minutes

With a flavor similar to fried chicken, these baked chicken parts are coated with a zesty, flavorful crust. The good news is that they are just as delicious as fried, but with a fraction of the fat.

¼ cup all-purpose flour

1 tablespoon crab-boil seasoning

½ teaspoon salt

2 eggs

¾ cup cornflake crumbs

3 tablespoons grated Parmesan cheese

1 broiler-fryer chicken (3 to 3½ pounds), cut into serving pieces and skin removed

1. Preheat the oven to 400°F. Coat a 13" × 9" baking pan with cooking spray.

2. In a shallow bowl, combine the flour, crab-boil seasoning, and salt. In another shallow bowl, beat the eggs. In a third shallow bowl, combine the cornflake crumbs and Parmesan.

3. Dip the chicken into the flour mixture, shaking off the excess. Dip it into the beaten eggs, then evenly coat it with the crumb mixture. Arrange the chicken in the prepared pan.

4. Bake for 40 minutes, or until the chicken is no longer pink in the center and the juices run clear.

Makes 4 servings

Ingredients Note

For a really delicious dish, buy Parmigiano-Reggiano or Pecorino Romano
and grate it yourself. Reggiano is expensive, but the flavor is well worth the
price, and it keeps well in the fridge if wrapped in foil (not plastic wrap).

Variation

Add a fresh or dried herb of your choice to the coating.

Chicken with Cranberry-Orange Sauce

Hands-On Time: 20 minutes ■ Total Time: 20 minutes

A sweet-tart sauce bathes these tender chicken thighs. For a fancier presentation, use boneless, skinless breasts in place of the thighs.

1 pound boneless, skinless chicken thighs	1½ cups fresh or frozen cranberries
½ teaspoon salt	¼ cup orange juice
¼ teaspoon cracked black pepper	⅓ cup packed brown sugar
2 tablespoons olive oil	⅛ teaspoon ground cinnamon
⅓ cup chicken broth	

1. Season the chicken with the salt and pepper.

2. In a large nonstick skillet, heat the oil over medium-high heat. Add the chicken and cook, turning occasionally, for about 6 minutes, or until browned. Add the broth and bring to a boil over high heat. Reduce the heat to low, cover, and simmer for 8 minutes, or until the chicken is no longer pink in the center and the juices run clear.

3. Meanwhile, in a medium saucepan, combine the cranberries, orange juice, sugar, and cinnamon. Bring to a boil over high heat. Reduce the heat to medium-low and simmer, stirring frequently, for about 4 minutes, or until the cranberries pop.

4. Remove the chicken from the skillet and place on a serving platter. Return the skillet to the heat and increase the heat to high. Add the cranberry mixture to the skillet and cook for 2 minutes, stirring constantly. Pour the sauce over the chicken.

Makes 4 servings

Nutri-Note

Cranberries are a rich source of procyanidins, phytochemicals that may offer protection against cancer and cardiovascular disease.

Freezing Tip

Fresh cranberries freeze well. You can put bags of cranberries in the freezer with no further preparation, and they don't need to be thawed before use.

Grilled Southwestern-Style Drumsticks

Hands-On Time: 25 minutes ■ Total Time: 35 minutes (plus marinating)

Kids will love this dinner—but use cider rather than dark beer, along with mild chili powder when you're making this dish for them. And since it's so easy to prepare, you'll love the convenience.

1 tablespoon chili powder	1 teaspoon ground cumin
1 tablespoon garlic powder	½ teaspoon salt
1 tablespoon onion powder	1 cup dark beer or apple cider
1 tablespoon paprika	8 chicken drumsticks, skin removed

1. In a zip-top plastic bag, combine the chili powder, garlic powder, onion powder, paprika, cumin, and salt. Shake the bag to mix. Add the beer and drumsticks. Shake well. Refrigerate for 20 minutes or up to 24 hours, turning occasionally.

2. Remove the drumsticks from the bag and place them on a plate. Reserve the marinade.

3. Coat a grill rack or broiler pan with cooking spray and heat to medium-high. Grill or broil the chicken for 20 minutes, or until it is well-browned and the juices run clear. Turn and baste with the reserved marinade occasionally during the first 15 minutes. Discard any remaining marinade.

Makes 4 servings

Accompaniments

Serve the drumsticks with Summery Pasta Salad (page 80) and lots of lemonade.
For dessert, have Four-Berry Pie (page 325).

Grilled Chicken Burgers
with Vegetable Salsa

Hands-On Time: 40 minutes ■ Total Time: 40 minutes

These burgers are terrific for lunch or a casual supper. If you like, you can lightly toast hamburger buns on the upper grill rack, then top the burgers with crispy greens and the vegetable salsa.

Burgers

1¼ pounds ground chicken

½ cup shredded mozzarella or Monterey Jack cheese

2 cloves garlic, minced

½ teaspoon salt

¼ teaspoon ground black pepper

4 hamburger buns (optional)

Salsa

1 tablespoon extra-virgin olive oil

1 tablespoon balsamic vinegar

¼ teaspoon salt

½ yellow bell pepper, chopped

½ small cucumber, peeled, seeded, and chopped

½ small red onion, finely chopped

½ tomato, seeded and diced

1. *To make the chicken burgers:* In a medium bowl, combine the chicken, cheese, garlic, salt, and black pepper just until blended. Shape into 4 patties.

2. *To make the salsa:* In a medium bowl, whisk together the oil, vinegar, and salt. Add the bell pepper, cucumber, onion, and tomato. Toss to coat well. Set aside.

3. Coat a grill rack or broiler pan with cooking spray and heat to medium-high.

4. Grill or broil the burgers for 20 minutes, or until the meat is no longer pink in the center and the juices run clear.

5. Serve the burgers on buns, if using. Top each patty with salsa.

Makes 4 servings

Ingredients Note

Cut a pound of boneless, skinless chicken breasts into chunks, place them in a food processor, and pulse until the chicken is ground as you like it. Be sure to use the pulse option, so the chicken retains some texture and does not turn into a paste.

Chicken Stew with Cider and Herbs

Hands-On Time: 30 minutes ■ Total Time: 1 hour 15 minutes

Although this stew is great any time of year, it's especially welcome in autumn, when cider is at its freshest. It's a really hearty one-dish meal that needs no extra accompaniment. You can serve the stew over rice instead of noodles, if you prefer.

3 tablespoons olive oil

1 broiler-fryer chicken (3 to 3½ pounds), cut into serving pieces and skinned

½ cup plus 3 tablespoons water

2 large onions, thinly sliced

2 cups sliced mushrooms

8 whole pitted prunes

1 teaspoon minced garlic

2 bay leaves

½ teaspoon ground nutmeg

½ teaspoon dried thyme

2 cups cider

8 ounces egg noodles

2 tablespoons cornstarch

1. Preheat the oven to 400°F. Bring a large pot of water to a boil.

2. In a large, heavy saucepan or Dutch oven, heat the oil over medium-high heat. Add the chicken and cook, turning, for 8 to 10 minutes, or until browned on all sides. Transfer to a plate.

3. Add ½ cup of the water to the pan and scrape the bottom with a wooden spoon to loosen any browned bits. Bring the water to a simmer and add the onions. Cover and simmer for 10 minutes, or until the onions are softened.

4. Add the mushrooms, prunes, garlic, bay leaves, nutmeg, and thyme. Cover and cook for 10 minutes, or until the vegetables are softened.

5. Add the cider and chicken to the pan. Cover and place in the oven. Bake for 25 minutes, or until the chicken is no longer pink in the center and the juices run clear.

6. Meanwhile, cook the noodles according to package directions until al dente. Drain them and keep them warm. In a cup, stir the cornstarch into the remaining 3 tablespoons water until smooth. Set aside.

7. Transfer the chicken to a serving platter and cover loosely with foil to keep it warm. Remove and discard the bay leaves. Add the reserved cornstarch mixture to the liquid in the pan. Stir over medium heat until thickened. Serve the chicken and sauce over the noodles.

Makes 4 servings

Ingredients Note

When fresh cider is out of season, you can use apple juice.

Chicken Potpie

Hands-On Time: 45 minutes ■ Total Time: 1 hour 10 minutes

What's homier than chicken potpie? Here buttermilk biscuits replace the traditional top crust.

Chicken Filling

3 cups plus 3 tablespoons chicken broth

1 cup thinly sliced celery

⅔ cup sliced green beans

⅔ cup thinly sliced carrots

⅔ cup diced red bell pepper

¼ to ½ cup 1% milk

1 tablespoon olive oil

½ cup chopped onion

⅓ cup whole wheat flour

2 tablespoons minced fresh parsley

1 teaspoon reduced-sodium soy sauce

½ teaspoon dried sage

½ teaspoon dried thyme

2 cups cubed cooked chicken breast

Biscuits

1 cup all-purpose flour

¾ cup whole wheat flour

2 teaspoons baking powder

½ teaspoon baking soda

3 tablespoons butter

¾ to 1 cup buttermilk

1 teaspoon honey

½ teaspoon reduced-sodium soy sauce

1. *To make the chicken filling:* Preheat the oven to 400°F. In a large saucepan, combine 3 cups of the broth with the celery, beans, carrots, and pepper. Bring to a boil over high heat and boil for 5 minutes. Strain the broth into a 4-cup glass measuring cup and add enough milk to make 3 cups. Reserve the vegetables.

2. In a large skillet, heat the oil over medium heat. Add the onion and cook for 2 to 3 minutes, stirring frequently. Stir in the remaining 3 tablespoons broth, then add the flour and cook for 1 minute. Gradually whisk in the milk mixture. Add the parsley, soy sauce, sage, and thyme. Cook over low heat, stirring constantly, until thickened. Add the chicken and the vegetables.

3. Coat 4 small casseroles (2 to 2½ cups each) with cooking spray. Divide the chicken mixture among the dishes.

4. *To make the biscuits:* Sift the all-purpose flour, whole wheat flour, baking powder, and baking soda into a large bowl. Using 2 knives, cut the butter into the flour until the mixture resembles coarse meal.

5. In a small bowl, whisk ¾ cup of the buttermilk with the honey and the soy sauce. Pour over the flour mixture and stir gently with a fork to moisten the flour. If the dough is too dry, mix in a little more buttermilk. Turn the dough out onto a lightly floured surface and divide it into 4 pieces. Pat each piece into a circle. Place over the chicken. Bake for 20 minutes.

Makes 4 servings

Cornish Hens
with Pineapple-Cornbread Stuffing

Hands-On Time: 25 minutes ■ Total Time: 1 hour 40 minutes

By halving the hens before roasting, you can serve each of your guests a generous portion of hen and stuffing without fussing with carving at the table.

2 teaspoons butter	¼ cup chopped water chestnuts
⅓ cup chopped celery	¼ teaspoon dried thyme
⅓ cup chopped scallions	1½ cups cornbread stuffing mix
1 can (8 ounces) crushed pineapple, packed in juice	4 Cornish game hens (1 to 1½ pounds each), split in half

1. Preheat the oven to 350°F.

2. In a medium nonstick skillet, melt the butter over medium heat. Add the celery and scallions, and cook until crisp-tender. Stir in the pineapple (with juice), water chestnuts, and thyme. Transfer the mixture to a large bowl. Add the stuffing mix and toss lightly to combine.

3. Spoon about ⅓ cup of the stuffing mixture into the cavity of each hen half.

4. Coat eight 9" × 6" pieces of foil with butter-flavored cooking spray. Cover the stuffing in each hen half with a piece of foil, crimping the edges to secure.

5. Place the hens, breast side up, on a rack in a shallow roasting pan.

6. Roast for 1 hour 5 minutes to 1 hour 15 minutes, or until the hens are tender and the juices run clear. Carefully remove the foil before serving.

Makes 8 servings

Kitchen Tip

Use kitchen shears to split the Cornish hens down the backbone.
Then turn the birds over and split them along the breastbone.

Ingredients Note

If you have leftover homemade cornbread, you can use it for the stuffing,
instead of the packaged mix. Season it to your liking.

Accompaniments

This game hen is delicious served with Balsamic Broccoli Rabe (page 289).

Grilled Garlic-Lime Game Hens

Hands-On Time: 10 minutes ■ Total Time: 30 minutes (plus standing)

Freshly squeezed lime juice and fresh garlic make all the difference in this recipe. Serve the hens with rice, potatoes, or couscous. Remove the skin before eating, if you are diet-conscious.

2 Cornish game hens (1½ pounds each), split in half

¼ cup plus 2 tablespoons fresh lime juice

1 tablespoon grated lime zest

3 cloves garlic, crushed through a press

1 teaspoon extra-virgin olive oil

¼ teaspoon ground black pepper

¼ teaspoon salt

⅛ teaspoon red pepper flakes

1. Place the hens in a shallow baking pan large enough to hold them in a single layer.

2. In a small bowl, mix the lime juice, lime zest, garlic, oil, black pepper, salt, and red pepper flakes.

3. Pour the mixture over the hens, rubbing it over both sides and especially under the skin. Cover and let stand for 10 minutes.

4. Meanwhile, preheat the broiler.

5. Broil the hens 5" to 6" from the heat for about 10 minutes per side, or until they're browned and the juices run clear. Baste the hens with the pan juices while they are roasting.

Makes 4 servings

Ingredients Note

If you don't have a garlic press, simply smash the cloves flat with the back of a chef's knife.

Orange and Sage Roast Turkey Breast with Pan Gravy

Hands-On Time: 20 minutes ■ Total Time: 3 hours 15 minutes

Why wait for Thanksgiving to eat roast turkey? It's a satisfying and healthy meal year-round. If you're not a fan of sage, use any herb you prefer.

1½ tablespoons rubbed sage

1 teaspoon salt

1 teaspoon coarsely ground black pepper

1 bone-in turkey breast (6½ to 7 pounds)

½ cup orange juice

1 tablespoon extra-virgin olive oil

1 cup plus 2 tablespoons water

1¾ cups chicken broth

2 tablespoons cornstarch

2 tablespoons butter, cut into small pieces

1 tablespoon balsamic vinegar

½ teaspoon freshly grated orange zest

1. Preheat the oven to 350°F. Place a rack in a roasting pan.

2. In a cup, combine the sage, salt, and pepper. Using your fingers, gently loosen the skin on the turkey breast and spread half of the herb mixture under the skin. Rub the remainder all over the turkey. Place the turkey breast on the rack in the roasting pan.

3. In another cup, combine the orange juice and oil.

4. Roast the turkey breast, basting with the orange juice mixture and the pan juices every 15 minutes, for 2 to 2½ hours, or until the turkey is no longer pink in the center and the juices run clear.

5. Remove the turkey from the oven and place on a cutting board. Let stand for 15 minutes.

6. Add 1 cup of the water to the roasting pan and stir to loosen any browned bits from the bottom of the pan. Strain the pan juices into a measuring cup. Let settle for 10 minutes, then skim off the fat that rises to the surface.

7. Pour the pan juices and the broth into the roasting pan. Place on the stove top and bring to a boil over high heat. Reduce the heat to medium-low and simmer for 5 minutes.

8. In a cup, combine the cornstarch with the remaining 2 tablespoons water. Add the mixture to the pan and bring to a boil, stirring constantly, until the sauce is thickened.

9. Whisk in the butter until it's melted and the gravy is smooth. Remove from the heat and stir in the vinegar and orange zest. Pour into a gravy boat. Slice the turkey and serve with the gravy.

Makes 12 servings

Turkey Cutlets with Apples

Hands-On Time: 35 minutes ■ Total Time: 35 minutes

Welcome autumn—the glorious season of apples—with this tangy turkey dish. You cook the apples with the skins on, so for extra color, use a selection of apples ranging from red to green to yellow. Try Empires, Granny Smiths, and Golden Delicious together; or combine Cortlands, Newtown Pippins, and Gravensteins.

3 tablespoons all-purpose flour	1 pound apples, cut into $\frac{1}{2}$"-thick wedges
1 teaspoon ground cumin	$\frac{3}{4}$ cup chicken broth
$\frac{1}{2}$ teaspoon ground black pepper	2 tablespoons honey
$\frac{1}{4}$ teaspoon salt	$\frac{3}{4}$ cup water
$\frac{1}{8}$ teaspoon ground cinnamon	1 teaspoon cider vinegar
4 thin turkey breast cutlets (1 pound)	2 tablespoons raisins
1 tablespoon olive oil	1 teaspoon unsalted butter

1. In a shallow bowl or pie plate, mix the flour, cumin, pepper, salt, and cinnamon. Dredge the turkey in the flour mixture, patting it into the surface. Set aside the excess flour mixture.

2. In a large, heavy nonstick skillet, warm the oil over medium-high heat. Add the turkey and cook for 2 to 3 minutes per side, or until golden brown and cooked through. Transfer the turkey to a platter and cover loosely with foil to keep warm.

3. Add the apples, $\frac{1}{2}$ cup of the broth, and 1 tablespoon of the honey to the skillet. Cook over medium heat for 8 to 10 minutes, or until the apples are tender and nicely glazed but not mushy. Turn the apples frequently and scrape any brown bits from the bottom of the skillet. Remove the skillet from the heat. Spoon the apples over the turkey.

4. In a medium bowl, combine the water, vinegar, the reserved seasoned flour, and the remaining $\frac{1}{4}$ cup broth and 1 tablespoon honey. Whisk until smooth. Pour this mixture into the skillet and bring to a boil over medium heat, stirring constantly. Stir in the raisins. Simmer, stirring frequently, for 2 minutes, or until the sauce is thickened.

5. Stir in the butter and remove the skillet from the heat. Pour the sauce over the turkey and apples.

Makes 4 servings

Kitchen Tip

If you find that your honey has crystallized, set the jar in hot water for 10 to 15 minutes.

Easy Make-Ahead Marinades for Poultry

Chicken breasts, bone-in or boneless thighs, and turkey cutlets take extremely well to marinating, and the flavor possibilities are endless. Use the marinades below to take your next make-ahead poultry meal to new heights of taste. Each of these recipes makes enough for 4 to 6 boneless, skinless chicken breasts or 4 turkey cutlets (about 1 pound). After removing the poultry from the marinade, grill it, broil it, or pan-fry it until the poultry is no longer pink and the juices run clear. Be sure to discard the marinade afterward, or bring it to a full boil before using it for basting.

Chinese Plum. In a zip-top plastic bag, combine 2 plums (peeled and finely chopped), $\frac{1}{3}$ cup cider vinegar, $\frac{1}{4}$ cup apple juice, 2 tablespoons honey, and 1 tablespoon minced garlic. Add the poultry and seal the bag. Turn to coat. Marinate in the refrigerator for 1 to 2 hours before cooking.

Indian Curry. In a food processor or blender, combine $\frac{3}{4}$ cup plain yogurt, $\frac{1}{2}$ cup chopped onion, 2 tablespoons fresh lemon juice, 1 tablespoon curry powder, 1 teaspoon minced garlic, and $\frac{1}{4}$ teaspoon ground red pepper. Process until smooth. Scrape into a zip-top plastic bag. Add the poultry and seal the bag. Turn to coat. Marinate in the refrigerator for 1 to 2 hours before cooking.

Italian. In a zip-top plastic bag, combine $\frac{1}{2}$ cup olive oil, 2 tablespoons fresh lemon juice, $1\frac{1}{2}$ tablespoons white wine vinegar, 3 crumbled bay leaves, $1\frac{1}{2}$ teaspoons garlic, $1\frac{1}{2}$ teaspoons dried oregano, $1\frac{1}{2}$ teaspoons salt, 1 teaspoon dried basil, 1 teaspoon dried thyme, and $\frac{1}{2}$ teaspoon ground black pepper. Add the poultry and seal the bag. Turn to coat. Marinate in the refrigerator for 24 hours before cooking. (Due to the long marinating time, the chicken may begin to turn white on the surface before cooking, which is okay.)

Mediterranean. In a zip-top plastic bag, combine $\frac{1}{4}$ cup shredded fresh basil, $\frac{1}{4}$ cup fresh lemon juice, $\frac{1}{4}$ cup olive oil, $\frac{1}{4}$ cup chopped fresh parsley, $\frac{1}{2}$ teaspoon dried oregano, $\frac{1}{2}$ teaspoon salt, $\frac{1}{4}$ teaspoon ground black pepper, and $\frac{1}{8}$ teaspoon ground red pepper. Add the poultry and seal the bag. Turn to coat. Marinate in the refrigerator for 1 to 4 hours before cooking.

Mexican. In a zip-top plastic bag, combine ¼ cup vegetable oil, 2 tablespoons fresh lime juice, 2 teaspoons chili powder, 1 teaspoon ground cumin, and 1 teaspoon minced garlic. Add the poultry and seal the bag. Turn to coat. Marinate in the refrigerator for 1 to 2 hours before cooking.

Moroccan. In a food processor, combine ½ cup fresh cilantro leaves, ½ cup fresh parsley leaves, 3 tablespoons vegetable oil, 1 tablespoon fresh lemon juice, 1 teaspoon minced garlic, ½ teaspoon ground cumin, ½ teaspoon paprika, ½ teaspoon salt, and ¼ teaspoon ground black pepper. Process until smooth and pour into a zip-top plastic bag. Add the poultry and seal the bag. Turn to coat. Marinate in the refrigerator for 2 to 6 hours before cooking.

Orange-Ginger. In a zip-top plastic bag, combine ½ cup orange juice, 1 teaspoon minced garlic, 1 teaspoon grated fresh ginger, 1 teaspoon grated orange zest, and ¼ teaspoon sesame oil. Add the poultry and seal the bag. Turn to coat. Marinate in the refrigerator for 1 to 2 hours before cooking.

Savory Horseradish. In a zip-top plastic bag, combine ½ cup dry sherry or chicken stock, 2 tablespoons fresh lemon juice, 1 teaspoon minced garlic, 1 teaspoon stone-ground mustard, and ½ teaspoon prepared horseradish. Add the poultry and seal the bag. Turn to coat. Marinate in the refrigerator for 1 to 2 hours before cooking.

Tarragon. In a zip-top plastic bag, combine ½ cup dry white wine, ¼ cup fresh lemon juice, ¼ cup olive oil, 2 teaspoons dried tarragon, ½ teaspoon minced garlic, ½ teaspoon salt, and ¼ teaspoon ground black pepper. Add the poultry and seal the bag. Turn to coat. Marinate in the refrigerator for 1 to 2 hours before cooking.

Teriyaki. In a zip-top plastic bag, combine ½ cup unsweetened pineapple juice, ¼ cup reduced-sodium soy sauce, 1 teaspoon minced garlic, and 1 teaspoon grated fresh ginger. Add the poultry and seal the bag. Turn to coat. Marinate in the refrigerator for 1 to 2 hours before cooking.

Turkey and Zucchini Parmigiana

Hands-On Time: 15 minutes ■ Total Time: 40 minutes

Broiling really brings out the flavor of vegetables, especially when they're cooked until lightly charred. The smoky savor of broiled onions and zucchini lends richness to this layering of turkey, vegetables, and luscious melted cheeses.

1 large Spanish onion, cut into ¼"-thick slices

1 tablespoon olive oil

2 cloves garlic, crushed

1 tablespoon water

½ teaspoon dried basil

½ teaspoon dried oregano

¼ teaspoon ground black pepper

¼ teaspoon red pepper flakes

⅛ teaspoon salt

4 thin turkey breast cutlets (1 pound)

2 medium zucchini, cut into ¼"-thick lengthwise slices

1 tablespoon unseasoned dried bread crumbs

1 can (14.5 ounces) no-salt-added stewed tomatoes, with juice

¾ cup shredded mozzarella cheese

1 tablespoon grated Parmesan cheese

1. Preheat the broiler. Coat a jelly-roll pan with cooking spray.

2. Arrange the onion slices in a single layer in the prepared pan and drizzle with 1 teaspoon of the oil. Broil 5" to 6" from the heat, turning once, for 10 minutes, or until the onions are softened and lightly charred.

3. Meanwhile, in a cup, mix the remaining 2 teaspoons oil with the garlic, water, basil, oregano, black pepper, red pepper flakes, and salt. Brush both sides of the turkey cutlets and zucchini slices with the oil mixture.

4. Using a metal spatula, push the onions toward the center of the pan, arranging them in four stacks. Place the turkey cutlets on top of the onions and arrange the zucchini slices around the edges. Broil for 7 to 9 minutes, or until the turkey is cooked through and the zucchini slices are softened. Remove from the broiler.

5. Reduce the oven temperature to 450°F.

6. Sprinkle the bread crumbs on the bottom of a 9" × 9" baking dish. Transfer the turkey and onions to the baking dish, then place the zucchini on top.

7. Spoon the tomatoes (with juice) over the turkey and vegetables. Sprinkle with the mozzarella and Parmesan. Bake for 10 minutes, or until the sauce is bubbly and the cheeses are melted.

Makes 4 servings

Turkey Tenderloin with Tomato-Mushroom Sauce

Hands-On Time: 25 minutes ▪ Total Time: 50 minutes

The addition of sun-dried tomatoes gives the sauce for the turkey an extra-tomatoey flavor. If you can't find dry-packed, you can use those packed in olive oil instead.

- 1 pound turkey tenderloin, cut into 4 pieces
- 2 tablespoons seasoned dried bread crumbs
- 1 teaspoon olive oil
- 1 cup sliced mushrooms
- 1 cup diced tomatoes
- 1/2 cup diced carrots
- 1/2 cup diced celery

- 1/2 cup chopped onion
- 1/4 cup chicken broth
- 2 ounces dry-packed sun-dried tomatoes, chopped
- 1 teaspoon minced garlic
- 1/4 teaspoon dried rosemary
- Salt
- Ground black pepper

1. Place the turkey and bread crumbs in a zip-top plastic bag. Shake well.

2. In a large nonstick skillet, heat the oil over medium-high heat. Add the turkey and cook for 2 minutes on each side. Transfer to a plate.

3. To the same skillet, add the mushrooms, diced tomatoes, carrots, celery, onion, broth, sun-dried tomatoes, garlic, and rosemary. Stir to combine. Cook for 5 minutes, then add the turkey. Cover and reduce the heat to medium. Cook for 20 minutes, or until the turkey is no longer pink and the juices run clear. Season with salt and pepper to taste.

Makes 4 servings

Kitchen Tip

For super flavor, make your own bread crumbs in a food processor with the metal blade. Lightly toast fresh bread slices, or use day-old bread (older than that tastes old). Tear the bread into pieces, place them in the machine, and pulse to the desired texture. To season, simply add dried herbs and salt and pepper to taste. Freeze the bread crumbs in zip-top bags for future use.

Accompaniment

Garlic-flavored mashed potatoes would be an ideal companion to this easy entrée.

Turkey Sausage Casserole

Hands-On Time: 30 minutes ■ Total Time: 2 hours (plus chilling)

This makes a wonderful brunch dish served with freshly squeezed orange juice, a light tossed salad, and fresh berries.

½ pound mild or spicy turkey sausage

½ cup minced onion

½ cup thinly sliced green bell pepper

½ cup thinly sliced yellow bell pepper

⅓ cup chopped drained pimiento

¼ cup shredded Cheddar cheese

1 tablespoon minced fresh parsley

½ teaspoon dried thyme

1½ tablespoons stone-ground mustard

2 teaspoons butter, softened

9 slices oat-bran bread, crusts removed

5 eggs

2½ cups milk

¼ teaspoon ground white pepper

1. Remove any casing from the sausage. Crumble the meat into a large nonstick skillet. Brown over medium heat, breaking up the pieces with a wooden spoon. With a slotted spoon, transfer to a large platter lined with several thicknesses of paper towels. Set aside.

2. Add the onion and bell peppers, and cook over medium heat, stirring occasionally, for about 5 minutes, or until the vegetables are softened. Remove from the heat and add the pimiento, cheese, parsley, and thyme.

3. Coat a 9" × 9" baking dish with cooking spray. In a small cup, mix the mustard and butter. Cut the slices of bread in half and spread each half with a thin layer of the mustard mixture. Set aside 4 halves. Place the remaining bread, coated side down, in the dish to cover the bottom and come up the sides.

4. Cover with the bell pepper mixture. Sprinkle with half the sausage. Top with the reserved bread, mustard side up.

5. In a large bowl, whisk the eggs. Whisk in the milk and white pepper. Pour over the bread. Top with the remaining sausage. Cover and refrigerate for at least 2 hours or overnight to allow the bread to soak up the milk mixture.

6. Preheat the oven to 325°F.

7. Uncover the casserole and bake it for 60 to 75 minutes, or until a knife inserted in the middle comes out clean. Let it stand for 10 to 20 minutes before serving.

Makes 6 servings

Baked Turkey Tetrazzini

Hands-On Time: 35 minutes ■ Total Time: 1 hour 20 minutes

A baked casserole is a great way to use leftovers from the Orange and Sage Roast Turkey Breast with Pan Gravy on page 116.

8 ounces spaghetti	3 cups milk
1 tablespoon olive oil	1 pound cooked turkey breast, cut into ¾" cubes
8 ounces mushrooms, sliced	
1 medium onion, chopped	10 large kalamata olives, sliced
1 large red bell pepper, chopped	½ cup grated Parmesan cheese
⅓ cup all-purpose flour	

1. Bring a large pot of water to a boil. Preheat the oven to 350°F. Coat a 3-quart baking dish with cooking spray.

2. Prepare the spaghetti according to package directions until al dente.

3. Meanwhile, in a large skillet, heat the oil over medium-high heat. Add the mushrooms, onion, and pepper. Cook for 5 minutes, or until the vegetables are softened.

4. In a large bowl, whisk together the flour and milk. Add it to the skillet. Reduce the heat to medium. Cook, stirring constantly, for 5 minutes, or until it's slightly thickened and bubbling.

5. Remove the pan from the heat. Add the spaghetti, turkey, olives, and Parmesan. Toss to coat well. Transfer the mixture to the prepared baking dish.

6. Cover and bake for 20 minutes. Uncover and bake for 10 minutes longer, or until it's hot and bubbly. Let the dish stand for 5 minutes before serving.

Makes 6 servings

Make-Ahead

You can prepare this dish to the point of baking, then cover and refrigerate it for up to 2 days before baking.

Variations

For a change of pace, sprinkle the top with seasoned bread crumbs, cracker crumbs, or even crushed potato chips before baking. Use 1% milk, if you prefer.

Tasty Herb Blends for Poultry

Spend a minute making these easy herb blends, then store them in small containers in a cool cupboard or in the freezer, where they'll keep for 6 months. Dress up ordinary chicken breasts or thighs—or turkey cutlets, tenderloins, or steaks—for only pennies a serving by seasoning with your favorite blend.

Cajun Blend. Combine equal amounts of ground anise seeds, dried basil, ground black pepper, ground red pepper, and dried thyme.

Greek Blend. Combine equal amounts of crushed fennel seeds, garlic powder, dried oregano, and dried thyme.

Indian Blend. Combine equal amounts of ground cumin, ground coriander, ground ginger, and turmeric. Add ground red pepper and ground black pepper to taste.

Italian Blend. Combine equal amounts of dried sage, dried savory, and crushed fennel seeds.

Mediterranean Blend. Combine equal amounts of crushed dried rosemary, dried thyme, dried orange rind, and ground black pepper.

Mexican Blend. Combine equal amounts of good-quality chili powder, dried cilantro, ground cumin, dried oregano, dried thyme, and ground black pepper. Add ground dried chiles for added heat.

South-of-France Blend. Combine equal amounts of dried basil, dried oregano, and dried thyme.

Turkey Stew with Biscuit Crust

Hands-On Time: 35 minutes ■ Total Time: 1 hour 5 minutes

Sometimes, old-fashioned is best—especially when it comes to stews. This turkey version is bursting with vegetables and sports a simple, home-style biscuit crust. Your family is sure to love it.

Biscuits

1 cup all-purpose flour

1 teaspoon baking powder

¼ teaspoon baking soda

¼ teaspoon salt

2 tablespoons cold butter, cut into small pieces

¼ cup buttermilk

3 tablespoons sour cream

Stew

1 tablespoon olive oil

2 cloves garlic, minced

1 small onion, chopped

2½ teaspoons cornstarch

1 teaspoon dried thyme

½ teaspoon rubbed sage

2 cups chicken broth

2 cups cooked turkey, cubed

1 small head cauliflower, cut into small florets

2 carrots, very thinly sliced

1 cup fresh peas or thawed frozen peas

¼ teaspoon ground black pepper

1. Preheat the oven to 425°F. Coat a 2-quart baking dish with cooking spray. Set aside.

2. *To make the biscuits:* In a medium bowl, combine the flour, baking powder, baking soda, and salt. Using 2 knives or a pastry blender, cut in the butter until the mixture forms crumbs. Add the buttermilk and sour cream. Mix and gather into a ball. Turn the dough onto a sheet of plastic wrap and flatten into a round. Wrap and refrigerate while you make the stew.

3. *To make the stew:* In a large saucepan, heat the oil over medium-high heat. Add the garlic and onion. Cook, stirring occasionally, for 2 minutes.

4. In a medium bowl, combine the cornstarch, thyme, and sage. Whisk in the broth. Add to the onion mixture. Bring to a boil and cook, stirring, for 1 minute, or until thickened. Remove from the heat. Stir in the turkey, cauliflower, carrots, peas, and pepper. Transfer to the prepared baking dish.

5. Cut the biscuit dough into 4 equal parts. Arrange on the turkey mixture.

6. Bake for 30 minutes, or until the biscuits are golden and the stew is bubbling.

Makes 4 servings

Great Turkey Burgers

Hands-On Time: 10 minutes ▪ Total Time: 20 minutes

Just a few spoonfuls of applesauce keep these lean turkey burgers juicy. Serve them on toasted whole grain buns garnished with sliced tomatoes, crisp spinach leaves, and sliced red onions or other fresh toppers.

2 pounds ground turkey breast	1 clove garlic, minced
½ cup minced onion	1 teaspoon lemon-pepper seasoning
¼ cup unsweetened applesauce	½ teaspoon chili powder
3 tablespoons ketchup	½ teaspoon ground black pepper
1 tablespoon Worcestershire sauce	8 whole wheat buns, toasted (optional)

1. Preheat the broiler.

2. In a large bowl, mix the turkey, onion, applesauce, ketchup, Worcestershire, garlic, lemon-pepper seasoning, chili powder, and black pepper. Shape into 8 patties.

3. Broil for 5 minutes on each side, or until the burgers are no longer pink in the center. Serve on the buns, if using.

Makes 8 servings

Kitchen Tip

When mixing the meat for burgers, don't overhandle it or the burgers will be tough.

Accompaniments

Serve the burgers with Cajun Potato Salad (page 78). For dessert, offer Blondies (page 337).

White Bean and Turkey Chili with Cilantro Yogurt

Hands-On Time: 55 minutes ■ Total Time: 55 minutes

Hot corn tortillas make a fine accompaniment to this Southwestern-style stew. To heat the tortillas, place an ungreased heavy skillet over medium-high heat and toast the tortillas for 1 to 2 minutes on each side. Keep them warm in a covered soufflé dish or bowl.

Cilantro Yogurt

8 ounces plain yogurt

2 to 3 tablespoons minced fresh cilantro

3 tablespoons minced fresh parsley

Chili

1½ cups chopped onion

1 can (14 ounces) reduced-sodium chicken broth

1 can (4.5 ounces) diced green chile peppers, drained

4 large cloves garlic, minced

2¼ teaspoons chili powder

2¼ teaspoons ground cumin

2¼ teaspoons dried oregano

½ teaspoon ground red pepper

2 cans (15 ounces each) great Northern beans, rinsed and drained

1 can (11 ounces) tomatillos, coarsely chopped

½ to ¾ cup chopped fresh cilantro

2 cups cubed cooked turkey breast

1 bunch scallions, white and light green parts, thinly sliced (½ cup)

2 tablespoons fresh lime juice

¼ teaspoon ground black pepper

Finely shredded Cheddar cheese (optional)

1. *To make the cilantro yogurt:* In a small bowl, stir together the yogurt, cilantro, and parsley. Cover and refrigerate while you make the chili.

2. *To make the chili:* Lightly coat a large saucepan or Dutch oven with cooking spray. Add the onion and 2 tablespoons of the broth. Cook, stirring, over medium heat for 5 minutes, or until the onions are softened.

3. Add the chile peppers, garlic, chili powder, cumin, oregano, and red pepper. Cook, stirring, for 5 minutes.

4. Stir in the beans, tomatillos, cilantro, and the remaining broth. Bring to a boil. Add the turkey, scallions, lime juice, and black pepper. Cook, stirring occasionally, for about 10 minutes, or until heated through.

5. Serve topped with dollops of the cilantro yogurt. Sprinkle with the Cheddar, if using.

Makes 6 servings

Turkey and Rice Stuffed Peppers

Hands-On Time: 40 minutes ■ Total Time: 1 hour

Food served in edible containers—like these striking red bell pepper cups—always makes a fun meal. When you've eaten the filling, be sure to polish off your "dish" as well: Red bell peppers are a good source of vitamin C.

4 large red bell peppers plus 1 small red bell pepper, or a mix of red and yellow peppers

2 cups water

½ cup long-grain white rice

¾ teaspoon salt

2 teaspoons olive oil

1 pound lean ground turkey

1 medium onion, chopped

2 cloves garlic, minced

1½ teaspoons dried thyme or 1 teaspoon chopped fresh

¼ teaspoon ground black pepper

1 pound fresh spinach, stemmed and coarsely chopped

½ cup dried currants

¼ cup chopped fresh parsley

1. Preheat the oven to 350°F. Bring a large saucepan of water to a boil.

2. Meanwhile, cut off and discard the tops of the 4 large bell peppers. Seed the large peppers, being careful not to puncture them. Seed and dice the small bell pepper and set aside.

3. Cook the whole peppers in the boiling water for 2 minutes, or until slightly softened. Drain the peppers on paper towels, then stand the peppers upright in an 8" × 8" baking dish. Set aside.

4. In a medium saucepan, combine 1 cup of the water, the rice, and ¼ teaspoon of the salt. Cover and bring to a boil over medium-high heat. Reduce the heat to low and cook, covered, for 15 to 17 minutes, or until the rice is tender and the liquid is absorbed.

5. Meanwhile, in a large nonstick skillet, heat the oil over medium-high heat until hot but not smoking. Add the turkey and cook, stirring, for about 3 minutes, breaking up any clumps with a spoon. Add the onion, garlic, thyme, black pepper, and the remaining ½ teaspoon salt. Cook for about 3 minutes, or until the onions are softened.

6. Add the spinach, currants, parsley, and the diced bell pepper. Cover and cook for 3 minutes, or until the spinach is wilted. Remove the pan from the heat.

7. Fluff the cooked rice with a fork. Add it to the spinach mixture and stir to combine. Spoon the mixture into the bell peppers. Pour the remaining 1 cup water into the baking dish around the peppers. Bake for 15 minutes, or until the peppers and filling are hot.

Makes 4 servings

Meaty Entrées

"Vegetables are interesting but lack a sense of purpose when unaccompanied by a good cut of meat."

—FRAN LEBOWTIZ

Marinated Tuscan Steak

Hands-On Time: 10 minutes ■ Total Time: 35 minutes

Here a simple orange-flavored marinade complements the rich flavors of flank steak, a lean and inexpensive cut of meat. The steak is just right served with Stuffed Baked Potatoes (page 308).

2 cups orange juice	3 cloves garlic, minced
2 tablespoons grated orange zest	1 teaspoon Dijon mustard
2 tablespoons chopped fresh sage	1 teaspoon ground black pepper
2 tablespoons red wine vinegar	1 pound flank steak

1. In a large bowl, mix the orange juice, orange zest, sage, vinegar, garlic, mustard, and pepper. Add the steak and turn to coat. Refrigerate for 15 minutes or cover and refrigerate for up to 24 hours, turning occasionally.

2. Coat a broiler-pan rack with cooking spray. Preheat the broiler.

3. Remove the steak from the marinade and broil about 5" from the heat for 5 minutes per side for medium-rare. (A thermometer inserted into the center registers 145°F for medium-rare, 160°F for medium, or 165°F for well-done.) Baste twice with the marinade while broiling and discard the remaining marinade.

4. To serve, slice thinly across the grain and at an angle.

Makes 4 servings

Variation

The marinade is also good with chicken breasts and turkey tenderloins.

Leftovers

Leftovers are delicious in a salad or sandwich with sharp mustard.

Mushroom Swiss Steak

Hands-On Time: 10 minutes ■ Total Time: 1 hour 10 minutes

This is a super-simple recipe that has barely any Hands-On time. If you're dieting, use 97% fat-free mushroom soup.

1   boneless round steak (1¼ pounds), cut ½" thick

1   teaspoon olive oil

¼   teaspoon ground black pepper

1   large onion, cut into 6 slices

1   can (10.75 ounces) condensed cream of mushroom soup

1. Preheat the oven to 350°F.

2. Using a meat mallet, pound the beef until it's about ¼" thick. Cut it into 6 equal pieces.

3. In a large nonstick skillet, heat the oil over medium heat. Add the beef and cook for 2 minutes. Turn the pieces over and cook for 2 minutes longer, or until browned.

4. Transfer the beef to an 11" × 7" baking pan. Sprinkle with the pepper and top each piece with an onion slice. Spoon the soup over the meat. Cover and bake for 50 to 60 minutes, or until the meat is tender.

Makes 6 servings

Variations

You could use a can of tomato soup instead of mushroom and add some diced green peppers.

For a colorful garnish, sprinkle a little chopped fresh parsley over each serving of meat.

Steak with Many Peppers

Hands-On Time: 30 minutes ■ Total Time: 35 minutes

You needn't give a moment's thought to garnishing this dish—the vivid colors of the bell peppers and tomatoes make it quite irresistible without any extra fuss or flourishes. Serve the steak with crusty Italian bread, rice pilaf, or potatoes.

- 2 cloves garlic, minced
- ¾ teaspoon coarsely ground black pepper
- ¼ teaspoon salt
- ¾ pound well-trimmed boneless sirloin steak
- 1 tablespoon balsamic vinegar
- 1 tablespoon olive oil
- 1 small red bell pepper, thinly sliced
- 1 small green bell pepper, thinly sliced
- 1 small yellow bell pepper, thinly sliced
- 1 medium onion, halved and cut into thin wedges
- 1 large tomato, cut into thin wedges
- 1 tablespoon chicken broth or water
- 1 tablespoon chopped fresh oregano

1. Coat a broiler-pan rack with cooking spray. Preheat the broiler.

2. In a small bowl, combine the garlic, pepper, and ⅛ teaspoon of the salt. Rub both sides of the steak with the mixture. Place the steak on the prepared rack and drizzle it with 1 teaspoon of the vinegar. Broil 5" to 6" from the heat for 5 minutes, then flip the steak and drizzle the second side with 1 teaspoon of the vinegar. Broil for 4 to 5 minutes longer for medium-rare. (A thermometer inserted into the center registers 145°F for medium-rare, 160°F for medium, or 165°F for well-done.) Transfer the steak to a warmed platter, cover loosely with foil, and let stand for 5 minutes.

3. While the steak is cooking, in a deep, medium-size nonstick skillet, heat the oil over high heat until hot but not smoking. Add the bell peppers and the onion. Toss to coat with the oil. Cook, stirring, for 1 minute. Reduce the heat to medium-high, add the tomato and broth, and toss to combine. Cover and cook, stirring frequently, for 8 to 10 minutes, or until the vegetables are softened.

4. Uncover the skillet and add the remaining 1 teaspoon vinegar, ⅛ teaspoon salt, and any juices that have collected on the steak platter. Simmer for 1 minute. Remove the pan from the heat and stir in the oregano.

5. Carve the steak into thin slices and arrange on the platter. Spoon the vegetables and pan juices around the steak.

Makes 4 servings

How to Grill a Steak

Sitting down to a perfectly grilled steak is one of life's great pleasures. Here's how to get grilled steak that's crisp and brown on the surface, yet juicy and cooked to your liking on the inside.

1. Choose the right cut. Tenderloin, T-bone, porterhouse, and sirloin are all excellent candidates. Look for steaks that are well-marbled with fat, which melts as the steak cooks and helps keep the meat moist. Steaks for grilling should be at least 1" but no more than 3" thick.

2. Trim the steak of excess fat at its edges to help prevent flare-ups.

3. Nick the border of the steak with the tip of your knife at ¾" intervals to help prevent the steak from curling as it cooks. If the steak has a thin "tail," wrap it around the steak and secure it with toothpicks or a wooden skewer that has been soaked in water for 10 minutes.

4. Rub a few drops of olive or vegetable oil into both sides of the steak, and season well with salt and ground black pepper.

5. Coat the grill rack with cooking spray and set the rack 4" to 6" over the heat for a few minutes to get it nice and hot. This will help sear the meat properly.

6. Put the steak on the rack, directly over the hottest part of a medium-hot fire. When small beads of juice rise to the surface, turn the steak over and cook the second side until the juices rise to the top again.

7. Using a pair of long-handled grilling tongs, hold the steak on one side to sear. Turn and continue to sear until all the edges until brown.

8. Move the steak to one side of the grill where the heat is less intense and continue cooking, turning once, until it's done to your liking. The total grilling time will depend on the thickness of the steak and the temperature of the fire. Generally, for each 1" thickness, allow 8 to 10 minutes for rare, about 12 minutes for medium, and 15 minutes for well-done. Test for doneness by pressing the steak with your fingertip and/or checking the internal temperature with an instant-read thermometer. If it's soft, the meat is medium-rare (145°F); a bit of spring to the meat indicates that it's cooked medium (160°F); and if the meat feels stiff, it's well-done (165°F). For the juiciest steak, let it stand 10 minutes before slicing.

Charred Flank Steak with Picadillo Relish

Hands-On Time: 20 minutes ■ Total Time: 30 minutes (plus marinating)

In many Spanish-speaking countries, picadillo is a dish of ground meat fried with vegetables and often raisins. In this variation, a whole cut of beef is grilled for added flavor, and the remaining picadillo ingredients are combined into a zesty relish.

2 pounds flank steak

½ cup bottled herb-garlic marinade

1 tablespoon minced garlic

2 tablespoons extra-virgin olive oil

1 cup thinly sliced onion

1 cup thinly sliced red bell pepper

¼ cup raisins

¼ teaspoon salt

1. In a large zip-top plastic bag, combine the steak, marinade, and garlic. Massage the bag to coat the steak evenly. Refrigerate, massaging occasionally, for at least 30 minutes or as long as 8 hours.

2. Coat a grill rack or broiler-pan rack with cooking spray. Preheat the grill or broiler.

3. Remove the steak from the bag, reserving the marinade. Grill or broil the steak, turning once, for 8 minutes per side, or until well browned. Continue cooking to the desired doneness. (A thermometer inserted into the center registers 145°F for medium-rare, 160°F for medium, or 165°F for well-done.) Let stand for 5 minutes before cutting into thin slices across the grain.

4. Meanwhile, in a medium skillet, heat the oil over medium-high heat. Add the onion, pepper, raisins, and salt. Cook, stirring occasionally, for about 5 minutes, or until the onion is golden. Add the reserved marinade. Bring to a boil. Serve the relish with the steak.

Makes 4 to 6 servings

Ingredients Note

Flank steak is the only steak in the beef carcass containing muscle fibers that run the full length of the steak. To help tenderize these long fibers, the butcher scores the meat across the cut. Even so, you still need to slice the steak across the grain to serve.

Not Your Mother's Meat Loaf

Hands-On Time: 30 minutes ■ Total Time: 1 hour 35 minutes

This delicious, moist meat loaf is made with a mix of beef and turkey. For a crowd, bake both this meat loaf and the spicy version, opposite.

1 tablespoon olive oil	1½ cups fresh bread crumbs (see page 121)
½ small onion, chopped	⅓ cup milk
1 stalk celery, chopped	⅓ cup chopped fresh parsley
⅓ cup finely chopped red or green bell pepper	1 egg
1 clove garlic, minced	2 teaspoons Italian seasoning
1 pound ground round	2 teaspoons Worcestershire sauce
1 pound ground turkey breast	1 can (14.5 ounces) diced tomatoes, drained

1. Preheat the oven to 350°F. Coat a 9" × 5" loaf pan with cooking spray.

2. In a medium skillet, heat the oil over medium heat. Add the onion, celery, bell pepper, and garlic. Cook, stirring frequently, for 4 to 5 minutes, or until the vegetables are softened. Transfer to a large bowl. Add the ground round, turkey, bread crumbs, milk, parsley, egg, Italian seasoning, Worcestershire, and 1 cup of the tomatoes. Stir until well-blended. Pat the mixture into the prepared loaf pan.

3. Bake for 1 hour, or until a thermometer inserted in the center registers 160°F and the meat is no longer pink. During the last 15 minutes of baking, spread the remaining tomatoes down the center of the meat loaf.

4. Remove the meat loaf from the oven and drain off any accumulated juices from the pan. Let stand for 5 minutes before slicing.

Makes 8 servings

Accompaniment

Make a creamy mustard gravy to go with the meat loaf or with mashed potatoes:
Place 2 tablespoons cornstarch or flour in a small saucepan. Gradually add 1 cup chicken broth, whisking until smooth. Cook, stirring, over medium heat for 2 to 3 minutes, or until thickened. Add 1 cup milk and 2 to 3 tablespoons Dijon mustard. Stir to blend. Season with a pinch each of salt and pepper. Cook for 2 minutes, or until heated through. Makes 8 servings.

Mexicali Meat Loaf

Hands-On Time: 15 minutes ■ Total Time: 1 hour 25 minutes

Here's a south-of-the-border take on meat loaf. Spicy salsa gives it character, and corn adds sweetness. You can use frozen corn or scrape the kernels off the cob.

1 pound ground round	1½ teaspoons chili powder
½ pound ground turkey breast	½ teaspoon ground cumin
¾ cup salsa	¼ teaspoon ground black pepper
¾ cup fresh bread crumbs (see page 121)	⅛ teaspoon salt
1 cup chopped onion	¼ cup tomato sauce
½ cup whole kernel corn	1 tablespoon ketchup
1 egg, lightly beaten	1 teaspoon sugar
2 cloves garlic, minced	

1. Preheat the oven to 350°F.

2. In a large bowl, combine the ground round, turkey, salsa, bread crumbs, onion, corn, egg, garlic, chili powder, cumin, pepper, and salt. Mix well. Form into a loaf. Place in a 9" × 5" nonstick loaf pan.

3. In a small bowl, combine the tomato sauce, ketchup, and sugar. Spread over the top of the meat loaf. Cover with foil and bake for 1 hour, or until a thermometer inserted into the center reads 160°F. Uncover and bake for 5 minutes longer, or until the top browns slightly. Let stand for 5 minutes before slicing.

Makes 8 servings

Ingredients Note

Be sure to use ground round for making meat loaf since it has less fat than regular ground beef and more fat than ground sirloin, which would produce a dry meat loaf.

Freezing Tip

If you double or triple this recipe to freeze, line the loaf pans before cooking with enough overhanging freezer-quality foil to wrap the baked loaves. To freeze, remove the cooled cooked loaves from their pans. Wrap in the original foil and another layer, as well. To use, thaw overnight in the refrigerator. Bake the foil-wrapped loaves at 350°F for 20 minutes, or until hot.

Braised Beef Brisket

Hands-On Time: 30 minutes ■ Total Time: 3 hours

Brisket typically comes with a large fat cap. To make this a leaner dish, have the butcher completely trim the fat. Because brisket is a tough cut, it requires long, slow cooking.

2 pounds beef brisket, trimmed of all visible fat

¼ teaspoon salt

¼ teaspoon ground black pepper

2 tablespoons olive oil

1 large onion, halved and thinly sliced

1 can (28 ounces) diced tomatoes

1 cup beef broth

½ cup water

5 carrots, sliced

2 stalks celery, sliced

1½ teaspoons dried thyme

1. Preheat the oven to 350°F.

2. Season the brisket on both sides with the salt and pepper.

3. In a Dutch oven, heat the oil over medium-high heat. When the oil is hot but not smoking, add the brisket. Cook for 2 minutes per side, or until browned. Remove the brisket to a plate.

4. Lower the heat to medium. Add the onion. Cook for 5 to 6 minutes, or until softened. Return the brisket to the pot. Add the tomatoes, broth, water, carrots, celery, and thyme. Cover tightly with a lid or foil. Place in the oven.

5. Bake for 1½ hours, turning the brisket after 45 minutes. Remove from the oven. Remove the brisket and place on a cutting board. Slice across the grain into ¼"-thick slices.

6. Return the sliced brisket to the pan and cover. Bake for 1 hour, or until the brisket and vegetables are fork-tender.

Makes 6 servings

Leftovers

Tender leftover beef brisket makes the best barbecued beef sandwiches, which can be served for lunch or dinner the following day. Shred 1½ cups cooked beef brisket and place in a medium bowl with ½ cup of your favorite barbecue sauce. Stir to mix. Heat in the microwave oven on high power for 2 minutes. Slice 2 kaiser rolls in half and lightly toast. Cover each of the roll bottoms with ⅓ cup shredded lettuce, half the beef mixture, and ⅓ cup coleslaw. Cover with the roll tops. Makes 2 sandwiches.

Pot Roast with Apple Cider

Hands-On Time: 40 minutes ■ Total Time: 1 hour 10 minutes (plus marinating)

Pot roast is ideal dinner-party fare when the weather starts to turn chilly in the fall. Browning the meat before slowly braising it produces a flavorful, tender result.

1 boneless beef chuck pot roast (2 pounds), trimmed of all visible fat

1 large onion, sliced

8 whole cloves

1 piece (1" long) fresh ginger, peeled and sliced

2 cinnamon sticks

½ teaspoon salt

2 cups cider or apple juice

2 tablespoons olive oil

8 to 10 small red or white potatoes

1 bag (16 ounces) frozen baby onions

16 baby carrots

1. In a large zip-top plastic bag, combine the pot roast, onion, cloves, ginger, cinnamon sticks, and salt. Pour in the cider. Seal the bag, place it in a large bowl, and refrigerate it for 12 to 24 hours, turning it over once.

2. Remove the meat from the bag, reserving the marinade and onion. Pat the meat dry with paper towels.

3. In a large, heavy pot or Dutch oven, heat the oil over medium heat. Add the pot roast and cook, turning, for 8 to 10 minutes, or until browned on all sides.

4. Add the reserved marinade. Bring to a boil, then reduce the heat to medium-low. Cover and cook for 40 minutes. Add the potatoes, baby onions, and carrots. Cover and cook for 50 minutes, or until the meat and vegetables are tender.

5. Remove the meat and vegetables to a warm platter. Bring the pan juices to a boil. Cook, stirring, until the juices are reduced by about half. Keep warm.

6. Thinly slice the meat. Serve with the pan juices.

Makes 8 servings

Beef Stroganoff

Hands-On Time: 35 minutes ■ Total Time: 35 minutes

Originating in Russia over a century ago, beef Stroganoff continues to be a dinnertime favorite around the world. Use any type of mushrooms you prefer.

8 ounces wide egg noodles	1½ teaspoons dried thyme
1 pound lean beef sirloin, cut into strips	1 large onion, sliced
½ teaspoon salt	8 ounces mushrooms, sliced
¼ teaspoon mustard powder	2 tablespoons minced garlic
¼ cup plus 1 tablespoon all-purpose flour	2 bay leaves
2 teaspoons olive oil	8 ounces sour cream
1½ cups beef broth	Salt
2 tablespoons balsamic vinegar	Ground black pepper

1. Bring a large pot of water to a boil. Add the noodles and cook according to package directions until al dente.

2. Meanwhile, in a zip-top plastic bag, combine the beef, salt, mustard, and ¼ cup of the flour. Shake well.

3. In a large nonstick skillet, heat the oil over medium-high heat. Shake any excess flour off the beef and add the beef to the pan. Cook, stirring, for about 5 minutes, or until browned on all sides. Transfer to a plate.

4. Add the broth, vinegar, and thyme to the pan. Bring to a boil, scraping the bottom of the pan to loosen any browned bits. Add the onion, mushrooms, garlic, and bay leaves. Cook, stirring frequently, for 5 minutes. Add the beef. Cover, reduce the heat to low, and simmer for 5 minutes longer.

5. In a small bowl, combine the sour cream and the remaining 1 tablespoon flour. Stir into the pan and heat through. Season with salt and pepper to taste. Remove and discard the bay leaves. Serve over the noodles.

Makes 4 servings

Variation

Add some Dijon mustard and a little fresh dill to the sour cream, if you like.

New-Fashioned Beef Stew

Hands-On Time: 25 minutes ■ Total Time: 50 minutes

Heating up a can of beef stew is one way of putting a quick hot meal on the table, but it's not the only alternative—and certainly not the best one—to spending hours over the stove. This chunky beef-and-vegetable stew is prepared in a streamlined fashion: The meat is browned quickly, then added to the already-cooked vegetables.

4 small red potatoes, cut into wedges	1 bay leaf
1 medium turnip, cut into chunks	2 cloves garlic, crushed
1 medium parsnip, cut into chunks	½ teaspoon dried thyme
1 cup frozen pearl onions, thawed	½ teaspoon ground black pepper
3 medium carrots, cut into chunks	¾ pound lean, trimmed beef top round or sirloin, cut into ½" cubes
1¾ cups beef broth	
1 cup drained canned tomatoes	1 tablespoon all-purpose flour
1 tablespoon red wine vinegar	1 tablespoon olive oil

1. In a large, heavy saucepan or Dutch oven, combine the potatoes, turnip, parsnip, onions, carrots, broth, tomatoes, vinegar, bay leaf, half the garlic, ¼ teaspoon of the thyme, and ¼ teaspoon of the pepper. Break up the tomatoes with the edge of a spoon. Cover and bring to a boil over high heat. Reduce the heat to medium and simmer for 25 minutes, or until the vegetables are just softened.

2. Meanwhile, toss the beef cubes with the remaining garlic and the remaining ¼ teaspoon each of the thyme and pepper. Dredge the seasoned beef cubes in the flour.

3. In a large, heavy skillet, heat the oil over high heat until hot but not smoking. Add the beef and cook, stirring occasionally, for 5 minutes, or until the beef is browned on the outside and medium-rare on the inside.

4. Add the beef to the vegetables, reduce the heat to medium-low, and simmer for 5 minutes, or until the vegetables are softened and the flavors are blended.

Makes 4 servings

Ingredients Note

Carrot-size parsnips (8" to 9" long) are likely to be tender throughout. Larger parsnips, which may be overmature, tend to have tough, woody cores that will need to be removed. Choose turnips that are heavy for their size, which are the youngest and most tender.

Mile-High Burgers

Hands-On Time: 10 minutes ■ Total Time: 30 minutes

You won't need sugary ketchup on these burgers. Tomato-infused mayonnaise flavors the meat from the inside out.

1½ ounces dry-packed sun-dried tomatoes

⅓ cup packed fresh basil leaves

2 tablespoons mayonnaise

1 clove garlic

1¼ pounds extra-lean ground beef

1 jarred roasted red pepper, quartered

2 slices (1 ounce each) mozzarella cheese, halved

4 large lettuce leaves

4 Italian-style sandwich buns

1. Coat a grill rack or broiler-pan rack with cooking spray. Preheat the grill or broiler.

2. Place the sun-dried tomatoes in a medium bowl. Cover with boiling water and soak for 10 minutes, or until very soft. Drain and discard the liquid. In a food processor, combine the tomatoes, basil, mayonnaise, and garlic. Process until smooth.

3. In a medium bowl, combine the beef and tomato mixture. Mix just until blended. Shape into 4 burgers.

4. Place the burgers on the prepared rack. Cook 4" from the heat for 4 minutes per side, or until a thermometer inserted in the center registers 160°F and the meat is no longer pink. Top each burger with a slice of pepper and half a slice of cheese. Cook for 30 seconds longer, or until the cheese melts.

5. Divide the lettuce among the buns. Top each with a burger.

Makes 4 servings

Accompaniments

Serve these burgers outdoors with two side salads. Try Picnic Potato Salad (page 76) and Sicilian Cauliflower-Olive Salad (page 73). Make Banana-Glazed Pecan Ice-Cream Sundaes (page 351) for dessert.

The Best Burgers

Typically made of ground beef, hamburgers are one of America's best-loved meals. The secret to making a good ground beef hamburger is to keep it simple. Use the best-quality ground beef, season it simply, handle it gently, and you can't go wrong. You can also make burgers with ground turkey or chicken, or make veggie burgers with vegetables and/or beans.

Basics

To choose beef for burgers: Buy the best meat you can, and don't skimp on fat. Meat with 10 to 15 percent fat makes the most flavorful, juicy burgers. Having it ground fresh by the butcher is best. A blend of ground sirloin and chuck makes tender burgers with a rich flavor.

To make juicy hamburgers: Avoid making the burgers too big. Oversize burgers need more time to cook, which can dry out the surface of the meat before the inside is done. Five ounces of raw beef makes a perfect burger.

To shape ground beef for hamburgers: Handle the meat as little as possible. Shape each patty by lightly passing 5 ounces of meat back and forth between your cupped hands until it's about ¾" thick and about 3½" in diameter. Handle the meat just as long as it takes to make the patty. Overhandling the meat will make the burger tougher.

To cook: Let the shaped hamburger patties sit at room temperature for about 5 minutes before cooking. The meat should feel cool but not cold to the touch. If the meat is too cold, the burgers will cook unevenly. Also, cook hamburgers on a flat surface. A well-seasoned cast-iron griddle is ideal. Some people prefer open grills, but these allow valuable juices to escape, and the flavor of the charcoal interferes with the pure beef taste of the meat. Avoid pressing down on the burger with a spatula as it cooks. This forces out the juices that keep the meat tender and give it flavor.

Problem Solvers

To form even-size burgers: Divide the total weight of the meat you are using by the number of burgers desired. Then use a scale to weigh out each burger.

To keep ground beef from sticking to your hands: Wet your hands with cold water.

To rescue a hamburger that is burnt on the outside: Gently saw off the crust with a bread knife.

To rescue an overcooked burger: Slice the burger in half horizontally and tuck a slice of cheese in the center. At least it's a distraction.

Time-Saver

To cook hamburgers faster: Add 1 tablespoon of ice water for every 5 to 6 ounces of ground meat used. Just a tablespoon of water per burger reduces the cooking time by 10 percent, regardless of the degree of doneness. As the burger cooks, the water trapped in the meat steams, increasing the speed at which heat will permeate the burger's center. Adding ice water also helps keep burgers juicier, even when cooking them through to well-done.

Hamburger Variations

Green Chile Hamburgers: Mix 1 drained can (4 ounces) chopped green chile peppers and ¼ cup chopped fresh cilantro into 1 to 1½ pounds ground beef. Shape into 4 patties and grill, broil, or pan-fry over medium heat for 4 to 6 minutes per side, or until the center registers 160°F on an instant-read thermometer (for medium) and the meat is no longer pink. Makes 4 burgers.

Onion Hamburgers: Chop 1 large onion. In a large nonstick skillet, cook the onion in 1 teaspoon olive oil over medium heat, stirring frequently, for about 5 minutes, or until the onion is softened and translucent. If the onion becomes dry, add 1 to 2 tablespoons water and continue cooking. Cool, then mix with 1 to 1½ pounds ground beef. Shape into 4 patties and grill, broil, or pan-fry over medium heat for 4 to 6 minutes per side, or until the center registers 160°F on an instant-read thermometer (for medium) and the meat is no longer pink. Makes 4 burgers.

Healthy Burgers

To make a more healthful burger: Replace one-eighth of the ground meat with an equal amount of finely chopped and cooked vegetables, such as onions, peppers, and/or zucchini. Or use equal amounts ground beef and ground turkey or chicken breast meat, mixing well. Or use a blend of chicken and turkey meat (see Poultry 'n' Vegetable Burgers, below). You can also soften ½ cup textured vegetable protein (TVP) in 2 tablespoons hot water and mix it into 1 pound ground beef. To go completely veggie, grill or roast a large portobello mushroom and use it in place of a burger. Or try a ready-made veggie burger from the supermarket.

Poultry 'n' Vegetable Burgers: Chop ¼ onion and ½ small bell pepper. In a large nonstick skillet, cook the onion and pepper in 2 teaspoons olive oil, stirring frequently, until softened. Cool, then mix with ½ pound ground chicken, ½ pound ground turkey breast, and 1 egg white. Shape into 4 patties and grill, broil, or pan-fry over medium heat for 5 to 6 minutes per side, or until the center registers 165°F on an instant-read thermometer and the meat is no longer pink. Makes 4 burgers.

Italian Meatball Sandwiches

Hands-On Time: 30 minutes ■ Total Time: 40 minutes

Stuffed with flavor, these subs will satisfy even the hungriest eaters. You'll save at least $3 a serving by making them at home rather than buying them at a fast-food restaurant.

1 pound lean ground round

¼ cup dried bread crumbs

1 cup coarsely chopped onion

1 tablespoon olive oil

4 cloves garlic, minced

1 can (14.5 ounces) diced tomatoes, with juice

2 tablespoons tomato paste

1 tablespoon sugar

1 teaspoon dried basil

½ teaspoon dried oregano

1 long loaf (16 ounces) Italian or French bread, halved horizontally

½ cup shredded mozzarella cheese

1. In a medium bowl, combine the ground round, bread crumbs, and ¼ cup of the onion. Mix just until blended. Form into 1" meatballs.

2. In a large nonstick skillet, heat the oil over medium-high heat. Add the garlic and the remaining ¾ cup onions. Cook, stirring occasionally, for 5 minutes, or until the onions are golden brown. Add the meatballs and cook for 5 minutes, or until the meatballs are browned on the bottom. Turn the meatballs, then add the tomatoes (with juice), tomato paste, sugar, basil, and oregano. Cover and cook for 10 minutes, or until the meatballs are no longer pink in the center. (Check by inserting the tip of a sharp knife in the center of a meatball.)

3. Scoop out the bread from the bottom half of the loaf. Spoon the meatballs and sauce into the bread shell. Top with the mozzarella and the top half of the bread. Cut into 8 sandwiches.

Makes 8 servings

Beef and Black Bean Chili

Hands-On Time: 30 minutes ■ Total Time: 45 minutes

Wake up your tastebuds with this lively, classic chili, an ideal dish for a family gathering. The snap comes from chili powder plus two chile peppers. The recipe is easily doubled or tripled for a larger party.

1 tablespoon olive oil	1 teaspoon cumin seeds
1½ pounds lean ground beef	1 teaspoon dried oregano
2 red onions, cut into thin wedges	½ teaspoon sugar
3 cloves garlic, minced	¼ teaspoon celery seeds
1 can (15 ounces) crushed tomatoes	1 tomato, diced
2 jalapeño peppers, seeded and chopped (wear plastic gloves when handling)	2 cans (15 ounces each) black beans, rinsed and drained
1 tablespoon chili powder	

1. In a large saucepan, heat the oil over medium-high heat. Add the beef and cook, stirring frequently, for 8 minutes, or until no longer pink. Add the onions and cook, stirring occasionally, for 5 minutes, or until softened. Add the garlic and cook for 1 minute.

2. Add the tomatoes, peppers, chili powder, cumin seeds, oregano, sugar, and celery seeds. Bring to a boil. Reduce the heat to low, cover, and simmer for 10 minutes. Add the tomato and beans. Cook for 3 minutes to heat through.

Makes 6 servings

Ingredients Note

For best flavor, make your own chili powder (see page 28 for a recipe). And, if you have the time, use dried black beans instead of canned. (See page 264 for soaking and cooking tips.)

Accompaniment

Serve the chili with Spinach Salad with Strawberry Mayonnaise (page 68).

Freezing Tip

You can freeze the chili for up to 1 month. Defrost it in the refrigerator the day before you plan to use it.

Tuscan Pork and Chickpeas with Spinach

Hands-On Time: 20 minutes ■ Total Time: 20 minutes

By buying pre-marinated pork tenderloin and prewashed spinach, you save yourself some time on this recipe. But you can easily make your own marinade at home with fresh lemon juice and minced garlic (and an herb of your choice, if you like). If you do, let the pork marinate for at least an hour or for up to 24 hours. Have plenty of robust Italian bread on hand to mop up the pan juices, and pass some red pepper flakes at the table.

¼ cup olive oil

½ cup chopped onion

1¼ pounds pre-marinated lemon-garlic pork tenderloin, cut into ½"-thick slices

1 can (15 ounces) chickpeas, rinsed and drained

1 can (15 ounces) Italian-seasoned tomato sauce

½ teaspoon salt

1½ bags (15 ounces total) baby spinach leaves

2 tablespoons fresh lemon juice

1. In a large skillet, heat the oil over medium-high heat. Add the onion. Cook, stirring occasionally, for about 2 minutes, or until fragrant. Scrape the onion to the side. Add the pork. Cook for about 4 minutes, turning once, until browned on both sides. Add the chickpeas, tomato sauce, and salt. Stir. Adjust the heat so the sauce is at a moderate simmer. Cover and cook for 5 minutes.

2. Add the spinach, one large handful at a time, covering the pan between each addition so the spinach wilts and you can fit more into the pan. Cook for about 3 minutes total, or until all the spinach wilts. Remove the pork to serving plates, leaving the chickpea and spinach mixture in the pan. Add the lemon juice to the pan and stir to combine. Serve the chickpea and spinach mixture with the pork.

Makes 4 to 6 servings

Ingredients Note

Canned chickpeas retain their shape and flavor better than most other canned legumes. Rinsing and draining them before using gets rid of most of the sodium. Rinse them even if you're using the no-salt variety, to get rid of any canned taste.

Leftovers

Use leftover pork tenderloin in stir-fries with your favorite veggies.

Orange Beef and Broccoli

Hands-On Time: 30 minutes ■ Total Time: 40 minutes

This delicious stir-fry will appeal to the whole family. If you're feeding kids, leave out the red pepper flakes or put some on the table for sprinkling. Serve it over brown or white basmati rice.

¼ cup chicken broth

½ cup orange juice

3 tablespoons dry sherry or chicken broth

2 tablespoons soy sauce

1 tablespoon grated fresh ginger

2 teaspoons cornstarch

1 teaspoon toasted sesame oil

½ teaspoon red pepper flakes

¾ pound sirloin, trimmed and cut into ¼"-thick strips

2 teaspoons olive oil

1 large bunch broccoli, cut into florets

1 bunch scallions, cut into ¼"-thick diagonal slices

3 cloves garlic, minced

2 tablespoons water

1. In a medium bowl, combine the broth, orange juice, sherry, soy sauce, ginger, cornstarch, sesame oil, and red pepper flakes. Add the sirloin, tossing to coat. Let stand for 10 minutes.

2. In a large skillet, heat 1 teaspoon of the olive oil over medium-high heat. Add the beef, reserving the marinade. Cook, stirring, for 3 minutes, or until browned. Transfer to a plate.

3. Add the remaining 1 teaspoon olive oil to the skillet. Add the broccoli, scallions, and garlic. Cook, stirring, for 2 minutes. Add the water. Cover and cook for 2 minutes, or until the broccoli is crisp-tender. Add the reserved marinade and cook, stirring, for 3 minutes, or until the mixture boils and thickens slightly.

4. Return the beef to the pan and cook, stirring, for 2 minutes, or until heated through.

Makes 4 servings

Sweet-and-Sour Pork

Hands-On Time: 25 minutes ■ Total Time: 25 minutes

This healthy recipe uses cooking spray rather than oil for stir-frying. The secret is to keep the food in perpetual motion so it doesn't stick to the pan. Use a wooden spoon or a metal stir-fry spatula to gently toss the pieces during cooking.

1 can (20 ounces) pineapple chunks, packed in juice

¼ cup packed brown sugar

2 tablespoons cornstarch

¼ teaspoon ground ginger

¼ cup red wine vinegar

2 tablespoons reduced-sodium soy sauce

1½ pounds boneless pork top loin, trimmed

2 green bell peppers, thinly sliced

1 large onion, thinly sliced

¼ cup water

1. Drain the pineapple, reserving the juice.

2. In a small bowl, combine the sugar, cornstarch, and ginger. Stir well. Stir in the vinegar, soy sauce, and reserved pineapple juice. Set aside.

3. Thinly slice the pork against the grain and cut it into bite-size pieces.

4. Coat a wok or large skillet with cooking spray and heat over medium-high heat. Add the pork and cook, stirring constantly, for 2 minutes. Add the peppers, onion, and water. Cook, stirring constantly, for 3 minutes, or until the pork is no longer pink and the vegetables are crisp-tender.

5. Stir the soy sauce mixture, then add it to the pan. Cook, stirring, just until thickened. Stir in the pineapple chunks and heat through.

Makes 6 servings

Ingredients Note

Look for organically fed pork at butcher shops and specialty food stores. It comes from pigs that eat natural feed without steroids, hormones, or antibiotics.

Accompaniment

The pork and vegetables are delicious served over Asian noodles.

Apple-Orchard Pork Chops

Hands-On Time: 15 minutes ■ Total Time: 25 minutes

The pork you buy today is more than 30 percent lower in fat than the pork that was available a decade ago. Pork sirloin chops are the leanest choice for this recipe, but if you can't find that cut, choose pork loin chops.

1 tablespoon olive oil

4 boneless pork sirloin chops (4 ounces each), trimmed

Ground black pepper

⅔ cup cider or apple juice

2 tablespoons Dijon mustard

2 tart apples, cored and sliced ¼" thick

½ cup raisins

1 bunch scallions, white and light green parts, thinly sliced (½ cup)

3 tablespoons cold water

2 teaspoons cornstarch

1. In a large skillet, heat the oil over medium-high heat. Add the pork and brown on both sides. Sprinkle with the pepper to taste.

2. In a small bowl, stir together the cider and mustard. Pour over the pork. Reduce the heat to low, cover, and cook for 5 minutes.

3. Add the apples, raisins, and scallions to the skillet. Cover and cook for 5 minutes. Use a slotted spoon to transfer the pork and apples to a serving platter. Keep warm. Leave the skillet on the heat.

4. In a small bowl, stir together the water and cornstarch. Add to the skillet, increase the heat to medium, and bring to a boil, stirring constantly. Reduce the heat and cook for 2 minutes. Serve the sauce over the pork chops and apples.

Makes 4 servings

Ingredients Note

Use any tart apples you like: Granny Smith, Empire, or Stayman are all good choices.

Accompaniments

These pork chops are delicious with Spiced Brown Rice with Cashews (page 256) and Balsamic Broccoli Rabe (page 289).

Chinese Barbecued Pork Chops

Hands-On Time: 25 minutes ■ Total Time: 25 minutes

These pork chops are especially good done on the grill. Keep an eye on them, though; cooking too long will dry them out.

⅓ cup tomato sauce

¼ cup hoisin sauce

3 tablespoons rice wine vinegar or white wine vinegar

2 tablespoons dry sherry or chicken broth

3 cloves garlic, minced

1 tablespoon grated fresh ginger

4 boneless center-cut pork chops (4 ounces each), trimmed

1. Coat a grill rack or broiler-pan rack with cooking spray. Preheat the grill or broiler.

2. In a small saucepan, combine the tomato sauce, hoisin sauce, vinegar, sherry, garlic, and ginger. Bring to a boil over medium-high heat. Cook, stirring often, for 3 minutes, or until reduced to a syrupy consistency. Set aside.

3. Meanwhile, grill or broil the pork chops 4" from the heat for 8 minutes, turning once. Continue to cook, brushing with the reserved sauce and turning occasionally, for 3 minutes longer, or until a thermometer inserted in the center of a chop registers 160°F and the juices run clear.

Makes 4 servings

Ingredients Note

Hoisin sauce, also called Peking sauce, is a sweet and spicy, thick, reddish-brown sauce made of soybeans, garlic, chile peppers, and various spices. Keep it refrigerated once opened.

Accompaniment

Serve the pork with Quinoa Pilaf with Toasted Pistachios (page 276).
It's a nice change of pace from rice.

Heartland Pork, Potato, and Apple Bake

Hands-On Time: 5 minutes ■ Total Time: 1 hour

This dinner is as versatile as it is easy. Golden Delicious is a good choice for the apples, or use Granny Smith for more tartness. If you don't care for the French onion flavor, frozen oven-roast potatoes are available in a number of other flavors.

1¼ pounds pre-marinated peppercorn pork tenderloin

1 pound frozen French onion oven-roast potatoes (4 cups)

1 cup chunky unsweetened applesauce

2 apples, cored and cut into walnut-size chunks

2 tablespoons stone-ground mustard

1. Preheat the oven to 375°F. Coat a 17" × 11" baking pan or other large, shallow baking pan with cooking spray.

2. Place the pork, potatoes, applesauce, and apples in the pan. Toss to coat with the applesauce. Clear a diagonal strip in the center of the pan. Place the pork in the cleared space.

3. Bake for about 45 minutes, or until a thermometer inserted into the center reaches 155°F and the juices run clear. Remove the pork to a cutting board. Let stand for 10 minutes. Cut the pork into thin slices. Stir the mustard into the potato-apple mixture and serve with the pork.

Makes 4 to 6 servings

Make-Ahead

Assemble the Heartland Pork, Potato, and Apple Bake, but don't bake it. Cover the baking pan tightly with plastic wrap and refrigerate for up to 3 days. Remove the plastic wrap before baking, or you can complete the cooking and refrigerate the dish to be eaten within a few days. Cool it completely, then store in an airtight container in the refrigerator. To reheat, place one serving on a microwaveable plate and cover with wax paper. Microwave on medium power for 2 minutes, then on high power for 1 minute. Let stand for 1 minute.

Bourbon-Barbecued Pork
with Mesquite Sweet Potato Fries

Hands-On Time: 15 minutes ■ Total Time: 1 hour 15 minutes

Convenient frozen sweet potato oven fries really spark up this barbecue plate. There's no need to thaw them before tossing on the grill.

1 pre-marinated onion-and-garlic or oven-roasted-flavor pork roast (2 pounds)

1 bag (1 pound) frozen sweet potato oven fries

¼ teaspoon mesquite seasoning

Salt (optional)

1 cup bottled barbecue sauce

2 tablespoons bourbon

1. Coat a grill rack and a large perforated grill topper with cooking spray. Preheat the grill.

2. Set the grill topper on the grill away from direct heat. Place the pork on the grill topper. Cook for about 30 minutes.

3. Scatter the fries on the grill topper in a single layer around the pork. Cook for about 15 minutes, tossing occasionally, or until heated. With mitts, move the grill rack over direct heat. Cook, watching carefully, for about 5 minutes, or until the potatoes are sizzling and browned. Remove the pork and potatoes from the grill, and sprinkle both with the mesquite seasoning and salt, if using, to taste. Transfer the potatoes to a platter and keep them warm.

4. Check the pork for doneness (a thermometer should register 155°F when inserted in the center and the juices should run clear). Return the pork to the grill, if necessary, to finish cooking. When the pork is done, let it stand for 10 minutes before carving.

5. Meanwhile, combine the barbecue sauce and bourbon in a microwaveable bowl. Cover with wax paper and microwave on high power for 2 minutes, or until hot.

6. Cut the pork into thin slices. Drizzle with the sauce. Serve with the potatoes on the side.

Makes 4 servings

Ingredients Note

Mesquite seasoning, available in the spice racks of many supermarkets, usually includes salt, garlic, onion, red bell pepper, sugar, and paprika in addition to the sweet "natural mesquite smoke" flavor. It's a great flavor complement to the sweet potatoes. Taste it before adding the optional extra salt.

Oven Pork Barbecue

Hands-On Time: 30 minutes ■ Total Time: 1 hour 10 minutes

For a summer picnic, serve this Southern-style barbecued pork on buns along with your favorite slaw, sliced tomatoes, corn on the cob, and watermelon.

1 chipotle chile pepper (wear plastic gloves when handling)

2 tablespoons olive oil

¾ pound pork tenderloin

¼ teaspoon ground black pepper

⅛ teaspoon ground red pepper

⅔ cup diced onion

1 tablespoon minced garlic

½ cup barbecue sauce

¼ cup ketchup

¼ cup water

1 teaspoon maple syrup

4 sandwich buns, split and warmed

1. Place the chipotle pepper in a small bowl. Cover with hot water and let stand for 5 minutes. Drain and remove the stem and seeds. Coarsely chop the pepper and set aside.

2. In a large nonstick skillet, heat 1 tablespoon of the oil over high heat until hot but not smoking. Add the pork and brown on all sides. Sprinkle with the black and red pepper. Transfer the pork to a large sheet of foil.

3. In a 2-quart saucepan, heat the remaining 1 tablespoon olive oil over medium heat. Add the onion and cook, stirring occasionally, for 5 minutes, or until softened. Add the garlic and cook for 1 minute longer. Add the barbecue sauce, ketchup, water, maple syrup, and the chopped chipotle pepper. Bring to a boil and simmer for 10 minutes.

4. Preheat the oven to 350°F.

5. Spoon one-third of the sauce over the pork. Wrap well in the foil and bake for 25 minutes, or until a thermometer inserted in the center reaches 155°F and the juices run clear.

6. Cut the pork into very thin slices, then cut again into thin strips. Add the pork to the remaining sauce in the saucepan and heat through. Serve on the buns.

Makes 4 servings

Ingredients Note

Chipotle peppers are smoked and dried jalapeño peppers. If you can't find a fresh chipotle, use a canned chipotle, which comes in adobo sauce (you can use a little of the sauce or rinse off the pepper). There's no substitute for the flavor of a chipotle, but if you have trouble finding one, you can use a fresh serrano or jalapeño pepper to add the needed spiciness.

Pork and Sweet Potato Stew

Hands-On Time: 35 minutes ■ Total Time: 2 hours

This is a version of a stew popular in South America. It combines lean pork loin with healthy sweet potatoes for a hearty main-course meal.

2 teaspoons olive oil

¾ pound lean pork loin, cut into ¾" cubes

2 cups diced onion

½ cup thinly sliced carrots

½ cup thinly sliced celery

1 tablespoon minced garlic

2 teaspoons ground cumin

1 can (28 ounces) diced Italian tomatoes, with juice

1 large sweet potato, cubed

2 tablespoons currants or raisins

2 cups packed chopped escarole

1 tablespoon water

¼ teaspoon ground black pepper

2 tablespoons minced fresh cilantro

1. In a Dutch oven, heat the oil over medium heat. Add the pork and cook for 10 minutes, turning to brown on all sides. Add the onion, carrots, celery, and garlic. Reduce the heat to low, cover, and cook for 10 minutes longer. Stir in the cumin. Cover and cook for 10 minutes longer, or until the vegetables are tender.

2. Add the tomatoes (with juice), sweet potato, and currants. Cover and cook over medium-low heat for 45 minutes to 1 hour, or until the meat and potatoes are tender.

3. Meanwhile, in a large nonstick skillet, combine the escarole and water. Cover and cook over low heat for about 12 minutes, or until the escarole is wilted and almost tender.

4. Stir the escarole and any pan juices into the stew. Add the pepper and stir. Cover and simmer for 10 minutes to meld the flavors. Serve sprinkled with the cilantro.

Makes 4 servings

Variation

Replace the pork with cubes of veal, lamb, beef, chicken, or turkey.
If you use chicken or turkey, reduce the cooking time to 30 minutes.

Stuffed Pork Loin

Hands-On Time: 30 minutes ■ Total Time: 1 hour 35 minutes (plus marinating)

To roast the pork loin, you will need a cooking bag that is big enough to contain the roast and a small rack. This cooking method keeps the pork nice and moist. Serve it with baked potatoes, steamed broccoli, and a fruit salad of apple and orange slices.

Pork

2 pounds pork tenderloin, trimmed of all visible fat

2 cloves garlic, minced

2 small chile peppers, seeded and minced

2 tablespoons fresh lime juice

1 tablespoon minced fresh oregano

½ teaspoon ground cumin

½ teaspoon honey

Pinch of ground cinnamon

1 tablespoon flour

½ cup chicken broth

Stuffing

1 cup cooked brown rice

½ cup corn

¼ cup diced red bell pepper

¼ cup diced onion

2 cloves garlic, minced

1 egg, lightly beaten

1. *To make the pork:* Make a long, deep, lengthwise slit in the meat as a pocket for the stuffing.

2. In a small bowl, combine the garlic, chile peppers, lime juice, oregano, cumin, honey, and cinnamon. Rub over the meat with the mixture, inside and out. Cover and refrigerate overnight.

3. *To make the stuffing:* Just before you're ready to stuff the pork, in a medium bowl, combine the rice, corn, bell pepper, onion, garlic, and egg.

4. Preheat the oven to 450°F. Pack the stuffing into the slit area. Tie the roast with kitchen string to contain the stuffing. Set the meat on a roasting rack.

5. Place the flour in an oven cooking bag and shake to coat the interior of the bag. Place the roast and rack in the bag. Add the broth. Tie the bag shut and follow the bag package directions for making slits for steam to escape. Place the bag in a shallow roasting pan.

6. Place the roast in the oven and reduce the temperature to 350°F. Bake for 50 minutes, or until a thermometer inserted in the center reaches 155°F and the juices run clear. Remove from the oven and let stand for 15 minutes for easier carving.

Makes 8 servings

Grilled Italian Sausage–Stuffed Zucchini

Hands-On Time: 10 minutes ■ Total Time: 45 minutes

This dish is marvelous to serve to company. Cover the zucchini with plastic wrap and refrigerate for up to 24 hours before grilling.

6 zucchini (6" long), halved lengthwise

1¼ pounds loose-pack mild or hot Italian sausage

¾ cup canned onion-garlic diced tomatoes

¾ cup shredded Parmesan and Romano cheese blend

1. Coat a grill rack with cooking spray. Preheat the grill to low.

2. Use a melon baller or a small spoon to scoop out the pulpy seeds in the zucchini halves. Discard the seeds.

3. In a large bowl, combine the sausage, tomatoes, and ½ cup of the cheese. Mix well with your hands. Press equal amounts of the mixture on top of each zucchini half to cover evenly. Sprinkle the remaining ¼ cup cheese over the tops.

4. Place on the grill away from direct heat. Cover and cook for about 45 minutes, or until the sausage is no longer pink.

Makes 4 to 6 servings

Ingredients Notes

Italian sausage links may replace the loose-pack sausage. Use kitchen scissors to quickly cut the casings for removal. You can use any seasoned diced tomatoes you prefer.

Rosemary-Fennel Lamb Chops

Hands-On Time: 15 minutes ■ Total Time: 30 minutes

Rubbing freshly ground herbs and spices into meat or poultry accomplishes the same purpose as marinating, but it does it more quickly and produces a more intense flavor.

1 teaspoon dried rosemary	¼ teaspoon ground black pepper
1 teaspoon dried thyme	¼ teaspoon salt
½ teaspoon garlic powder	4 rib lamb chops (1½ pounds)
¼ teaspoon fennel seeds	

1. In a clean coffee or spice mill, or in a mortar and pestle, grind the rosemary, thyme, garlic powder, fennel seeds, pepper, and salt to a fine powder. Rub the spice mixture over both sides of the lamb chops and place them on a plate. Cover and let stand at room temperature for 15 minutes.

2. Preheat the broiler. Place the chops on a broiler-pan rack and broil 4" to 5" from the heat for 6 to 8 minutes, turning once, or until browned and a thermometer inserted in the center registers 145°F for medium-rare. (The cooking time will depend on the thickness of the chops.)

Makes 4 servings

Kitchen Tip

Handheld electric coffee mills (also sold as spice mills) are perfect for grinding spices. It's best, however, not to use the same mill for coffee and spices: Both have pervasive aromas, and you may end up with coffee-flavored spices or spice-scented coffee.

Make-Ahead

Grind the herbs and spices in advance and store them in a small jar with a tight-fitting lid in a cool, dry place.

Accompaniments

Complement the full-flavored lamb with a salad of tart-bitter greens such as chicory, arugula, or mizuna (Japanese mustard greens). Rice pilaf, orzo (rice-shaped pasta), or couscous provides a fine foil for the meat's richness.

Easy Marinades, Rubs, and Herb Crusts for Meat

Marinades are an effective way to flavor and moisten extra-lean cuts of meat, which can be dry. Use about 1 pound of lean beef or pork with any of these marinades. For best results, marinate in the refrigerator for at least 1 hour. During cooking, baste meats frequently with the marinade. Another easy way to increase flavor while cutting back on fat is to rub meat with spices or herbs. Rubs can be put on dry, though adding a teaspoon of water or broth will help them spread more evenly. Always use fresh herbs, unless otherwise indicated.

CITRUS GLAZE MARINADE

¼ cup fresh lemon juice

1 tablespoon honey

1 teaspoon grated lemon zest

¼ teaspoon ground black pepper

¼ teaspoon salt

Makes about ⅓ cup

CURRY YOGURT MARINADE

½ cup nonfat plain yogurt

1 tablespoon brown sugar

1 teaspoon curry powder

1 teaspoon olive oil

Makes about ½ cup

HONEY AND SPICE MARINADE

3 tablespoons honey

2 tablespoons Dijon mustard

1 tablespoon fresh lemon juice

1 tablespoon frozen orange juice concentrate

1 teaspoon ground cinnamon

Makes about ⅓ cup

LATIN SALSA MARINADE

⅓ cup mild salsa

1 tablespoon brown sugar

½ teaspoon ground cumin

¼ teaspoon ground red pepper

Pinch of salt

Makes about ⅓ cup

TOMATO BLISS MARINADE

¼ cup tomato purée

¼ cup nonfat plain yogurt

1 tablespoon reduced-sodium soy sauce

1 teaspoon chili powder

1 teaspoon minced garlic

1 teaspoon sugar

Makes about ½ cup

ZIPPY MUSTARD MARINADE

¼ cup fresh lemon or lime juice

1 tablespoon Dijon mustard

1 tablespoon chopped fresh parsley or cilantro

1 teaspoon minced garlic

1 teaspoon grated lime or lemon zest

Makes about ⅓ cup

CAJUN SPICE RUB

1 tablespoon paprika

1 teaspoon garlic powder

1 teaspoon onion powder

½ teaspoon dried oregano

½ teaspoon dried thyme

⅛ teaspoon ground black pepper

⅛ teaspoon ground red pepper

Makes about 2½ tablespoons

MEXICAN SPICE RUB

1 tablespoon chili powder

1 tablespoon chopped fresh cilantro

2 cloves garlic, minced

½ teaspoon ground cumin

⅛ teaspoon ground red pepper

Makes about 2½ tablespoons

MOROCCAN SPICE RUB

1 tablespoon chopped fresh mint

2 cloves garlic, minced

2 teaspoons grated fresh ginger

½ teaspoon ground cinnamon

½ teaspoon ground cumin

Makes about 2 tablespoons

FRENCH HERB CRUST

3 tablespoons chopped fresh parsley

1 tablespoon chopped fresh chives

2 cloves garlic, minced

2 teaspoons chopped fresh thyme

2 teaspoons grated orange zest

Makes about 5 tablespoons

GREEK HERB CRUST

2 tablespoons chopped fresh parsley

1 tablespoon grated lemon zest

2 cloves garlic, minced

1 tablespoon chopped fresh oregano

Make about 4 tablespoons

ITALIAN HERB CRUST

3 tablespoons chopped fresh parsley

2 tablespoons chopped fresh basil

2 cloves garlic, minced

2 teaspoons grated lemon zest

Makes about 5½ tablespoons

TRADITIONAL HERB CRUST

2 tablespoons chopped fresh parsley

1½ tablespoons chopped fresh rosemary

2 cloves garlic, minced

Greek Lamb Kebabs with Confetti Rice

Hands-On Time: 40 minutes ■ Total Time: 55 minutes

Lamb kebabs, which are often cooked over a charcoal brazier, are traditional picnic fare in Greece. Topping the cooked lamb with a yogurt sauce gives it a delicious tangy flavor.

1   cup long-grain white rice

1   pound boneless leg of lamb, well-trimmed and cut into 16 cubes, 1" each

1   green bell pepper, cut into 1" pieces

1   cup plain yogurt

½   cup minced red onion

1   tablespoon honey

2   cloves garlic, minced

1   teaspoon curry powder

¼   cup chicken broth

2   tablespoons diced carrots

2   tablespoons whole kernel corn

2   tablespoons chopped scallions

½   teaspoon salt

½   teaspoon ground black pepper

4   cherry tomatoes

1. Cook the rice according to the package directions.

2. Meanwhile, thread the lamb and bell pepper onto 4 skewers, each 12" long.

3. In a medium bowl, combine the yogurt, onion, honey, garlic, and curry powder. Stir well. Let stand at room temperature, stirring occasionally.

4. When the rice is done, in a large nonstick skillet, combine the broth, carrots, corn, and scallions. Cook over medium heat, stirring occasionally, for 5 minutes, or until the carrots are soft. Add the cooked rice. Cover and cook for 3 minutes, stirring occasionally. Add the salt and black pepper. Remove from the heat, cover, and keep warm.

5. Coat a grill rack or broiler-pan rack with cooking spray. Preheat the grill or broiler to medium. Grill or broil the lamb skewers 4" from the heat for 5 minutes. Turn and cook for 2 minutes longer, or until the lamb has browned on all sides. Carefully add the tomatoes to the skewers and cook for 1 minute, or until the tomatoes are hot.

6. Serve the kebabs over the confetti rice. Top with the yogurt sauce.

Makes 4 servings

Ingredients Note

For a richer sauce, use Greek-style yogurt, available in many markets. It's been strained for several hours before being packaged, reducing its water content and resulting in a creamier product.

Braised Provençal Lamb Shanks

Hands-On Time: 25 minutes ■ Total Time: 1 hour 20 minutes

Here's an amazing way to get incredible "all-day-in-the-kitchen" flavor in about an hour. But you'll need a pressure cooker to do so. There are a variety of pressure cookers on the market, usually ranging from 4 to 8 quarts. A 6-quart model is good for most jobs, but go larger if you have a big family. Don't worry, they're far safer than those of yesteryear. If you prefer, you can make the recipe the traditional way. See Variation, below.

2 tablespoons extra-virgin olive oil

8 carrots, cut into sticks

8 stalks celery, cut into sticks

1 cup chopped onion

2 tablespoons garlic

1 cup dry red wine

6 lamb shanks (3½ to 4 pounds)

1 can (14.5 ounces) diced tomatoes with Burgundy wine and olive oil, with juice

1 teaspoon herbes de Provence

½ teaspoon ground black pepper

½ teaspoon salt

1. In a pressure cooker pot, heat the oil over medium-high heat. Add the carrots, celery, onion, and garlic. Cook, stirring occasionally, for 5 minutes, or until softened. Add the wine. Allow the mixture to come to a boil.

2. Add the lamb, tomatoes (with juice), herbes de Provence, pepper, and salt. Stir to combine. Cover the pot and lock the lid. Bring to high pressure over high heat. Reduce the heat to maintain high pressure. Cook for 20 minutes.

3. Allow the pressure to release naturally. Remove the lid. Transfer the meat to a platter. Let stand for 15 minutes, or until the meat is cool enough to handle. Remove the meat from the bones. Discard the bones and any fat or gristle. Return the meat to the pot and serve with the sauce.

Makes 4 to 6 servings

Variation

To prepare the recipe by the conventional stove-top method in a large pot,
follow the recipe to the point where the lamb, tomatoes, and seasonings are added.
Cover and bring almost to a boil. Reduce the heat so the mixture simmers gently.
Cook for about 2 hours, or until the lamb is fork-tender.

Herb-Crusted Roast Leg of Lamb

Hands-On Time: 15 minutes ■ Total Time: 2 hours 25 minutes (plus marinating)

A flavorful herb rub and a crusty bread-crumb topping give this leg of lamb a company-special touch. Serve the lamb with Artichoke Gratin (page 282) and Root Vegetable Mash (page 312). For dessert, bring out Heavenly Orange Cake (page 318).

3 cloves garlic, minced

1 teaspoon dried rosemary

1 teaspoon dried thyme

½ teaspoon ground black pepper

¼ teaspoon salt

2 teaspoons plus 1 tablespoon olive oil

1 boneless leg of lamb (3 pounds), trimmed, rolled, and tied by the butcher

½ cup fine, dried, plain bread crumbs

¼ cup minced fresh parsley

⅓ cup water

1. In a small bowl, stir together the garlic, rosemary, thyme, pepper, and salt. Rub 2 teaspoons of the oil into the lamb. Spread the garlic mixture over the lamb. Cover and refrigerate for 3 to 4 hours.

2. Preheat the oven to 300°F. Coat a roasting rack with cooking spray and place the rack in a roasting pan. Place the lamb on the rack and roast for 1 hour.

3. In a small bowl, combine the bread crumbs and parsley. Stir in the water and the remaining 1 table-spoon oil to make a paste. Spread the paste over the lamb.

4. Bake for 55 to 70 minutes, or until a meat thermometer registers 145°F for medium-rare or 160°F for medium.

Makes 8 servings

Ingredients Note

If you have the time, make your own bread crumbs (see page 121).

Pastitsio

Hands-On Time: 40 minutes ■ Total Time: 1 hour

A not-too-distant cousin of lasagna, *pastitsio* is a Greek pasta casserole with layers of macaroni, cheese sauce, and meat. Rather than making the traditional béchamel, this recipe uses a ricotta-based sauce that's thick and rich-tasting but low in fat. And, for a contemporary look, fettuccine is used instead of macaroni.

1 cup 1% milk	¾ pound boneless leg of lamb, well-trimmed and cut into chunks
½ cup chicken broth	8 ounces eggplant, diced
3 tablespoons all-purpose flour	8 ounces zucchini, diced
¼ teaspoon freshly grated nutmeg	½ cup coarsely chopped onion
3 tablespoons grated Parmesan cheese	3 tablespoons chopped fresh mint
½ cup part-skim ricotta cheese	¼ teaspoon ground black pepper
1 tablespoon chopped fresh dill	1 can (15 ounces) tomato sauce
8 ounces fettuccine	

1. Preheat the oven to 375°F. Bring a large covered pot of water to a boil over high heat.

2. Meanwhile, in a large nonstick skillet over medium-high heat, whisk together the milk, broth, flour, nutmeg, and 2 tablespoons of the Parmesan. Cook, whisking constantly, for 3 minutes, or until thickened. Whisk in the ricotta and dill, then transfer the mixture to a large bowl. Rinse and dry the skillet.

3. Add the fettuccine to the boiling water and cook according to package directions until al dente. Drain the pasta in a colander, then add to the cheese mixture and toss well. Set aside.

4. While the pasta is cooking, place the lamb in a food processor and process until finely ground.

5. In the same large skillet, combine the lamb, eggplant, zucchini, and onion. Cook over medium-high heat for 5 minutes, or until the vegetables are tender and the lamb is browned on all sides. Stir in the mint and pepper. Stir in the tomato sauce and simmer, stirring occasionally, for 2 minutes. Remove the skillet from the heat.

6. Coat an 11" × 7" baking dish with cooking spray. Spoon half of the pasta-cheese mixture into the bottom. Spoon the lamb mixture over the pasta and then top with the remaining pasta-cheese mixture. Bake for 10 minutes. Sprinkle with the remaining 1 tablespoon Parmesan. Bake for 5 minutes longer, or until heated through.

Makes 4 servings

Irish Stew

Even Irish people don't agree on what exactly constitutes an authentic Irish stew. Like any peasant dish, it varies depending on the season and what is on hand. Most, like this one, feature lamb and a variety of vegetables.

¾ pound boneless leg of lamb, well-trimmed and cut into 1" cubes

¾ pound small red potatoes, quartered

6 cups water

3 cups beef broth

3 carrots, sliced

3 parsnips, sliced

8 ounces green or red cabbage, shredded

1 large onion, halved and sliced

1 bay leaf

1 teaspoon dried thyme

½ teaspoon salt

¼ cup chopped fresh parsley

1. In a Dutch oven, combine the lamb, potatoes, water, broth, carrots, parsnips, cabbage, onion, bay leaf, thyme, and salt. Cover and bring to a boil over high heat. Reduce the heat to medium-low. Partially cover and simmer for 45 minutes.

2. Remove the lid and cook, stirring occasionally, for 45 minutes longer, or until the lamb is fork-tender.

3. Stir in the parsley. Remove and discard the bay leaf.

Makes 4 servings

Make-Ahead

This dish only improves with time. Make it a day ahead and reheat it. A sprinkling of lemon zest and additional chopped parsley just before serving will heighten the flavors.

Lamb Curry

Hands-On Time: 30 minutes ■ Total Time: 50 minutes

Cooks in India designed this dish to use up leftover lamb by combining it with a rainbow of spices and vegetables.

2 tablespoons olive oil

1 medium eggplant, thinly sliced

1 onion, diced

⅓ cup apple juice

1 teaspoon minced garlic

1 pound boneless leg of lamb, well-trimmed and cut into 1" cubes

1 can (14.5 ounces) diced tomatoes, with juice

¼ cup chicken broth

3 tablespoons curry powder

1 teaspoon ground black pepper

½ teaspoon ground coriander

½ cup plain yogurt

2 tablespoons minced fresh cilantro

1. In a large nonstick skillet, heat the oil over medium-high heat. Add the eggplant, onion, apple juice, and garlic. Cook, stirring, for 5 minutes.

2. Add the lamb, tomatoes (with juice), broth, curry powder, pepper, and coriander. Bring to a boil. Reduce the heat to medium. Cook, stirring occasionally, for 20 minutes, or until the curry is thick and the lamb is no longer pink in the center.

3. Serve topped with the yogurt and sprinkled with the cilantro.

Makes 4 servings

Freezing Tip

To freeze, pack the cooled cooked curry in a freezer-quality plastic container. To use, thaw overnight in the refrigerator. Cover and microwave on high power for 5 minutes, or until hot.

Fisherman's Catch

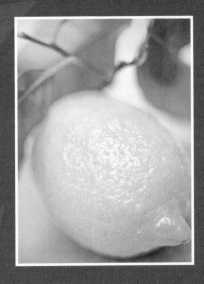

"Give a man a fish and he'll eat for a day.
Teach a man to fish and he'll eat for a lifetime."

—CHINESE PROVERB

Cornmeal-Crusted Catfish

Hands-On Time: 15 minutes ■ Total Time: 30 minutes

A crisp cornmeal coating, sparked with lime, enhances pan-fried catfish. The fish is especially delicious served with a fresh salsa cruda (see Accompaniments, below).

½ cup buttermilk

1 tablespoon fresh lime juice

⅓ cup cornmeal

⅓ cup all-purpose flour

4 scallions, minced

¼ teaspoon ground cumin

¼ teaspoon salt

4 catfish fillets (5 ounces each)

2 tablespoons olive oil

1. Line a large plate with wax paper.

2. In a medium, shallow bowl, combine the buttermilk and lime juice. In another shallow bowl, combine the cornmeal, flour, scallions, cumin, and salt. Stir to mix.

3. Dip the fillets into the buttermilk mixture, then into the cornmeal mixture, pressing gently to help it adhere. Place on the prepared plate. Refrigerate for 15 minutes.

4. In a large nonstick skillet, heat the oil over medium-high heat. Add the fillets and cook for 4 to 5 minutes, or until golden brown on the bottom. Turn and cook 4 to 5 minutes longer, or until the fish flakes easily.

Makes 4 servings

Accompaniments

A fresh salsa cruda is a zesty partner for crispy pan-fried catfish. In a small bowl, combine 4 chopped plum tomatoes, ¼ cup chopped red onion, 2 minced cloves garlic, 2 tablespoons fresh lime juice, 2 tablespoons chopped fresh cilantro, 1 seeded and minced jalapeño pepper (wear plastic gloves when handling), 1 teaspoon sugar, and a pinch each of salt and pepper. Allow the salsa to sit at room temperature for 15 to 20 minutes for the flavors to develop.

Baked Cod with Lemon and Herbs

Hands-On Time: 10 minutes ■ Total Time: 20 minutes

You won't miss those restaurant meals with this gourmet recipe. We use a foolproof French-inspired method—cooking in a sealed packet—for keeping fish flavorful and moist. You can also use a very tightly covered pan to achieve the same moisture-sealing effect; it turns ordinary fish into an extraordinary dinner with only the simplest seasonings.

¼ cup chopped scallions

3 tablespoons chopped fresh parsley

2 tablespoons fresh lemon juice

1 tablespoon grated lemon zest

2 cloves garlic, minced

1 teaspoon olive oil

4 cod fillets (4 ounces each)

1. Preheat the oven to 450°F. Arrange 4 sheets of foil (12" × 12" each) on a work surface.

2. In a small bowl, combine the scallions, parsley, lemon juice, lemon zest, garlic, and oil. Place 1 fillet in the center of each piece of foil. Top each with one-quarter of the lemon mixture. Fold the sides of the foil over the fish, creating a sealed packet. Place the packets on a baking sheet.

3. Bake for 8 minutes. The fish should flake easily with a fork. Check for doneness by opening the packets very carefully (steam will be released). Serve with the cooking liquid.

Makes 4 servings

Variation

You could use haddock, scrod, or hake instead of cod for this recipe.

Maryland Crab Cakes

These Chesapeake-style crab patties make a delicious appetizer or light lunch, served with a mélange of greens.

⅓ cup mayonnaise	2 tablespoons olive oil
1 tablespoon Worcestershire sauce	1½ cups lump crab meat, flaked
1 teaspoon fresh lemon juice	½ cup seasoned dried bread crumbs
⅛ teaspoon ground ginger	1 egg white, lightly beaten
⅛ teaspoon paprika	¼ cup minced onion
⅛ teaspoon ground black pepper	¼ cup minced celery
¼ teaspoon hot pepper sauce	Lemon wedges (optional)

1. In a food processor, combine the mayonnaise. Worcestershire, lemon juice, ginger, paprika, black pepper, hot pepper sauce, and 1 teaspoon of the oil. Process until smooth. Transfer to a large bowl.

2. Add the crab meat, bread crumbs, egg white, onion, and celery to the bowl. Mix well. Chill for 30 minutes to make handling easier.

3. Form the crab mixture into 4 large or 8 small patties.

4. In a large nonstick skillet, heat the remaining 5 teaspoons oil over medium heat. Add the patties and cook for 4 to 5 minutes per side, or until brown. Serve with the lemon wedges, if desired.

Makes 4 servings

Ingredients Note

You may use fresh or canned crab or crab substitute.

Accompaniments

Serve with a light tartar sauce (pickle relish mixed with yogurt), Three-Bean Salad with Mustard Dressing (page 64), and Herbed Oven Fries (page 307).

White Clam Pizzas

Hands-On Time: 10 minutes ■ Total Time: 30 minutes

These pizzas are superquick because you buy prepared pizza dough, minced garlic, and shredded Parmesan. To save even more time, at your next patio party, invite guests to shape and top their own pizzas. You'll cut your prep time to nothing.

1 tube (10 ounces) refrigerated pizza dough

All-purpose flour

Extra-virgin olive oil

2 teaspoons minced garlic

1 container (3 ounces) whole clams, rinsed, drained, and patted dry, or ½ cup canned whole clams, rinsed and drained

2 tablespoons shredded Parmesan cheese

1. Preheat the grill.

2. Remove the dough from the package, but don't unroll it. Cut it into 8 pieces. Fold the edges under and pinch to form balls. Let them stand for 5 minutes.

3. On a lightly floured surface, roll or pat each piece into a 4" circle. Place each circle on a piece of aluminum foil. Brush with the oil. Spread each round with ¼ teaspoon of the garlic. Scatter the clams and the Parmesan evenly over each round.

4. Place the pizzas on the grill away from direct heat. Grill, in batches if necessary, for about 15 minutes, or until browned and sizzling.

Makes 8 small pizzas

Variations

You could add chopped cooked oysters or shrimp to this recipe and a sprinkling of crispy bacon, if you like.

Mediterranean Flounder

Hands-On Time: 10 minutes ■ Total Time: 25 minutes

Like the cod on page 173, flounder also lends itself to packet cooking. The feta and olives provide a vibrant sauce for this delicately flavored fish.

4 flounder fillets (5 ounces each)

1 teaspoon dried oregano

¼ teaspoon salt

½ cucumber, halved, peeled, seeded, and sliced

3 plum tomatoes, sliced

⅓ cup crumbled feta cheese

2 tablespoons chopped pitted kalamata olives

6 tablespoons chicken broth

1. Preheat the oven to 350°F. Arrange 4 sheets of foil (12" × 12" each) on a work surface.

2. Place 1 fillet in the center of each piece of foil. Combine the oregano and salt in a small bowl. Then season the fillet. Bring the sides of the foil pieces up slightly to cup each fillet.

3. Top each fillet with equal amounts of the cucumber, tomatoes, feta, and olives. Add 1½ tablespoons of the broth to each packet. Bring the edges of each piece of foil together and crimp to seal. Place the packets on a baking sheet.

4. Bake for 15 minutes, or until the fish flakes easily. Check for doneness by opening 1 packet very carefully (steam will be released) and flaking with a fork. To serve, transfer the contents of each packet to a plate.

Makes 4 servings

Accompaniments

Serve with Millet Pilaf (page 274) as a side dish and Honey-Baked Pears (page 330) for dessert.

Halibut with Tropical Salsa

Hands-On Time: 25 minutes ■ Total Time: 35 minutes

Fruit salsa is delicious on any type of fish but particularly good on strong-flavored halilbut. This one is made from canned pineapple and mandarin oranges, which are often on sale at the supermarket.

1 can (8 ounces) unsweetened crushed pineapple, with juice

1 can (8 ounces) mandarin oranges, drained

½ cup minced green bell pepper

¼ cup minced red onion

¼ cup fresh lime juice

2 tablespoons minced fresh cilantro or parsley

2 cloves garlic, minced

1 teaspoon ground cumin

4 halibut steaks (3 ounces each)

1. In a medium bowl, combine the pineapple (with juice), oranges, pepper, onion, lime juice, cilantro, garlic, and cumin. Stir well. Cover and let stand at room temperature for 10 minutes.

2. Coat a grill rack or broiler-pan rack with cooking spray. Preheat the grill or broiler.

3. Grill or broil the halibut 4" from the heat for 5 minutes. Turn and cook for 5 to 7 minutes longer, or until the fish is opaque in the center. Top with the salsa.

Makes 4 servings

Ingredients Note

When buying halibut steaks, use the same freshness test you would for a whole fish. The steaks should look recently cut and firm, and their color should be translucent. Avoid any with red spots or browning around the edges.

Poaching Fish and Shellfish

Poaching refers to the technique of cooking food slowly and gently in a simmering, but not boiling, liquid. This moist-heat cooking method is ideal for preparing delicate foods such as fish and shellfish. The poaching liquid may be flavored or seasoned with any herbs or spices you like (or use the recipes below). This flavor will then transfer to the seafood. Here are some poaching pointers.

Equipment: If you don't poach fish often, you can improvise with a large saucepan or skillet, a roasting pan, or an oval sauté pan. Be sure it is deep enough to cover the fish with the poaching liquid. If you plan to poach whole fish, the most convenient piece of equipment is a fish poacher with a rack, which helps keep the fish from falling apart.

The poaching liquid: The poaching liquid should hover between 160°F and 170°F. The surface of the water should look like it's just about to bubble, without ever reaching a simmer. Keep the food completely submerged in the poaching liquid by pressing a sheet of parchment paper directly onto the surface of the cooking liquid—but don't cover the pot, because that will increase the cooking temperature. Check frequently and adjust the burner temperature to maintain a bare simmer. If you're using a fish poacher, you can place it over the span of two burners on the stove for more even heating.

Cooking times: Cooking times vary for different thicknesses of fish. A general rule is to allow 3 to 4 minutes for fresh fish ¼" to ½" thick (4 to 6 minutes for frozen), 4 to 6 minutes for fresh fish ½" to ¾" thick (6 to 10 minutes for frozen), and 8 to 12 minutes for fresh fish 1" to 1½" thick (13 to 22 minutes for frozen). Cook until the fish flakes easily when tested with a fork. Lift the cooked fish carefully from the liquid with a wide spatula. Drain well, patting excess moisture from the fish with paper towels. Shrimp overcook quickly and become very tough. Small shrimp take only about 1 minute to poach; medium shrimp (2 or 3 inches long) take about 2 minutes; larger shrimp take 3 to 4 minutes. If possible, poach shrimp in their shells, which protect the delicate meat as it cooks. When the shrimp are cooked, they will be pink, firm, and opaque in the center. Cut one to check. If it still looks translucent, poach for another 30 seconds, then check again. When the shrimp are done, drain them.

Seasoned Poaching Broths

Wine broth: In a large saucepan or skillet, simmer 6 cups water, 3 cups white wine, 2 chopped celery stalks, 2 chopped carrots, 2 chopped onions, and 2 teaspoons salt for 20 minutes. Strain and use to poach fish or shellfish.

Orange spice broth: In a large saucepan or skillet, simmer 3 cups each water and orange juice, 2 cups white wine, 1 large sliced leek, 4 star anise, and 6 allspice berries for 15 minutes. Strain and use to poach fish or shellfish.

Mahi Mahi with Mustard-Caper Sauce

Hands-On Time: 15 minutes ■ Total Time: 15 minutes (plus marinating)

Mahi mahi is a lean, firm, and fine-textured fish. The savory mustard-caper sauce need not be reserved for this fish, however. Try it with other "steak-type" seafood such as swordfish, shark, and halibut.

2 pounds mahi mahi steaks	2 tablespoons Dijon mustard
½ cup bottled French vinaigrette dressing	2 tablespoons capers, rinsed and drained
⅓ cup dried bread crumbs	

1. In a large zip-top bag, combine the fish and dressing. Massage the bag to coat evenly. Refrigerate for 30 minutes.

2. Coat a grill rack or broiler-pan rack with cooking spray. Preheat the grill or broiler.

3. Remove the fish from the bag, pouring the marinade into a microwaveable bowl. Cover the bowl with wax paper. Microwave on high power for 2 minutes, or until boiling. Set aside.

4. Sprinkle both sides of the fish with the bread crumbs to coat. Grill or broil the fish, turning once, for 3 to 4 minutes per side, or until just opaque.

5. Meanwhile, whisk the mustard and capers into the reserved marinade. Drizzle over the fish just before serving.

Makes 4 to 6 servings

Variations

For a change of pace, use pompano, snapper, or cod in this recipe.

Salmon Burgers

Hands-On Time: 25 minutes ■ Total Time: 25 minutes (plus chilling)

Canned salmon is a convenient and cheap way to get good fish protein into your menus. It makes delicious burgers when combined with lemon-ginger seasoning.

1	can (16 ounces) salmon, flaked	$\frac{1}{2}$	teaspoon ground black pepper
$\frac{1}{2}$	cup dried bread crumbs	2	tablespoons plain yogurt
3	scallions, chopped	1	tablespoon mayonnaise
2	eggs, lightly beaten	1	teaspoon Dijon mustard
1	teaspoon minced fresh ginger	$\frac{1}{2}$	teaspoon honey
1	teaspoon fresh lemon juice	4	hamburger buns (optional)
$\frac{1}{8}$	teaspoon paprika		

1. In a medium bowl, combine the salmon, bread crumbs, scallions, eggs, ginger, lemon juice, and paprika. Form into 4 burgers. Sprinkle with the pepper. Cover and refrigerate for 10 minutes.

2. Coat a large nonstick skillet with cooking spray and set it over medium-high heat. When the skillet is hot, add the burgers. Cook for 5 minutes, turn, and cook for 3 minutes longer, or until the burgers are firm and golden brown.

3. In a small bowl, combine the yogurt, mayonnaise, mustard, and honey.

4. Place the burgers on the buns, if using, and top with the yogurt sauce.

Makes 4 servings

Pesto Salmon

Hands-On Time: 20 minutes ■ Total Time: 35 minutes

Homemade pesto is delicious on this salmon, but you can use one of the prepared pestos, found in most supermarkets, when you're in a rush.

1¼ cups loosely packed fresh basil

3 tablespoons chicken broth

1 clove garlic

1 tablespoon slivered almonds

1 tablespoon fresh lemon juice

2 teaspoons extra-virgin olive oil

2 teaspoons grated Parmesan cheese

¼ teaspoon ground black pepper

¼ teaspoon salt

1 pound skinless salmon fillet, cut into 4 pieces

Lemon wedges (optional)

Basil sprigs (optional)

1. In a blender, combine the basil, broth, garlic, almonds, lemon juice, oil, Parmesan, pepper, and salt. Blend until puréed.

2. Place the salmon on a plate. Spoon 3 tablespoons of the pesto over the salmon and turn to coat both sides. Cover with plastic wrap and let stand for 15 minutes. Reserve the remaining pesto.

3. Meanwhile, preheat the broiler. Coat a jelly-roll pan with cooking spray.

4. Place the salmon in the prepared pan. Spread any of the pesto remaining on the plate on top of each piece. Broil the salmon 4" to 5" from the heat for 6 to 8 minutes, or just until opaque.

5. Place the salmon pieces on 4 plates and top each piece with some of the reserved pesto. Garnish with lemon wedges and basil sprigs, if using.

Makes 4 servings

Variations

Make the pesto with cilantro or parsley instead of basil, if you prefer.

Penne with Salmon and Roasted Vegetables

Hands-On Time: 15 minutes ■ Total Time: 1 hour

When you're in the mood for seafood and pasta, this recipe fits the bill. Roasting the vegetables in a hot oven gives them a rich flavor that beautifully complements the salmon.

2 pounds leeks	1 tablespoon olive oil
1 red bell pepper, cut into strips	1 yellow summer squash, halved and cut into ¼" slices
¼ cup chicken broth	¼ cup pitted kalamata olives
2 tablespoons fresh lemon juice	1 skinless salmon fillet (8 ounces)
2 teaspoons dried thyme	12 ounces penne
¼ teaspoon ground black pepper	

1. Bring a large pot of water to a boil. Preheat the oven to 400°F.

2. Meanwhile, cut the leeks into 2" lengths and quarter them lengthwise. Rinse them completely. Place the leeks and the bell pepper in a 13" × 9" baking dish. Add the broth, lemon juice, thyme, black pepper, and 2 teaspoons of the oil. Cover with foil and bake for 15 minutes.

3. Add the squash, olives, and salmon to the baking dish, and drizzle with the remaining 1 teaspoon oil. Cover and bake for 30 minutes, or until the salmon is opaque and the vegetables are softened.

4. Meanwhile, cook the penne according to package directions until al dente.

5. Place the penne in a large serving bowl. Break the salmon into bite-size pieces and add to the penne with the vegetables. Toss to combine.

Makes 4 servings

Baked Scallops Newburg

Hands-On Time: 30 minutes ■ Total Time: 40 minutes

Elegant Newburg sauce is said to have been created by a chef at the famous Delmonico Restaurant in New York City. Typically, it is composed of butter, cream, egg yolks, sherry, and seasonings, and it's used over cooked shellfish such as lobster, crab, shrimp, or, as here, scallops. We didn't add sherry to this version, but you can if you like.

¼ cup fresh bread crumbs

2 teaspoons butter, melted

1 tablespoon olive oil

1 pound bay scallops

8 ounces mushrooms, sliced

3 scallions, sliced

2 tablespoons chopped fresh tarragon or 2 teaspoons dried

2 tablespoons pastry flour

¼ teaspoon salt

⅛ teaspoon ground red pepper

1½ cups light cream or half-and-half

1 egg yolk

1. Preheat the oven to 400°F. Place 4 small 1-cup baking dishes (8 ounces each) or ramekins on a baking sheet. Coat the dishes with cooking spray.

2. In a small bowl, combine the bread crumbs and butter, and set aside.

3. In a large skillet, heat the oil over medium heat. Add the scallops and cook, stirring, for 3 minutes, or until opaque. Remove them to a plate with a slotted spoon and keep them warm.

4. Add the mushrooms and cook, stirring occasionally, for 3 minutes, or until they release their liquid. Add the scallions and tarragon. Cook for 1 minute, or until the mushrooms are softened. Transfer to the plate with the scallops.

5. Add the flour, salt, and pepper to the skillet. Cook, stirring constantly, for 1 minute. Gradually whisk in the cream until blended. Cook, stirring often, for 5 minutes, or until thickened. Add the egg yolk and cook, stirring constantly, for 2 minutes, or until the mixture bubbles.

6. Return the scallops and mushroom mixture to the pan and stir to coat well. Spoon into the prepared baking dishes. Sprinkle with the bread crumb mixture.

7. Bake for 8 minutes, or until golden and bubbly.

Makes 4 servings

Cape Cod Scallops with Tomatoes

Hands-On Time: 35 minutes ■ Total Time: 35 minutes

This dish has the consistency of a chunky stew. Serve it over rice or pasta accompanied by an arugula salad and crusty bread.

1 tablespoon olive oil	3 tablespoons minced fresh parsley
2 cups sliced mushrooms	2 tablespoons fresh lemon juice
1 cup sliced onions	1 clove garlic, minced
1½ cups diced tomatoes	½ teaspoon dried basil
1 cup chicken broth	¼ teaspoon dried rosemary
1¼ pounds sea scallops	

1. In a large nonstick skillet, heat the oil over medium heat. Add the mushrooms and onions. Cook, stirring occasionally, for 5 minutes. Add the tomatoes and broth. Bring to a boil.

2. Add the scallops, parsley, lemon juice, garlic, basil, and rosemary. Reduce the heat and simmer for 5 minutes, or until the scallops are opaque. Using a slotted spoon, transfer the scallops and vegetables to a serving bowl.

3. Increase the heat to high and boil the broth for 5 minutes, or until reduced by half. Pour over the scallop mixture and serve.

Makes 4 servings

Shrimp Tips

Most of the shrimp eaten in the United States is harvested from relatively warm, shallow tropical waters. Though there are literally hundreds of species of shrimp, only a few varieties appear in our markets, where they are usually labeled by size rather than by their species name.

To choose: Most shrimp is frozen at sea right after it is caught. The fish markets then buy it frozen and usually thaw it before selling. Shrimp freezes well, so frozen shrimp is generally the best buy. Of course, if you can find very fresh shrimp (sometimes called day boat shrimp) that have never been frozen—or better yet, live shrimp—the flavor and texture will be a revelation.

When buying frozen shrimp, press on the bag or box. If you hear a crunchy covering of ice crystals, the shrimp have thawed partially and been refrozen. Look for a box or bag without a crunchy sound. It also helps to feel around for areas that are soft or empty, a sign that the package is beginning to thaw or may have been refrozen. When buying thawed shrimp, always smell before you buy: Shrimp should smell sweetly of the ocean. A stale ammonia scent indicates that the shrimp has begun to deteriorate. Black spots along the sides of shrimp are another sign that the shrimp is past its prime. Also avoid shrimp with a pinkish cast—those have been sprayed with a fine mist of hot water for purely cosmetic reasons. Go for the gray shrimp instead, which will turn pink when cooked. Buy unpeeled shrimp whenever possible. The peels help keep the shrimp moist and flavorful. When buying cooked shrimp, make sure they look plump, moist, and succulent.

To store: Store fresh or thawed shrimp in a colander that is filled with ice and set over a bowl (to provide for drainage) in the refrigerator. Thawed shrimp will keep for up to 1 day. Wrap frozen shrimp in plastic wrap and then in aluminum foil, and freeze for up to 2 months.

To peel and devein at the same time: With kitchen shears or a small knife, cut the shrimp shell along its outer curve, just deep enough into the flesh to expose the dark vein. Peel back the shell under running water, loosening the vein (the intestine) with your fingertips. If it's really stuck, use the tip of the shears or knife to pull it out. If the vein is light in color, it's empty, and there's no reason to bother pulling it out.

Sizing Up Shrimp

Shrimp is usually sold by "count" or size. The count, such as 16/20, refers to the number of shrimp you'll get per pound according to size. It can be a little confusing. Here's how to make sense of it.

SIZE	SHRIMP PER POUND
Small	41–50
Medium	31–40
Large	26–30
Extra large	21–25
Jumbo	16–20

Shrimp and Rice Enchiladas

Hands-On Time: 1 hour ■ Total Time: 1 hour 30 minutes

This festive south-of-the-border dish is well worth the time it takes to make it.

Salsa

1 teaspoon extra-virgin olive oil	1 can (28 ounces) plum tomatoes, with juice
2 tablespoons minced onion	2 tablespoons minced fresh cilantro
1 clove garlic, minced	¼ teaspoon ground black pepper
1 teaspoon ground cumin	

Enchiladas

1 teaspoon extra-virgin olive oil	1 cup cooked rice
½ cup chopped green bell pepper	¼ cup chopped red onion
½ teaspoon cumin seeds	2 teaspoons minced jalapeño pepper
½ cup canned diced tomato, with juice	½ cup shredded Monterey Jack cheese
½ cup diced zucchini	8 corn tortillas
½ pound shrimp, peeled, deveined, and coarsely chopped	2 tablespoons minced fresh cilantro

1. *To make the salsa:* In a large saucepan, heat the oil over medium heat. Add the onion and cook, stirring, for about 5 minutes, or until softened. Add the garlic and ground cumin. Stir to combine. Stir in the tomatoes (with juice). Use the side of a spoon to break up the tomatoes. Bring to a boil, then reduce the heat to a simmer. Cook, stirring frequently, for about 15 minutes, or until the sauce thickens. Add the cilantro and pepper. Remove from the heat and set aside.

2. *To make the enchiladas:* In a large nonstick skillet, heat the oil over medium heat. Add the bell pepper and cumin seeds. Cook, stirring, for 2 minutes. Add the tomato and zucchini. Cook, stirring, for 1 minute. Increase the heat to high. Add the shrimp and cook, stirring constantly, for 1 to 2 minutes, or until they turn opaque. Stir in the rice, onion, jalapeño pepper, and ¼ cup of the Monterey Jack. Mix well. Remove from the heat and set aside. Preheat the oven to 300°F.

3. Wrap the tortillas in foil. Bake for 5 to 7 minutes, or until they're soft enough not to crack when rolled.

4. Divide the rice filling among the tortillas, spooning it down the center of each. Roll up the tortillas.

5. Increase the oven temperature to 350°F. Coat a 13" × 9" baking dish with cooking spray. Add the tortillas, seam side down. Top with about half of the salsa. Sprinkle with the remaining ¼ cup cheese. Bake for 20 minutes, or until heated through. Sprinkle with the cilantro and serve with the remaining salsa.

Makes 4 servings

Garlic-Scented Broiled Shrimp

Hands-On Time: 30 minutes ■ Total Time: 30 minutes (plus marinating)

To make it easier to turn the shrimp, thread them onto skewers before broiling. If you're using wooden skewers, soak them in warm water for 10 minutes before threading on the shrimp to reduce the likelihood of burning the wood. Be sure to leave a little space between the shrimp so they cook evenly.

¾ cup apple cider or apple juice

2 tablespoons chopped fresh parsley

1 tablespoon plus 1 teaspoon Worcestershire sauce

1 clove garlic, minced

¼ teaspoon ground black pepper

2 pounds large shrimp, peeled and deveined

1. In a large bowl, combine the cider, parsley, Worcestershire, garlic, and pepper. Stir in the shrimp. Cover and marinate in the refrigerator for at least 2 hours.

2. Drain the shrimp, reserving the marinade.

3. Coat a broiler-pan rack with cooking spray. Preheat the broiler.

4. Broil the shrimp 4" to 5" from the heat for 3 minutes. Turn and brush with the marinade. Broil for 2 minutes, or until the shrimp turn pink.

Makes 6 servings

Kitchen Tip

If you purchase the shrimp already peeled and deveined rather than in the shell, you'll need to buy only 1½ pounds.

Orange Roughy Veracruz

Orange roughy is a firm-fleshed white fish available in specialty fish markets and some supermarkets. You can use red snapper if orange roughy is unavailable.

4 orange roughy or red snapper fillets (6 ounces each)

1 tablespoon fresh lime juice

1 teaspoon dried oregano

2 teaspoons olive oil

1 medium onion, chopped

1 clove garlic, minced

1 can (14.5 ounces) Mexican-style diced tomatoes, with juice

12 pimiento-stuffed olives, coarsely chopped

2 tablespoons chopped parsley

1. Preheat the oven to 350°F. Coat an 8" × 8" baking dish with cooking spray.

2. Place the fillets in the baking dish. Sprinkle with the lime juice and oregano. Set aside.

3. In a medium skillet, heat the oil over medium heat. Add the onion and garlic. Cook, stirring occasionally, for 5 to 6 minutes, or until softened. Add the tomatoes (with juice), olives, and parsley. Cook, stirring occasionally, for 5 to 7 minutes, or until thickened. Spoon over the fillets. Cover the baking dish tightly with foil.

4. Bake for 15 to 18 minutes, or until the fish flakes easily.

Makes 4 servings

Variations

This oven-baked fish dish can be changed according to your taste or the ingredients that you have on hand. If you like hot chile peppers, you can add 1 seeded and minced jalapeño pepper (wear plastic gloves when handling) or ½ teaspoon hot pepper sauce to the tomato mixture. If you don't have olives, you can replace them with 1 tablespoon drained capers. And instead of parsley, try chopped fresh cilantro leaves.

Oven-Fried Orange Roughy

Hands-On Time: 10 minutes ■ Total Time: 20 minutes

Adding only shelf staples, you can create this satisfying oven-baked entrée in minutes.

¼	cup dried bread crumbs	⅛	teaspoon salt
1	tablespoon grated Parmesan cheese	¼	cup all-purpose flour
½	teaspoon baking powder	¼	cup low-fat buttermilk
¼	teaspoon dried marjoram	4	orange roughy fillets (6 ounces each)
¼	teaspoon dried thyme	2	teaspoons olive oil
⅛	teaspoon ground red pepper		

1. Preheat the oven to 450°F. Coat a large baking sheet with cooking spray.

2. In a medium bowl, combine the bread crumbs, Parmesan, baking powder, marjoram, thyme, pepper, and salt. Mix well.

3. Place the flour on a plate. Place the buttermilk in a shallow bowl. Brush both sides of the fillets with the oil. Dip the fish into the flour, then into the buttermilk, and then into the bread crumb mixture. Place on the prepared baking sheet.

4. Bake for 10 to 12 minutes, or until the fish is crisp, golden brown, and opaque in the center.

Makes 4 servings

Accompaniments

This dish is delicious served with Mashed Sweet Potatoes with Honey (page 304)
and Garlicky Green Beans (page 286).

Blackened Snapper

Hands-On Time: 15 minutes ▪ Total Time: 15 minutes

Red snapper is so named because of its reddish-pink skin and red eyes. It's suitable for almost any cooking method, including blackening in a hot skillet. You could use homemade Cajun spice mix (page 45) to replace all of these spices.

1 teaspoon paprika	¼ teaspoon salt
½ teaspoon dried oregano	⅛ teaspoon ground red pepper
¼ teaspoon garlic powder	4 red snapper fillets (5 ounces each)
¼ teaspoon onion powder	2 teaspoons olive oil
¼ teaspoon ground black pepper	

1. In a small bowl, combine the paprika, oregano, garlic powder, onion powder, black pepper, salt, and red pepper.

2. Coat a large cast-iron skillet with cooking spray and heat over high heat. Brush both sides of each snapper fillet with the oil and rub with the spice mixture.

3. Place in the skillet and cook, turning once, for 6 minutes, or until the fish flakes easily.

Makes 4 servings

Ingredients Note

Almost any firm, white-fleshed fish can be used in this recipe. Try grouper, sea bass, redfish (red drum), or pompano in place of the snapper.

Red Snapper with Fruit Salsa

Hands-On Time: 20 minutes ■ Total Time: 35 minutes

This is a delicious early summer dish, best made when nectarines are at their peak. Serrano peppers can be considerably hotter than jalapeño peppers, so consider how much "heat" you want in the sauce.

4 red snapper fillets (5 ounces each)

½ cup plus 2 tablespoons orange juice

2 nectarines, cut into small pieces

1 banana, cut into small pieces

½ small red onion, minced

1 serrano or jalapeño pepper, seeded and minced (wear plastic gloves when handling)

2 tablespoons chopped fresh cilantro

1 tablespoon brown sugar

⅛ teaspoon salt

1. Coat a grill rack or broiler-pan rack with cooking spray. Preheat the grill or broiler.

2. Place the snapper in a shallow dish. Pour ½ cup of the orange juice over the fillets, turning to coat. Cover and refrigerate for 15 minutes.

3. Meanwhile, in a medium bowl, combine the nectarines, banana, onion, pepper, cilantro, sugar, salt, and the remaining 2 tablespoons orange juice. Toss gently to mix.

4. Remove the snapper from the orange juice. Discard the juice. Place the fillets on the prepared rack. Grill or broil 4 to 5 minutes per side, or until the fish flakes easily. Serve topped with the fruit salsa.

Makes 4 servings

Variation

If you can't find good nectarines, use plums instead.

Sole with Stir-Fried Vegetables

Hands-On Time: 20 minutes ■ Total Time: 35 minutes

When you're in the mood for a light Chinese-inspired meal, consider this stir-fry. Using shiitake mushrooms rather than the white button type will give the dish extra flavor.

3 tablespoons dry sherry or reduced-sodium chicken broth

3 tablespoons soy sauce

2 cloves garlic, minced

2 teaspoons cornstarch

2 teaspoons grated fresh ginger or ½ teaspoon ground

1½ teaspoons sugar

2 teaspoons vegetable oil

¼ pound shiitake or button mushrooms, sliced

¼ pound snow peas

1 small red bell pepper, cut into strips

1 cup bean sprouts

1 teaspoon toasted sesame oil

4 sole fillets (5 ounces each)

1. In a small bowl, combine the sherry, soy sauce, garlic, cornstarch, ginger, and sugar. Stir well. Set aside.

2. In a large skillet or wok, heat the vegetable oil over high heat. Add the mushrooms, snow peas, and pepper. Cook, stirring constantly, for 3 to 4 minutes, or until the pepper starts to soften. Add the bean sprouts and sesame oil. Toss to combine.

3. Reduce the heat to medium. Add the cornstarch mixture. Cook, stirring, for 2 to 3 minutes, or until thickened. Place the fillets in a single layer over the vegetables. Cover tightly.

4. Cook for 10 to 12 minutes, or until the fish flakes easily.

Makes 4 servings

Ingredients Note

Be sure to remove the stems from shiitakes. They can be very tough.

5 Flavored Butters for Fish—And More

Nothing could be simpler than flavored butter. You soften a stick of butter in a bowl, stir in some flavorings, then shape the butter into a log in a piece of plastic wrap. Refrigerate the plastic-wrapped butter, and when it's cold, you have a time-saving flavor enhancer right there in the butter bin. Slice off a pat to top a baked, broiled, or grilled fish fillet or fish steak. Or use the butters on beef, chicken breasts, pork chops, or baked potatoes. Here are five flavor combinations to try. Each recipe makes about ½ cup.

1. **Chipotle Butter.** Combine 1 stick softened butter, 1 tablespoon finely chopped canned chipotle chile pepper packed in adobo sauce, and ¼ teaspoon salt.

2. **Ginger Butter.** Combine 1 stick softened butter, 1½ tablespoons grated ginger, 2 teaspoons fresh lime juice, ¼ teaspoon ground black pepper, and ¼ teaspoon salt. As an Asian variation, omit the salt and add 2 to 3 teaspoons soy sauce and ½ teaspoon toasted sesame oil.

3. **Tomato-Herb Butter.** Combine 1 stick softened butter, ¼ cup tomato paste, ½ teaspoon dried basil, ½ teaspoon dried oregano, ¼ teaspoon ground black pepper, and ¼ teaspoon salt.

4. **Watercress Butter.** Combine 1 stick softened butter, ¼ cup chopped watercress leaves, 1 to 2 teaspoons fresh lemon juice, ¼ teaspoon ground black pepper, and ¼ teaspoon salt.

5. **Paprika Butter.** Combine 1 stick softened butter, 1 tablespoon paprika, 1 teaspoon orange juice, and ¼ teaspoon salt.

Teriyaki Tuna with Pineapple

Hands-On Time: 30 minutes ■ Total Time: 45 minutes

Fresh tuna has a tender, firm texture and rich flavor. There are several types available: the high-fat, mild, white-fleshed albacore; the pale-pink yellowfin; the moderately flavored bluefin; and the strongly flavored bonito. Ask the fishmonger which is freshest.

¼ cup soy sauce

3 tablespoons dry sherry or reduced-sodium chicken broth

1 tablespoon grated fresh ginger or 1 teaspoon ground

1 tablespoon sugar

3 cloves garlic, chopped

4 tuna steaks (5 ounces each)

1 pineapple, peeled, halved, cut lengthwise into 8 wedges, and cored

1 red bell pepper, quartered lengthwise

1. In a small bowl, combine the soy sauce, sherry, ginger, sugar, and garlic. Stir to blend. Divide the marinade into 2 medium, shallow bowls.

2. Place the tuna in one bowl and the pineapple and bell pepper in the other. Turn the tuna, pineapple, and bell pepper to coat. Cover and refrigerate for 15 minutes.

3. Coat a grill rack or broiler-pan rack with cooking spray. Preheat the grill or broiler.

4. Arrange the tuna, pineapple, and bell pepper on the rack. Discard the marinade from the tuna bowl. Grill or broil, basting occasionally with the marinade from the pineapple bowl, for 4 to 5 minutes per side for the tuna, or until the tuna is just opaque and the pineapple and bell pepper are heated through and glazed.

Makes 4 servings

Ingredients Note

In a rush? Buy fresh sliced pinapple or use canned slices.

Tuna Burgers with Dill Sauce

Hands-On Time: 30 minutes ■ Total Time: 30 minutes

These tuna burgers are simple to prepare, so you can whip them up quickly for lunch or a light dinner. They're as satisfying as regular hamburgers but much lower in fat and cholesterol. And they have a bonus that beef lacks: heart-healthy omega-3s.

Dill Sauce

⅓ cup mayonnaise

2 tablespoons minced gherkin pickles

1 tablespoon minced fresh dill or
1 teaspoon dried

1 tablespoon minced fresh parsley

2 teaspoons snipped chives

1 teaspoon fresh lemon juice

½ teaspoon Dijon mustard

Tuna Burgers

1 can (12.5 ounces) tuna, drained and flaked

½ cup wheat germ

2 scallions, minced

1 tablespoon minced fresh parsley

½ teaspoon dried oregano

½ teaspoon ground black pepper

⅛ teaspoon ground red pepper

¼ cup mayonnaise

1 egg

1 tablespoon ketchup

2 teaspoons olive oil

4 kaiser rolls or crusty hamburger rolls

4 thick tomato slices

Boston or romaine lettuce

1. *To make the dill sauce:* In a small bowl, combine the mayonnaise, pickles, dill, parsley, chives, lemon juice, and mustard. Refrigerate until needed.

2. *To make the tuna burgers:* In a medium bowl, combine the tuna, wheat germ, scallions, parsley, oregano, black pepper, and red pepper.

3. In a cup, combine the mayonnaise, egg, and ketchup. Pour over the tuna and mix well.

4. Form the tuna into 4 patties.

5. In a large nonstick skillet, heat the oil over medium heat. Add the patties and cook for about 3 minutes per side, or until they're browned and heated through.

6. Serve on the rolls, topped with the tomatoes, lettuce, and dill sauce.

Makes 4 servings

Bouillabaisse

Hands-On Time: 35 minutes ■ Total Time: 50 minutes

Bouillabaisse is a traditional French stew brimming with seafood. It's ideal for wintry evenings, served in crockery bowls with crusty bread and a tossed salad.

1 tablespoon olive oil	1 pound halibut, cut into 2" cubes
2 bottles (8 ounces each) clam juice	½ pound bay scallops
¾ pound small red potatoes, quartered	½ pound large shrimp, peeled and deveined
1 cup chopped onion	2 to 3 tablespoons chopped fresh tarragon or basil
2 leeks, thinly sliced	Salt
5 cloves garlic, minced	Ground black pepper
1 can (28 ounces) diced tomatoes, with juice	

1. In a large, heavy saucepan or Dutch oven, bring the oil and ¼ cup of the clam juice to a boil over medium-high heat. Add the potatoes, onion, leeks, and garlic. Cook for 3 to 5 minutes, or until the onion is lightly browned.

2. Add the tomatoes (with juice) and the remaining clam juice. Bring to a boil. Cook for 10 minutes.

3. Add the halibut, scallops, and shrimp. Cook for 5 minutes, or until the fish is opaque and flakes easily. Stir in the tarragon. Add salt and pepper to taste. Serve hot.

Makes 4 servings

Ingredients Note

You can use any firm-fleshed fish instead of halibut, and sea scallops instead of bay (just quarter them).

Seafood Creole

Hands-On Time: 30 minutes ■ Total Time: 40 minutes

We trimmed the cost—but kept the zesty appeal—of this traditional New Orleans one-pot meal by using cod along with the shrimp. Serve it with cooked brown or white rice.

2 teaspoons olive oil

1 can (28 ounces) diced tomatoes, with juice

2 cups chopped onions

1 cup chopped green bell pepper

1 cup chopped celery

2 teaspoons minced garlic

1 cup fish stock or chicken broth

¼ cup white wine (optional)

1 tablespoon paprika

1 teaspoon ground red pepper

2 bay leaves

½ pound cod fillets, cut into 1" cubes

¼ pound peeled and deveined medium shrimp

1 tablespoon cornstarch

¼ cup water

¼ teaspoon salt

¼ teaspoon ground black pepper

1. In a large, heavy saucepan, heat the oil over medium-high heat. Add the tomatoes (with juice), onions, bell pepper, celery, and garlic. Cook, stirring occasionally, for 5 minutes, or until the onions are soft. Add the stock, wine (if using), paprika, red pepper, and bay leaves. Bring to a boil. Cook, stirring occasionally, for 5 minutes.

2. Add the cod. Cover and cook for 3 to 5 minutes, or until the fish is opaque in the center. Add the shrimp. Cover and cook for 1 minute, or until the shrimp turn pink.

3. In a small bowl, combine the cornstarch and water. Add to the pan. Cook, stirring, for 1 minute, or until the sauce thickens slightly. Add the salt and pepper. Remove and discard the bay leaves before serving.

Makes 4 servings

Perfect Pasta

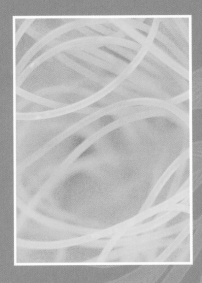

"Life is a combination of magic and pasta."

—FEDERICO FELLINI

Chicken Bow-Ties

Hands-On Time: 35 minutes ■ Total Time: 35 minutes

This pasta stir-fry will proceed most smoothly if you have all the ingredients chopped, measured, and lined up next to your stove before you begin cooking.

8 ounces bow-tie pasta

2 teaspoons olive oil (optional)

1 pound boneless, skinless chicken breasts

1 cup water

2 tablespoons cornstarch

2 tablespoons reduced-sodium soy sauce

1 tablespoon sesame or peanut oil

1 pound sugar snap peas or snow peas, cut into 1" pieces

1 green bell pepper, cut into 1" pieces

1 red bell pepper, cut into 1" pieces

½ cup canned sliced water chestnuts

8 scallions, cut into 1" pieces

1 stalk celery, thinly cut on the diagonal

1 tablespoon grated fresh ginger

1 clove garlic, minced

¼ cup minced fresh cilantro

1. Bring a large pot of water to a boil. Cook the pasta according to package directions until al dente. Do not overcook. Drain. If desired, in a large nonstick skillet or wok, heat the olive oil over medium heat. Add the noodles and cook for a few minutes to lightly brown. Transfer to a platter and keep warm.

2. Meanwhile, place the chicken between sheets of wax paper. Use a mallet to lightly pound the breasts to a uniform thickness, about ½". Cut into bite-size pieces.

3. In a cup, combine the water, cornstarch, and soy sauce until smooth. Set aside.

4. In the skillet or wok, heat 1½ teaspoons of the sesame oil over medium heat. Add the chicken and cook, stirring constantly, for 4 minutes, or until opaque. Remove with a slotted spoon and keep warm.

5. Add the remaining 1½ teaspoons sesame oil to the pan. Add the peas, green and red bell peppers, water chestnuts, scallions, celery, ginger, and garlic. Cook, stirring constantly, for about 4 minutes, or until the vegetables are crisp-tender.

6. Return the chicken to the pan and cook, stirring constantly, for 1 minute.

7. Add the cornstarch mixture to the pan. Cook, stirring, for 2 minutes, or until the sauce thickens. Stir in the cilantro. Serve over the warm pasta.

Makes 4 to 6 servings

Variations

Replace the chicken with thin strips of round steak, lean pork, or whole shrimp. Use other vegetables, such as yellow squash, mushrooms, cucumbers, carrots, or baby corn.

Penne with Chicken Marengo

Hands-On Time: 30 minutes ■ Total Time: 30 minutes

Legend has it that Napoleon's chef created Chicken Marengo for the general after a battlefield victory. Despite its glorious history, it differs very little from a traditional peasant dish of chicken braised with tomatoes and garlic. This version is enlivened with a touch of citrus in the sauce. Served over pasta, it makes a well-rounded meal fit for a victorious soldier—or a hungry family.

8	ounces penne	3	cups sliced mushrooms
½	cup dry-packed sun-dried tomatoes	½	cup chicken broth
½	pound boneless, skinless chicken breasts, cut into ½" cubes	1	can (15 ounces) crushed tomatoes in purée
1	tablespoon all-purpose flour	½	cup orange juice
½	teaspoon dried thyme	1	teaspoon grated orange zest
¼	teaspoon ground black pepper	1	teaspoon brown sugar
1	tablespoon olive oil	⅛	teaspoon salt

1. Bring a large pot of water to a boil. Cook the pasta according to package directions until al dente. Drain in a colander and transfer to a warmed serving bowl.

2. Meanwhile, in a small bowl, cover the sun-dried tomatoes with boiling water and soak for 5 minutes. When softened, drain and chop coarsely. Set aside.

3. Toss the chicken with the flour, thyme, and pepper. In a large, heavy skillet, heat the oil over high heat until hot but not smoking. Add the chicken and cook, stirring occasionally, for 2 to 3 minutes, or until golden brown. Add the mushrooms and 2 tablespoons of the broth. Cook, stirring occasionally, for 2 to 3 minutes, or until the mushrooms are barely softened and have begun to release their juices.

4. Add the crushed tomatoes (with purée), orange juice, orange zest, sugar, salt, the sun-dried tomatoes, and the remaining broth. Bring to a boil, scraping the bottom of the pan with a wooden spoon to release the browned bits. Reduce the heat to medium-low and simmer for 8 minutes, or until the sauce is thickened and the flavors are blended.

5. Pour the mixture over the pasta and toss to coat well.

Makes 4 servings

Pasta Tips

One of the world's most versatile and popular foods, pasta is simple to make and pleases almost everyone. The major difference between fresh and dried pasta is that fresh pasta contains egg and most dried pasta does not. Dried egg noodles are a notable exception.

Basics

To choose dried pasta: Look for pastas made from durum wheat. Many of the best brands are imported from Italy.

To choose ready-made fresh pasta: Do a trial tasting of several different ones to find one that you like. When choosing fresh filled pastas, look closely at the dough. It should be sheer enough to see the filling inside.

To measure out a single portion of pasta: For each portion, use approximately ½ cup dried pasta or measure ½" diameter of dried strand pasta such as spaghetti (about the size of a dime). This will yield approximately 1 cup cooked pasta.

To cook: Whether fresh or dried, pasta should be cooked in a large pot of rapidly boiling salted water. Bring the water to a boil, then add about 1 teaspoon of salt per quart of water. Add the pasta, or place it in a pasta insert and submerge it in the water (avoid cooking more than 2 pounds of pasta at a time; it will cook unevenly). Stir once. Cover the pot and return to a boil. Uncover and boil the pasta, following the package directions.

To test for doneness: Frequently taste-test the pasta before it is scheduled to be done. Start timing as soon as the water returns to a boil. Begin testing fresh pasta and very thin shapes after about 30 seconds and dried pasta after about 7 minutes. Lift a piece of the pasta out of the boiling water using tongs or a long-handled fork. Let cool slightly, then bite into it. It should be tender but slightly resistant to the tooth (al dente). Drain the pasta immediately once it's done. Pasta continues to cook from residual heat and can easily overcook. Remove from the heat and drain, but leave a little water clinging to the surface of the pasta to help the sauce flow.

To prepare pasta for casseroles or soups: Reduce the cooking time by about one-third. The pasta will finish cooking while baking or simmering in the dish.

To serve: Never rinse pasta unless it will be baked or used in a salad. The starch on the surface of the pasta will help the sauce cling to the pasta. For best results, warm the serving dishes. Also, pasta will stay warm longer when served in shallow bowls rather than on flat plates.

To substitute one for another: Many pastas are interchangeable, within reason. You can certainly substitute one long, thin pasta for another or one macaroni shape for another. You can also substitute rice noodles or lo mein for angel hair or spaghetti, and use wonton skins or egg roll wrappers to make ravioli or tortellini.

Problem Solvers

To prevent pasta from sticking: Perhaps the most common mistake in making pasta is not using enough water. Keep in mind that about a quart of water will be lost during the cooking process due to absorption and evaporation. Use about 4 quarts for every pound of pasta and stir occasionally. When the pasta is finished, drain and place it in a warmed serving bowl. Toss it with the sauce as soon as possible after draining. Pasta will begin to stick as soon as it cools; keeping it warm will help keep the pieces separate. As for the sauce itself, always prepare it before cooking the pasta so that the pasta never has to sit (and turn sticky and gluey) while the sauce finishes cooking. If the pasta finishes cooking before the sauce is ready, toss the warm pasta with a small amount of olive oil and keep it warm while the sauce finishes cooking.

To unstick stuck pasta: Submerge it in hot water and separate.

To prevent lasagna noodles from clinging during assembly: Rinse them with cold water after draining to remove surface starch.

To prevent boilovers: Before the pasta pot gets hot, rub a thin layer of oil around the interior lip of the pot. If the pot isn't too heavy and a boil-over is imminent, simply remove the pot from the heat and transfer it to another burner. If the pot is too heavy, you can blow over the water's surface to keep the boilover at bay while you lower the heat on the stove. You can also plunge a wooden spoon into the water, which helps control foaming.

To salvage overdone pasta: Skip the step of tossing the pasta with the sauce. In this situation, it's best to just spoon it on top. A rinse in tepid water will also help minimize the stickiness of overdone pasta. If the pasta is a real failure, just cook up a second batch of it. Pasta is easy and cheap enough. Save the overcooked pasta to use in another dish, such as an omelet.

Time-Savers

To cook pasta ahead of time: Cook the pasta until just slightly underdone. Cool the cooked pasta in a bowl of ice water. As soon as it reaches room temperature, drain it and toss it with oil to prevent sticking. Refrigerate it in a zip-top plastic bag. To reheat, plunge the pasta into a large pot of boiling water. Stir until the pieces of pasta separate, about 20 seconds, and drain. Toss with sauce.

To save cooking time: Use fresh pasta, which cooks in a few seconds (for thin pasta such as angel hair) to just 3 minutes (for large stuffed ravioli or tortellini). You can also save on cooking and cleanup time by cooking vegetables in the same pot with pasta. Trim and chop the vegetables and add them to the boiling pasta so that they are done cooking at the same time as the pasta. Add diced potatoes to the water when the pasta is added; broccoli florets 3 minutes before the noodles will be ready; asparagus 2 minutes before; and delicate leaves, such as spinach, about 30 seconds before. Drain the vegetables right along with the pasta.

Curried Chicken, Broccoli, and Penne Pasta Bake

Hands-On Time: 20 minutes ■ Total Time: 1 hour 20 minutes

Here's an interesting twist on an Italian favorite. Curry powder lends a wonderful color to the pasta.

16	ounces mini penne	½	teaspoon ground black pepper
1	pound broccoli florets	2	cups cooked chicken breast strips
1	cup chopped onion	1	carton (16 ounces) creamy small-curd cottage cheese
2	tablespoons olive oil	½	cup grated Parmesan cheese
1	teaspoon curry powder		
1	teaspoon dried thyme		

1. Bring a large pot of water to a boil. Cook the pasta for half the cooking time given on the package directions. Add the broccoli during the last 2 minutes of cooking. Reserve 1 cup of the cooking water. Drain and rinse with cold water. Set aside.

2. Meanwhile, preheat the oven to 375°F. Coat a 13" × 9" glass or ceramic baking dish with cooking spray.

3. In a glass measuring cup, combine the onion, oil, curry powder, thyme, and pepper. Cover with plastic wrap, leaving a small corner vent. Microwave on high power, stirring once, for 5 minutes, or until sizzling. Using a rubber spatula, carefully scrape the spice mixture into the prepared baking dish.

4. Add the chicken, cottage cheese, Parmesan, pasta, broccoli, and the reserved cooking water to the baking dish. Mix completely. Cover with aluminum foil. Bake for 30 minutes. Remove the foil. Bake for about 20 minutes longer, or until golden and bubbling.

Makes 4 servings

Make-Ahead

Prepare the recipe up to the point of baking and allow to cool completely. Cover tightly with plastic wrap. Refrigerate for up to 3 days. To serve, remove the plastic and bake according to the recipe directions.

Southwestern Chicken Lasagna

Hands-On Time: 15 minutes ■ Total Time: 1 hour 40 minutes

Make this kid-friendly lasagna for your next fiesta. You can purchase shredded mixed cheese, if you like. Look for Mexican or taco varieties to keep with your flavor theme, but any mix of cheeses will do.

8 ounces lasagna noodles

2 eggs

4 ounces ricotta cheese

1 can (4 ounces) chopped green chile peppers, drained

¼ cup chopped fresh cilantro, stems included

2 cups grated yellow and white cheeses, such as sharp Cheddar and Monterey Jack

1 jar (16 ounces) mild chunky salsa

1 can (15 ounces) tomato sauce

4 cups chopped cooked chicken

1. Preheat the oven to 350°F. Coat a 13" × 9" baking dish with cooking spray.

2. Bring a large pot of water to a boil. Prepare the lasagna noodles according to package directions.

3. Meanwhile, in a large bowl, combine the eggs, ricotta, peppers, cilantro, and ½ cup of the grated cheese.

4. In a small bowl, combine the salsa and tomato sauce.

5. Pour 1 cup of the sauce mixture into the prepared baking dish. Spread to cover the bottom. Top with a single layer of lasagna noodles. Top with half of the ricotta mixture, one-third of the chicken, and one-third of the remaining grated cheese. Top with one-third of the sauce mixture. Repeat the layers.

6. Cover with the remaining lasagna noodles, the remaining sauce, the remaining chicken, and the remaining shredded cheese.

7. Cover with foil and bake for 45 minutes, or until hot and bubbly. Remove the foil and bake for 10 minutes longer. Let stand for 10 minutes before serving.

Makes 8 servings

Make-Ahead

If you want to make the dish ahead of time and freeze it, line the baking dish with heavy-duty foil before filling it with the lasagna. Bake as directed, then after cooling, wrap the lasagna tightly in the foil (plus an extra layer) and freeze. Reheat (covered and without thawing) in a 300°F oven for 30 to 35 minutes, or until piping hot.

Lasagna Bolognese with Two-Tomato Sauce

Hands-On Time: 25 minutes ■ Total Time: 50 minutes

This homey dish comes from the city of Bologna, nicknamed *Bologna la grassa*—"Bologna the fat"—because of its inhabitants' lavish use of the local agricultural bounty, including cheeses, meats, milk, butter, and eggs. You can use 1% milk and part-skim mozzarella, if you prefer.

2¼ ounces dry-packed sun-dried tomatoes	½ teaspoon salt
2 tablespoons cornstarch	¼ teaspoon ground black pepper
¼ cup water	1 can (15 ounces) crushed tomatoes
1 pound lean ground beef	½ cup water
3 medium carrots, diced	1 bay leaf
1 medium onion, chopped	1 cup milk
½ pound mushrooms, sliced	½ cup chicken broth
2 stalks celery, diced	6 ounces no-cook lasagna noodles
1 teaspoon fresh rosemary, chopped	½ cup shredded mozzarella cheese
1 teaspoon fresh thyme, chopped	

1. Preheat the oven to 375°F. In a small bowl, cover the sun-dried tomatoes with boiling water and soak for 5 minutes. When softened, drain and chop coarsely. Set aside.

2. Dissolve the cornstarch in the water and set aside.

3. In a large nonstick skillet, combine the beef, carrots, onion, mushrooms, celery, rosemary, thyme, ¼ teaspoon of the salt, and ⅛ teaspoon of the pepper. Cook over medium-high heat, breaking up the meat with a spoon, for about 5 minutes, or until the beef is browned.

4. Add the crushed tomatoes, water, bay leaf, and the sun-dried tomatoes. Reduce the heat to medium and cook, stirring occasionally, for 2 minutes to blend the flavors. Transfer the meat sauce to a large bowl.

5. Pour the milk, broth, and the cornstarch mixture into the skillet. Cook over medium heat, stirring, for 2 minutes, or until the white sauce thickens. Add the remaining ¼ teaspoon salt and ⅛ teaspoon pepper. Remove the skillet from the heat.

6. Spoon one-fourth of the meat sauce into an 11" × 7" baking dish. Place one-third of the noodles over the meat sauce, then pour one-third of the white sauce over the noodles. Repeat with two more layers of noodles and sauces, ending with the meat sauce.

7. Sprinkle the mozzarella on top and bake for 15 to 20 minutes, or until the cheese is bubbly.

Makes 6 servings

Spaghetti with Garlic-Lemon Shrimp

Hands-On Time: 35 minutes ■ Total Time: 45 minutes

Shelling shrimp is a simple process. As a bonus, the shells will yield a tasty broth once the job is done (see Kitchen Tip, below).

1 pound medium shrimp, peeled and deveined, tails left on

3 garlic cloves, crushed

1 teaspoon grated lemon zest

¾ teaspoon dried oregano

¾ teaspoon dried thyme

½ teaspoon ground black pepper

¼ teaspoon salt

10 ounces spaghetti

2 teaspoons olive oil

3 cups sliced mushrooms

3 cans (8 ounces each) tomato sauce

¼ cup chopped fresh Italian parsley

2 tablespoons grated Parmesan cheese

1. Bring a large pot of water to a boil.

2. Meanwhile, in a medium bowl, toss the shrimp with the garlic, lemon zest, oregano, thyme, ¼ teaspoon of the pepper, and ⅛ teaspoon of the salt. Cover and let stand at room temperature for 10 minutes.

3. Cook the pasta according to package directions until al dente. Drain in a colander and transfer to a warmed serving bowl.

4. While the pasta is cooking, in a large, deep nonstick skillet, heat the oil over medium-high heat until very hot but not smoking. Add the mushrooms and cook for 2 to 3 minutes, tossing frequently. The pan will be dry at first, but the mushrooms will begin to release their juices as they cook.

5. Add the tomato sauce and the remaining ¼ teaspoon pepper and ⅛ teaspoon salt to the mushrooms, and bring to a boil. Stir in the shrimp and reduce the heat to medium. Simmer, stirring frequently, for 4 to 5 minutes, or until the shrimp are pink and opaque.

6. Pour over the spaghetti. Add the parsley and toss. Sprinkle with the Parmesan just before serving.

Makes 4 servings

Kitchen Tip

The shrimp shells can become the basis of a delicious broth to use when making seafood soups, chowders, or sauces. Place the shells in a saucepan with enough cold water to cover. Bring to a boil and simmer, covered, for half an hour. Let the shells cool in the broth, then strain them out and freeze the broth in an airtight container for up to 6 months.

Spaghetti with Meatballs

Hands-On Time: 45 minutes ■ Total Time: 1 hour 10 minutes

Comfort food doesn't get any better than spaghetti with meatballs. A mix of ground meats creates the most tender, flavorful meatballs.

2 tablespoons olive oil

2 medium onions, chopped

3 cloves garlic, minced

1 pound ground meat-loaf mix

⅔ cup seasoned dried bread crumbs

¼ cup milk

1 egg, lightly beaten

2 teaspoons chopped fresh sage or 1 teaspoon dried

½ teaspoon salt

1 can (28 ounces) whole tomatoes, with juice

2 teaspoons Italian seasoning

12 ounces spaghetti

1. In a large saucepan, heat the oil over medium heat. Add the onions and garlic and cook, stirring often, for 8 minutes, or until the onions are very soft. Remove ¼ cup of the onion mixture to a large bowl. Set aside the remaining onions in the saucepan.

2. Coat a broiler-pan rack with cooking spray. Preheat the broiler.

3. Add the ground meat, bread crumbs, milk, egg, sage, and salt to the bowl with the onions. Mix well. Shape into 12 meatballs, each about 2" in diameter. Place the meatballs on the prepared rack. Broil, turning occasionally, for 10 minutes, or until browned.

4. Add the tomatoes (with juice), Italian seasoning, and cooked meatballs to the reserved onions in the saucepan. Bring to a boil over high heat. Reduce the heat to low and cook, breaking up the tomatoes with the back of a spoon, for 25 minutes, or until the meatballs are no longer pink in the center.

5. Meanwhile, bring a large pot of water to a boil. Prepare the spaghetti according to package directions until al dente.

6. Drain in a colander and transfer to a serving bowl. Top with the meatballs and sauce.

Makes 6 servings

Ingredients Note

If you can't find prepackaged meat-loaf mix, ask the butcher to combine the meats for you. Not a fan of veal? Just ask for more beef and pork.

Linguine with Chili Scallops

Hands-On Time: 15 minutes ■ Total Time: 30 minutes

Not only will you love the flavor of the sweet-and-sour–accented scallops, you will also be amazed at how something so delicious can be made so quickly.

12 ounces linguine	½ cup chili sauce
2 tablespoons peanut oil	1½ tablespoons rice wine vinegar
1½ pounds sea scallops	1 tablespoon honey
4 large cloves garlic, minced	1 teaspoon ground ginger
8 scallions, cut into 1" pieces, including green tops	½ teaspoon salt

1. Bring a large pot of water to a boil. Cook the linguine according to package directions until al dente.

2. Meanwhile, in a large skillet, heat the oil over medium heat. Add the scallops and garlic and cook for 2 minutes. Stir in the scallions, chili sauce, vinegar, honey, ginger, and salt. Cook, stirring often, for 3 minutes, or until the scallops are opaque.

3. Drain the linguine and transfer to a serving bowl. Add the scallop mixture and toss.

Makes 6 servings

Linguine with Clam Sauce

Hands-On Time: 35 minutes ■ Total Time: 35 minutes

You can make this Italian seafood dish in multiple batches and freeze it for up to 2 months (see Kitchen Tip, below). If desired, you can make just the sauce to freeze and add freshly cooked linguine at serving time.

1 pound linguine	1 cup diced tomatoes
¼ cup apple juice	¼ teaspoon red pepper flakes
1 teaspoon olive oil	¼ cup chopped fresh parsley
1 cup chopped onion	¼ cup grated Parmesan cheese
6 large cloves garlic, minced	½ teaspoon ground black pepper
1 cup dry white wine	
3 cans (6 ounces each) chopped clams, with juice	

1. Bring a large pot of water to a boil. Cook the linguine according to package directions until al dente. Drain.

2. Meanwhile, in a large nonstick skillet, bring the apple juice and oil to a boil over medium-high heat. Add the onion and garlic. Cook, stirring, for 5 to 8 minutes, or until the onions are very soft but not browned. Add the wine and bring to a boil. Cook, stirring occasionally, for 10 minutes, or until the liquid is reduced to ¼ cup.

3. Add the clams (with juice), tomatoes, and red pepper flakes. Cook for 2 minutes, or until heated through.

4. Toss the linguine with the clam sauce. Sprinkle with the parsley, Parmesan, and black pepper.

Makes 6 servings

Kitchen Tip

To freeze, pack the cooled cooked linguine with clam sauce in a freezer-quality plastic container. To use, thaw overnight in the refrigerator. Cover and microwave on high power for 3 to 5 minutes, or until hot.

Pesto: The World's Most Adaptable Pasta Sauce

Pesto originated in Genoa, Italy, as an easy, no-cook fresh basil and olive oil sauce for pasta. But the basic method lends itself to many variations, which are often lower in fat, like those below. To use the following pestos as a pasta sauce, cook 16 ounces of pasta according to package directions. Reserve ¼ cup of the cooking water. Place the pasta in a serving bowl. Add the pesto and about 2 tablespoons of the reserved cooking water. Toss and add up to 2 tablespoons more water to make the pesto cling nicely to the pasta.

Asian Pesto. In a blender or food processor, combine 1 can (16 ounces) rinsed and drained water chestnuts, ½ cup soy sauce, ⅓ cup rice wine vinegar or white wine vinegar, ¼ cup honey, 3 large garlic cloves, 1 tablespoon peanut butter, and 1 tablespoon toasted sesame oil. Process until puréed. Makes 1½ cups.

Olive Pesto. In a blender or food processor, combine 1½ cups loosely packed fresh basil leaves, ½ cup chopped fresh or drained canned tomatoes, ¼ cup chicken broth, 3 tablespoons pitted olives, 2 large garlic cloves, 1 tablespoon balsamic vinegar, 1 tablespoon olive oil, and a pinch each of salt and ground black pepper. Process until puréed. Makes 1 cup.

Roasted Red Pepper Pesto. In a blender or food processor, combine 1⅓ cups diced roasted red peppers (patted dry), ¾ cup fresh parsley, ⅓ cup toasted pine nuts, 2 large garlic cloves, 1 tablespoon grated Parmesan cheese, 1 tablespoon wine vinegar, and a pinch each of salt and ground black pepper. Process until puréed. Makes 1 cup.

South-of-the-Border Pesto. In a blender or food processor, combine 1 can (19 ounces) rinsed and drained black beans, ½ cup loosely packed fresh cilantro leaves, 1 seeded jalapeño chile pepper (wear plastic gloves when handling), 2 garlic cloves, 2 tablespoons reduced-fat sour cream, and 1 teaspoon chili powder. Process until coarsely puréed. Makes 1½ cups.

Sun-Dried Tomato Pesto. In a blender or food processor, combine 1 cup fresh oregano leaves, ⅔ cup reconstituted dry-packed sun-dried tomatoes, 1 small coarsely chopped onion, 2 large garlic cloves, 1 tablespoon olive oil, 1 tablespoon vegetable broth, 1 tablespoon wine vinegar, and a pinch each of salt and ground black pepper. Process until puréed. Makes 1 cup.

Mediterranean-Style Tuna and Pasta

Hands-On Time: 25 minutes ■ Total Time: 45 minutes

This meal is almost like a salad in a skillet—light and fresh and full of vegetables. In fact, you needn't rush to the table with the dish, as it would be delicious served at room temperature, in the manner of many stylish dinner salads. The fresh tuna, tomatoes, feta, garlic, olive oil, and capers reflect its Mediterranean roots.

1 pint (8 ounces) cherry tomatoes, stemmed and halved

2 tablespoons rinsed and drained capers

2 tablespoons chopped fresh dill

2 cloves garlic, minced

2 teaspoons grated lemon zest

3 teaspoons extra-virgin olive oil

½ teaspoon salt

½ teaspoon ground black pepper

8 ounces penne

1½ pounds spinach, trimmed and chopped

½ pound tuna steak, cut into 1" cubes

½ cup crumbled feta cheese

1. Bring a large pot of water to a boil over high heat.

2. Meanwhile, in a large bowl, combine the tomatoes, capers, dill, garlic, lemon zest, 2 teaspoons of the oil, ¼ teaspoon of the salt, and ¼ teaspoon of the pepper.

3. Cook the penne according to package directions until al dente. During the last 1 minute of cooking, add the spinach. Drain the pasta and spinach together in a colander.

4. Add the pasta and spinach to the tomato mixture, and toss gently to combine.

5. Heat the remaining 1 teaspoon oil in a large nonstick skillet. Add the tuna and cook over medium-high heat for 3 to 5 minutes, or just until browned. Add the remaining ¼ teaspoon salt and ¼ teaspoon pepper, and toss.

6. Add the pasta and spinach mixture to the tuna in the skillet. Stir in the feta, tossing well. Cook until the cheese is melted and the pasta is heated through.

Makes 4 servings

Variation

Scallops are a delicious variation on this recipe. Use ½ pound of sea scallops; halve any that are very large. Cook the scallops, stirring occasionally, for 4 to 5 minutes, or until opaque. You can vary the seasonings: Fresh dill is wonderful with fish and shellfish, but you could try other fresh herbs, such as tarragon or oregano, when available.

Smoked Salmon with Creamy Dill Linguine

Hands-On Time: 15 minutes ■ Total Time: 35 minutes

Smoked salmon paired with fresh dill in a creamy sauce is a simple dinner that's hard to beat. Enjoy it at the height of summer, when the tomatoes are bursting with flavor.

8 ounces linguine	½ teaspoon ground black pepper
½ pound asparagus, trimmed and cut into 1½" pieces	½ teaspoon salt
¾ cup sour cream	1½ cups halved yellow or red cherry tomatoes
½ cup milk	3 ounces smoked salmon, cut into thin strips
1 tablespoon white wine vinegar	
2 tablespoons chopped fresh dill	

1. Bring a large pot of water to a boil. Cook the linguine according to package directions until al dente. Add the asparagus during the last 30 seconds of cooking.

2. Meanwhile, in a large bowl, whisk together the sour cream, milk, vinegar, dill, pepper, and salt. Add the tomatoes and salmon, and toss.

3. Drain the pasta and asparagus and add to the bowl. Toss to coat well.

Makes 4 servings

Kitchen Tip

Asparagus spears will snap off naturally where they become tough if you hold both ends and bend the spear. You can also use a vegetable peeler to trim off the outer layer.

Easy Salmon and Rotini Casserole

Hands-On Time: 25 minutes ■ Total Time: 1 hour

In this takeoff on tuna tetrazzini, canned salmon is the star. The vegetables cook with the pasta to save a pot.

8 ounces rotini

1½ cups broccoli florets

1½ cups cauliflower florets

1 small onion, finely chopped

1 stalk celery, thinly sliced

2 tablespoons butter

2 tablespoons all-purpose flour

1½ cups milk

¾ cup shredded Cheddar cheese

¾ teaspoon dried marjoram

1 can (7 ounces) salmon, drained and flaked

2 tablespoons seasoned dried bread crumbs

1. Preheat the oven to 350°F. Coat an 11" × 7" baking dish with cooking spray. Bring a large pot of water to a boil.

2. Cook the rotini according to package directions until al dente, adding the broccoli, cauliflower, onion, and celery during the last 5 minutes of cooking. Drain the pasta and vegetables together in a colander.

3. Meanwhile, in a large saucepan, melt the butter over medium heat. Stir in the flour and cook, stirring, for 1 minute, or until the flour is lightly browned. Stir in the milk until smooth. Cook, stirring often, for 5 minutes, or until thickened.

4. Remove the pan from the heat. Stir in the Cheddar and marjoram. Continue stirring until the cheese is melted and the mixture is smooth. Gently stir in the salmon and the pasta and vegetables.

5. Pour into the prepared baking dish. Top with the bread crumbs. Bake for 25 minutes, or until hot and bubbly.

Makes 6 servings

Ingredients Note

The name *rotini* derives from the Italian, meaning "twists." These tight little spirals are ideal for holding the sauce in this dish. You can use fusilli, if you prefer.

Zesty Tortellini with Sausage

Hands-On Time: 25 minutes ■ Total Time: 35 minutes

Jalapeño pepper jelly and wine vinegar combine with chicken broth in this sweet-and-sour sauce. Tossed with sweet sausage and tortellini, this colorful, hearty meal is a perfect, quick-to-fix family meal any night of the week.

12 ounces spinach and/or cheese tortellini	1 tablespoon red wine vinegar
½ pound bulk sweet Italian sausage	1 tablespoon jalapeño pepper jelly
1 red bell pepper, thinly sliced	1 teaspoon Italian seasoning
6 scallions, cut into ½" lengths	½ cup shredded Parmesan cheese
½ cup chicken broth	¼ cup pine nuts, toasted

1. Bring a large pot of water to a boil. Prepare the tortellini according to package directions until al dente.

2. Meanwhile, in a large skillet over medium-high heat, cook the sausage for 5 minutes, or until it's no longer pink. Drain off any fat. Reduce the heat to medium. Add the bell pepper and scallions. Cook, stirring occasionally, for 3 minutes, or until the vegetables are just softened.

3. Add the broth, vinegar, jelly, and Italian seasoning. Cook for 5 minutes, or until the liquid is slightly reduced. Drain the pasta and add it to the pan. Toss to coat well.

4. Transfer to 6 serving bowls and top with the Parmesan and nuts.

Makes 6 servings

Orzo Milanese

Hands-On Time: 15 minutes ■ Total Time: 30 minutes

In this variation of risotto Milanese, orzo takes the place of Arborio rice. You'll be happy with far less stirring.

1 teaspoon olive oil	½ cup frozen peas
1 small onion, minced	⅛ teaspoon crushed saffron threads
1 clove garlic, minced	2 tablespoons grated Parmesan cheese
¾ cup orzo pasta	
3 cups chicken broth	

1. In a medium saucepan, heat the oil over medium heat. Add the onion and garlic. Cook, stirring frequently, for 3 minutes, or until softened.

2. Add the orzo. Cook, stirring constantly, for 2 minutes, or until the orzo is well-coated. Stir in the broth, peas, and saffron. Increase the heat to high and bring to a boil. Reduce the heat to medium-low, cover, and simmer, stirring occasionally, for 10 minutes, or until the orzo is tender but still holds its shape.

3. Remove the pan from the heat and allow the mixture to rest for 3 minutes. Stir in the Parmesan.

Makes 6 servings

Ingredients Note

A little saffron goes a long way, which is good because it's expensive.
Be sure to crush the threads just before using. Store saffron in an airtight
container in a cool, dry place for up to 6 months.

Ruffled Pasta with Four Cheeses

Hands-On Time: 35 minutes ■ Total Time: 1 hour

Don't let the number of ingredients in this dish stop you from making this delicious variation on standard macaroni and cheese. The rich flavors are outstanding. You can use reduced-fat milk and cheeses, if you like. For a festive presentation, bake the pasta in individual containers, as we did in the photo, opposite. The baking time remains the same.

8 ounces ruffled pasta, elbow macaroni, or other medium pasta

1 tablespoon butter

3 tablespoons all-purpose flour

¼ teaspoon mustard powder

2½ cups milk

1 teaspoon minced garlic

1½ teaspoons reduced-sodium soy sauce

¼ teaspoon ground black pepper

Dash of hot pepper sauce

½ cup coarsely chopped mushrooms

¼ cup minced onion

½ cup finely diced red bell pepper

1 tablespoon water

½ cup ricotta cheese

¼ cup diced Cheddar cheese

¼ cup diced Monterey Jack cheese

2 tablespoons grated Parmesan cheese

4 teaspoons minced fresh basil

1 to 2 teaspoons minced pickled jalapeño pepper (optional; wear plastic gloves when handling)

1½ cups seasoned dried bread crumbs

1. Bring a large pot of water to a boil. Cook the pasta according to package directions until al dente. Drain in a colander.

2. Meanwhile, in a large saucepan, melt the butter over medium heat. Stir in the flour and mustard. Cook, stirring constantly, for 1 minute. Slowly whisk in the milk until smooth. Stir in the garlic, soy sauce, black pepper, and hot pepper sauce. Cook, whisking often, until the sauce thickens. Remove from the heat and set aside.

3. In a large nonstick skillet, combine the mushrooms, onion, bell pepper, and water. Cook over medium-high heat for about 5 minutes, or until the vegetables are softened. Fold into the sauce.

4. Preheat the oven to 400°F.

5. Add the pasta, ricotta, Cheddar, Monterey Jack, Parmesan, basil, and jalapeño pepper, if using, to the sauce.

6. Coat a 9" × 9" baking dish with cooking spray. Transfer the pasta mixture to the dish and top with the bread crumbs. Bake at 400°F for 20 minutes, or until heated through and golden on top.

Makes 6 servings

Bacon and Onion Macaroni

Hands-On Time: 40 minutes ■ Total Time: 40 minutes

Even bacon can have a place in a healthful diet, if it is eaten in moderation. Canadian bacon has about one-fifth the fat (and less than half the calories) of regular bacon. Just 3 ounces of Canadian bacon can add big flavor to this simple, hearty dish. This dish also includes Italian pepperoncini. These slender pickled peppers are slightly hot, so canned green chiles make a good substitute.

1 tablespoon plus 1 teaspoon olive oil

2 large onions, sliced

4 cloves garlic, minced

½ teaspoon dried basil

8 ounces ribbed elbow macaroni

1 can (14.5 ounces) whole tomatoes, with juice

3 ounces Canadian bacon or lean ham, cut into ¼" pieces

¼ cup drained, seeded, sliced pepperoncini or drained, canned, chopped green chiles

⅛ teaspoon red pepper flakes

2 tablespoons tomato paste

1. Bring a large pot of water to a boil.

2. In a large, heavy nonstick skillet, heat the oil over medium-high heat. Add the onions, garlic, and basil. Cook, stirring occasionally, until the onions just begin to soften. Reduce the heat to medium. Cover and cook, stirring frequently, for 10 minutes, or until the onions are very soft. (Reduce the heat if the onions seem to be sticking to the pan.)

3. Cook the macaroni according to package directions until al dente. Drain in a colander.

4. While the macaroni is cooking, drain and reserve the juice from the tomatoes. Coarsely chop the tomatoes and set aside.

5. Add the Canadian bacon, pepperoncini, and red pepper flakes to the skillet. Increase the heat to medium-high and cook, stirring frequently, for 2 to 3 minutes, or until heated through.

6. Stir in the tomato paste and tomatoes (with juice). Bring to a boil. Reduce the heat to medium, cover, and simmer, stirring occasionally, for 5 minutes, or until the flavors are blended.

7. Add the drained macaroni to the sauce. Toss until well mixed and heated through.

Makes 4 servings

Kitchen Tip

You can easily remove the seeds from the pepperoncini with the tip of a teaspoon.

Speedy Skillet Macaroni

Hands-On Time: 20 minutes ■ Total Time: 45 minutes

This is the perfect meal to make when you are short on time and big on hunger. Your kids will love the great taste of this wholesome one-dish meal, and you will love how easy it is to make.

1 pound lean ground beef

1 onion, chopped

2 cloves garlic, minced

2 cans (14.5 ounces each) Mexican-style stewed tomatoes, with juice

1 can (19 ounces) red kidney beans, rinsed and drained

1 cup elbow macaroni

1 tablespoon taco seasoning

½ cup shredded Cheddar cheese

1. In a large skillet, combine the beef, onion, and garlic. Cook over medium heat, stirring frequently, for 8 minutes, or until the beef is no longer pink. Drain off any fat.

2. Return the skillet to the heat and stir in the tomatoes (with juice), beans, macaroni, and taco seasoning. Increase the heat to high and bring to a boil. Reduce the heat to low, cover, and simmer, stirring occasionally, for 25 minutes, or until the macaroni is tender. Top with the Cheddar.

Makes 4 servings

Ingredients Note

Canned Mexican-style tomatoes, seasoned with spices and jalapeño peppers, are available at most grocery stores. Look for them near the other canned tomato products.

Rigatoni Carbonara with Peas

Hands-On Time: 10 minutes ■ Total Time: 35 minutes

Using ready-cooked real bacon in this family-friendly pasta saves you time two ways. It eliminates the need to cook the bacon *and* the minutes spent scrubbing the griddle. Since you're buying the bacon bagged, you might as well pick up some minced garlic and shredded cheese, as well.

12 ounces rigatoni	1 tablespoon minced garlic
2 cups frozen petite peas	4 eggs
2 tablespoons olive oil	1 cup shredded Parmesan-and-Romano cheese blend
½ cup (2 ounces) bagged crumbled bacon	

1. Bring a large pot of water to a boil. Cook the rigatoni according to package directions until al dente. Before draining, set aside 1 cup of the cooking water. Place the peas in a large colander. Drain the rigatoni over the peas. Set both aside.

2. Return the pot to medium-low heat. Add the oil, bacon, and garlic. Cook, stirring occasionally, for 2 minutes, or until the garlic is golden. Add the rigatoni and peas. Toss to coat with the garlic mixture.

3. In a medium bowl, beat the eggs. Stir in ½ cup of the reserved pasta cooking water.

4. Increase the heat under the pot to medium. Add the eggs and quickly stir them into the pasta mixture. Cook, stirring constantly, for about 4 minutes, or just until the eggs thicken and coat the pasta. (Take the pot off the burner if the eggs start to curdle.) Remove the pot from the heat. Add the cheese and stir to mix. Add a few more tablespoons of the cooking water to thin the sauce, if needed.

Makes 4 servings

Accompaniments

Precede the pasta with Mushroom-Stuffed Mushrooms (page 2),
and serve Pumpkin Panna Cotta (page 348) for dessert.

Rigatoni Alfredo

Hands-On Time: 20 minutes ■ Total Time: 45 minutes

This simple cream sauce, bursting with basil and Parmesan cheese, turns pasta into an elegant dinner that can be prepped in 20 minutes. For a change of pace, substitute pecans and Asiago for the walnuts and Parmesan.

12 ounces rigatoni

1 cup milk

½ cup sour cream

2 cloves garlic, minced

½ teaspoon freshly grated nutmeg

½ teaspoon salt

½ teaspoon ground black pepper

⅔ cup shredded Parmesan cheese

½ cup walnuts, toasted and coarsely chopped

¼ cup thinly sliced fresh basil

1. Bring a large pot of water to a boil. Prepare the rigatoni according to package directions. Drain and return it to the pot.

2. Stir in the milk, sour cream, garlic, nutmeg, salt, pepper, and ⅓ cup of the Parmesan. Cook over low heat, stirring constantly, for 3 minutes, or until thick and bubbling.

3. Add the walnuts and basil. Toss to combine. Place in a serving bowl and top with the remaining ⅓ cup cheese.

Makes 6 servings

Meatless Mains

"The one who constantly eats vegetable roots can do anything."

—CHINESE PROVERB

Spinach and Mushroom Pie

Hands-On Time: 20 minutes ■ Total Time: 1 hour 40 minutes

There's something comforting about a spinach and mushroom pie. This lighter take on the Mediterranean classic eliminates the crust to cut fat. You won't even miss it.

1 cup long-grain white rice	3 egg whites
10 ounces frozen chopped spinach	1 egg
½ cup shredded part-skim mozzarella cheese	2 teaspoons Dijon mustard
¼ cup minced red bell pepper	¼ teaspoon hot pepper sauce
¼ cup minced scallions	¼ teaspoon ground white pepper
2 tablespoons minced fresh dill or 1½ teaspoons dried	½ cup thinly sliced mushrooms
1½ cups 2% milk	1 tablespoon grated Parmesan cheese

1. In a large covered saucepan, cook the rice according to package directions. Remove from the heat, transfer to a large bowl, and let cool briefly.

2. Meanwhile, cook the spinach according to package directions. Transfer to a strainer to cool. Press with the back of a spoon, then squeeze with your hands to remove as much liquid as possible.

3. Preheat the oven to 350°F.

4. Add the spinach, mozzarella, bell pepper, scallions, and dill to the rice. Stir to blend thoroughly.

5. In a small bowl, whisk together the milk, egg whites, egg, mustard, hot pepper sauce, and white pepper.

6. Coat a 10" pie plate with cooking spray. Add the rice mixture in a smooth layer. At even intervals, tuck mushrooms into the rice in a decorative pattern. Pour the egg mixture over the rice and sprinkle with the Parmesan.

7. Bake for 45 to 50 minutes, or until the custard is set and the top is golden. Cool for 10 minutes before cutting it into wedges.

Makes 6 servings

Ingredients Note

You can use 2 cups of leftover white rice to make this recipe.
Bring it to room temperature before using. Or, for
more fiber, use high-fiber brown rice.

Vegetable Pot Pies with Johnnycake Crust

Hands-On Time: 25 minutes ■ Total Time: 45 minutes

Pioneers called the cornmeal bread they made on a griddle "johnnycakes." In this recipe, cornmeal crusts top individual vegetable casseroles. For a spicier dish, add ⅛ teaspoon ground red pepper to the vegetable mixture.

Vegetable Filling

1 teaspoon olive oil

3 cups frozen mixed vegetables (such as carrots, corn, and peas)

2 tablespoons butter

2 tablespoons all-purpose flour

2 cups milk

½ teaspoon salt

½ teaspoon dried thyme

¼ teaspoon ground black pepper

Johnnycake Crust

½ cup yellow or white cornmeal

½ cup all-purpose flour

1 teaspoon baking powder

½ cup buttermilk

1 egg

1 tablespoon honey

1. Preheat the oven to 350°F.

2. *To make the vegetable filling:* In a large nonstick skillet, heat the oil over medium-high heat. Add the vegetables and cook, stirring occasionally, for 5 minutes, or until just softened. Remove the skillet from the heat and set aside.

3. In a medium saucepan, heat the butter over medium heat. Add the flour and whisk for 2 to 3 minutes, or until smooth. Slowly add the milk and stir for 5 to 7 minutes, or until thickened. Stir in the salt, thyme, and pepper.

4. Pour the thickened sauce over the vegetables in the skillet and mix well. Divide the mixture among 4 individual casseroles.

5. *To make the johnnycake crust:* In a medium bowl, mix the cornmeal, flour, and baking powder.

6. In a small bowl, mix the buttermilk, egg, and honey. Pour over the cornmeal mixture and stir until blended.

7. Spoon the crust mixture over the vegetables. Bake for 20 minutes, or until the top is browned and the vegetables are bubbling.

Makes 4 servings

Vegetarian Shepherd's Pie

Hands-On Time: 40 minutes ■ Total Time: 1 hour

Shepherd's pie, as the name suggests, is traditionally made with lamb or mutton (or sometimes with beef). This wonderfully warming rendition of the British favorite is quite different: It's a vegetarian dish, with a savory filling of beans in tomato sauce, a layer of corn, and a cheese-crowned mashed potato crust. To dress it up a bit, you can pipe the potato topping through a pastry bag.

1½ pounds small baking potatoes, cut into 1" cubes

1 cup canned black beans, rinsed and drained

1 cup canned kidney beans, rinsed and drained

1 can (15 ounces) no-salt-added tomato sauce

1 cup chopped onion

2 cloves garlic, minced

½ teaspoon salt

½ teaspoon ground black pepper

½ cup milk

2 tablespoons butter

2 tablespoons chopped fresh cilantro

1 package (10 ounces) frozen corn kernels, thawed

¼ cup shredded Cheddar cheese

1. Preheat the oven to 375°F.

2. In a large saucepan, combine the potatoes and water to cover. Bring to a boil over high heat. Reduce the heat to medium, cover, and simmer for 10 minutes, or until the potatoes are just softened.

3. Meanwhile, in a medium saucepan, combine the black beans, kidney beans, tomato sauce, onion, garlic, ¼ teaspoon of the salt, and ¼ teaspoon of the pepper. Bring to a boil over medium-high heat. Reduce the heat to medium and simmer for 2 to 3 minutes, or just until heated through. Spread the bean mixture in an 11" × 7" baking dish and set aside.

4. When the potatoes are cooked, drain them in a colander and return them to the saucepan. Add the milk, butter, cilantro, and the remaining ¼ teaspoon salt and ¼ teaspoon pepper. Mash with a potato masher until smooth.

5. Spread the corn over the bean mixture, then spread (or pipe) the mashed potatoes on top. Sprinkle with the Cheddar.

6. Bake for 20 minutes, or until the top is golden. Increase the oven temperature to broil and place under the broiler for about 1 minute, or until the top is browned slightly.

Makes 4 servings

Vegetable Chili

Hands-On Time: 30 minutes ■ Total Time: 50 minutes

This quick vegetarian chili takes less than half an hour and can be made largely from pantry staples. If you're feeding kids, leave out the jalapeño pepper and use mild salsa.

2 tablespoons olive oil	½ cup mild or medium salsa
1½ cups chopped onion	2½ teaspoons chili powder
2 tablespoons minced garlic	1 teaspoon ground cumin
2 cups diced red bell peppers	⅛ teaspoon dried basil
2 teaspoons minced jalapeño pepper (wear plastic gloves when handling)	1 can (15 ounces) red kidney beans, rinsed and drained
1 can (28 ounces) whole tomatoes, with juice	1½ cups frozen corn
1 cup vegetable broth	

1. In a large, heavy saucepan, heat the oil over medium-high heat. Add the onion and garlic. Cook, stirring occasionally, for 3 to 4 minutes, or until softened.

2. Stir in the bell peppers and jalapeño pepper. Cook, stirring occasionally, for 3 to 4 minutes, or until softened.

3. Drain the tomatoes, reserving ½ cup of the juice. Add the tomatoes and juice to the pan, crushing the tomatoes with the back of a wooden spoon. Stir in the broth, salsa, chili powder, cumin, and basil. Bring to a boil. Reduce the heat to medium-low and simmer for 10 minutes, stirring occasionally, or until the mixture has thickened slightly.

4. Add the beans and corn, increase the heat to medium, and simmer for 6 to 8 minutes, or until the beans and corn are heated through.

Makes 4 servings

Variations

Use other beans, such as pintos, great Northern, or black beans. If using dried beans, soak and cook them ahead. You'll need 2 cups of cooked beans to make this recipe. (For a quick-soaking method, see page 264.)

The Power of Nuts

Take nuts off your taboo list! People who eat nuts four or five times a week have far less incidence of heart disease than people who don't, several large studies reveal. Just a few nuts deliver a jolt of heart-healthy monounsaturated or omega-3 fats, vitamin E, magnesium, and copper.

But here's a nutty problem: How do you eat "just a few"? Nuts are high in calories and fat, so you need to stay in control. One ounce is the perfect serving and can be easily added to many meatless dishes, as well as to breads and desserts. Here are some suggestions.

- Toss nuts into salads, soups, and stews.

- Use nuts as a topping for casseroles.

- Add finely ground nuts to sauces, such as tomato or pesto, to thicken.

- Add finely chopped nuts to bread batter.

- Add finely chopped nuts to the batter for baked goods such as scones, muffins, and quick breads.

- Sprinkle nuts on cereal or yogurt.

- Sprinkle nuts over fresh or canned fruit.

Calorie Counts for Common Nuts

To help you avoid getting too many calories from nuts, check the list below to find the calorie counts for 1-ounce servings of some of the most common nuts.

NUTS	CALORIES
3 chestnuts	70
18 cashews	160
20 peanuts	160
47 pistachios	160
24 almonds	170
12 hazelnuts	180
14 walnut halves	180
8 Brazil nuts	190
15 pecan halves	190
12 macadamia nuts	200

Spicy Black Bean Stew

Hands-On Time: 35 minutes ■ Total Time: 1 hour 35 minutes

This delicious vegetarian stew gets its kick from chili powder and ground red pepper. We recommend that you make your own chili powder for the best flavor. (See page 28 for directions.)

¼ cup orange juice

1½ cups chopped onion

1 small red bell pepper, chopped

2 tablespoons minced garlic

3 cups vegetable broth

3 cups diced canned tomatoes, with juice

2 cups cooked or canned black beans

1 cup diced carrot

1 cup diced red potatoes

1 cup tomato juice

1 stalk celery, diced

1 tablespoon chili powder

½ teaspoon ground red pepper

⅓ cup minced fresh parsley

½ cup crushed tortilla chips

¼ cup shredded mozzarella cheese

1. In a Dutch oven, combine the orange juice, onion, bell pepper, and garlic. Cook, stirring occasionally, over medium-high heat for 5 minutes.

2. Add the broth, tomatoes (with juice), beans, carrot, potatoes, tomato juice, celery, chili powder, and ground red pepper. Bring to a boil. Reduce the heat to medium, cover, and cook for 1 hour, or until the stew is thickened. Add the parsley.

3. Top each serving with the chips and mozzarella.

Makes 4 servings

Hearty Cheddar-Vegetable Stew

Hands-On Time: 15 minutes ■ Total Time: 15 minutes

Imagine a smooth, rich cheese fondue with the dipping vegetables already mixed in, and you'll have a mental taste of this pleasing meatless meal. The stew is especially appealing served over a baked potato or steamed brown rice.

2 tablespoons butter

3 bags (8 ounces each) broccoli florets

1 bag (12 ounces) frozen pearl onions, thawed

1 teaspoon paprika

1 teaspoon poultry seasoning

¼ cup water

3 tablespoons flour

2 cups whole milk

2 cups finely shredded sharp Cheddar cheese

1. In a large saucepan, heat the butter over medium-high heat. Add the broccoli, onions, paprika, and poultry seasoning. Cook, stirring, for about 1 minute, or until the vegetables are well coated with the seasonings.

2. Add the water, cover, and reduce the heat to medium. Cook, stirring occasionally, for about 4 minutes, or until the broccoli is bright green and partially cooked.

3. Add the flour. Stir to mix well. Add the milk. Cook, stirring frequently, for 4 minutes, or until thickened. Add the Cheddar, stirring constantly, until melted.

Makes 4 to 6 servings

Make-Ahead

Prepare the stew to the point where the milk is thickened. Pack in an airtight container and refrigerate for up to 3 days. To finish cooking, place the stew in a large pot. Cover and heat over medium-high heat, until bubbling. Add the cheese and cook, stirring constantly, until the cheese is melted.

Rice-Stuffed Peppers

Hands-On Time: 30 minutes ■ Total Time: 1 hour 15 minutes

For any meat eaters in the family, you can add sautéed ground poultry, such as turkey breast or Italian-style turkey sausage (removed from the casings), to the rice mixture.

1²⁄₃ cups vegetable broth

¾ cup brown rice

¼ cup wild rice

4 red, yellow, and/or green bell peppers

2 tablespoons water

1 tablespoon olive oil

½ cup diced onion

1 clove garlic, minced

½ cup minced carrot

½ cup frozen corn

½ cup frozen peas

½ cup shredded part-skim mozzarella cheese, plus 4 thin slices

¼ teaspoon dried oregano

2 cups tomato sauce, warmed

1. Combine the broth, brown rice, and wild rice in a 1-quart saucepan. Bring to a boil over medium heat. Cover, reduce the heat to medium-low, and simmer for about 40 minutes, or until the rice is tender and all the broth has been absorbed. Set aside.

2. Meanwhile, preheat the oven to 350°F. Cut the tops off the peppers near the stem ends. Discard the stems, seeds, and inner membranes.

3. Coat a deep 3-quart casserole dish with cooking spray. Place the peppers upside down in the dish. Add the water. Cover with the lid or foil and bake for 20 minutes.

4. Heat the oil in a large nonstick skillet over medium heat. Add the onion and garlic. Cook, stirring, for 5 minutes, or until softened. Add the carrot, corn, and peas. Cover and cook over low heat for 5 minutes. Stir in the shredded cheese, oregano, and the rice.

5. Remove the peppers from the oven. Carefully turn them right side up and fill them with the rice mixture, mounding the tops slightly. Top each with a slice of mozzarella.

6. Cover and bake for 15 minutes. Remove the lid or foil and bake for 5 minutes longer. Serve with the tomato sauce.

Makes 4 servings

Make-Ahead

Bake the peppers ahead. Then reheat them either in the oven at 350°F for 10 minutes, in a skillet with a little water, or in the microwave (for about 1 minute per half).

Baked Potatoes: A Fun Meatless Meal

Potatoes make a filling and healthy meal when served with toppings like those below.

If you have the time, you can bake potatoes in a conventional oven at 400°F for about 1 hour. Serve them straight from the oven or reheat them later.

A quicker alternative is to microwave the potatoes. Scrub 4 large baking potatoes (about 2 pounds) and pierce them with a fork in several places. Arrange them in a square or spoke pattern on a paper towel placed in the microwave. Microwave on high power for 5 minutes, then turn the potatoes and microwave on high power for 7 to 10 minutes longer, or until the potatoes are tender. Cover with paper towels and let them stand for 3 minutes to finish cooking.

Each of the following recipes makes enough for 4 baked potatoes. Split the hot potatoes and add your choice of topping.

- **Creamy Shrimp Topping.** In a large nonstick skillet, combine ¼ cup chicken broth, ½ cup sliced mushrooms, ¼ cup diced red bell peppers, and 2 chopped scallions. Cook over medium heat, stirring occasionally, for about 8 minutes, or until the vegetables are softened. Add ½ cup frozen cooked shrimp and cook for 1 to 2 minutes, or until thawed. Remove from the heat and stir in ¼ cup shredded part-skim mozzarella cheese and 2 tablespoons reduced-fat yogurt.

- **Summer Garden Topping.** In a large nonstick skillet, combine ⅓ cup diced red bell pepper, ⅓ cup diced red onion, ⅓ cup diced yellow squash, ⅓ cup diced zucchini, and ¼ cup fat-free chicken broth. Cook over medium heat, stirring occasionally, for about 8 minutes, or until the vegetables are softened. Stir in ¼ cup chopped parsley and 2 minced garlic cloves. Cook for 1 minute. Remove from the heat and stir in ⅓ cup reduced-fat cream cheese. Season with chopped fresh herbs or salt and pepper.

- **Southwestern Salsa Topping.** In a medium bowl, combine ½ cup mild prepared salsa, ½ cup reduced-fat sour cream, ½ cup reduced-fat yogurt, and ¼ cup chopped scallions. Stir well.

- **Pesto Topping.** Preheat the broiler. Remove half of the potato flesh from the baked potatoes. In a medium bowl, combine the potato flesh with ½ cup pesto sauce, ¼ cup grated Parmesan cheese, and ½ teaspoon minced garlic. Spoon back into the potatoes and broil until golden.

- **Tonnato.** In a medium bowl, combine 8 ounces drained canned water-packed tuna, ½ cup light mayonnaise, 2 tablespoons drained capers, 2 tablespoons Dijon mustard, 2 teaspoons fresh lime juice, and chopped fresh herbs to taste.

Mediterranean Eggplant Casserole

Hands-On Time: 25 minutes ▪ Total Time: 1 hour 20 minutes

Eggplant Parmesan is traditionally made by breading eggplant and frying it in a great deal of oil. By microwaving the eggplant before assembling the casserole, we've slimmed down the fat and calories considerably. Yet this dish is every bit as tasty as the classic.

2 eggplants, peeled	½ teaspoon ground black pepper
½ cup water	2½ cups tomato sauce
4 ounces mushrooms, sliced	1½ cups shredded part-skim mozzarella cheese
1 onion, thinly sliced	½ cup grated Parmesan cheese
1 clove garlic, minced	
3 tablespoons minced fresh basil or 1 teaspoon dried	

1. Cut the eggplants crosswise into ⅜"-thick slices. Layer the slices in an 11" × 7" glass baking dish. Sprinkle with ¼ cup of the water. Cover loosely with wax paper and microwave on high power for 7 minutes. Redistribute the pieces, moving the soft ones to the center of the dish. Cover with wax paper and microwave on high power for 8 minutes longer, or until all the slices are softened.

2. Drain the eggplants. Transfer to a platter lined with several layers of paper towels. Cover with more towels and press out the excess liquid. Set aside.

3. In a 2-quart casserole, combine the mushrooms, onion, and garlic. Add the remaining ¼ cup water. Cover with a lid and microwave on high power for 4 minutes. Stir well, cover, and microwave on high power for 4 minutes longer, or until softened. Drain well and stir in the basil and pepper.

4. Preheat the oven to 350°F. Coat the 11" × 7" baking dish with cooking spray.

5. Spread 1 cup of the tomato sauce on the bottom of the baking dish. Top with half of the eggplant slices and all of the onion mixture. Add 1 cup of the remaining tomato sauce, ¾ cup of the mozzarella, and ¼ cup of the Parmesan. Top with the remaining eggplant, the remaining ½ cup tomato sauce, the remaining ¾ cup mozzarella, and the remaining ¼ cup Parmesan.

6. Bake for 20 minutes, or until bubbly. Let the casserole stand for 10 minutes before serving.

Makes 6 servings

Variations

Serve the eggplant over cooked pasta. Or add a layer of lasagna noodles or other cooked pasta to the casserole itself. For a spicy dish, add minced hot chile peppers or red pepper flakes.

Asparagus Quesadillas

This particular recipe showcases asparagus in crispy tortilla "sandwiches." For a really hearty meal, serve with side dishes of beans and rice. Or make the quesadillas an accompaniment to grilled fish, such as halibut or flounder.

Asparagus Filling

1 tablespoon olive oil	⅛ teaspoon ground red pepper
1 large red onion, diced	1 pound asparagus spears, trimmed, cut into 2" pieces, and lightly steamed
2 cloves garlic, minced	
½ teaspoon chili powder	6 cherry tomatoes, quartered
½ teaspoon ground cumin	¼ cup minced fresh cilantro
⅛ teaspoon ground cinnamon	

Quesadilla

6 flour tortillas	6 cherry tomatoes, halved or quartered
½ cup shredded Monterey Jack cheese	¼ cup minced fresh cilantro
1 cup green or red salsa	

1. *To make the asparagus filling:* In a large nonstick skillet, heat the oil over medium heat. Add the onion and cook, stirring occasionally, for 3 to 4 minutes, or until softened. Add the garlic, chili powder, cumin, cinnamon, and pepper. Stir for 1 minute.

2. Add the asparagus, tomatoes, and cilantro. Cook, stirring occasionally, for 3 minutes, or until the flavors are blended. Transfer the mixture to a large bowl.

3. *To assemble the quesadillas:* Divide the asparagus filling among the tortillas, positioning it on one half of each. Sprinkle with the Monterey Jack. Fold the tortillas in half.

4. Clean the skillet and coat it with cooking spray. Heat over medium-high heat. Add 2 tortillas and cook for 2 minutes per side, or until golden. Press with a spatula to flatten slightly. Repeat with the remaining tortillas.

5. To serve, cut each quesadilla in half and top with the salsa, tomatoes, and cilantro.

Makes 6 servings

Variation

Replace the asparagus with green beans or bell pepper strips.

Macaroni and Cheese with Vegetables

Hands-On Time: 15 Minutes ■ Total Time: 45 Minutes

A steaming pot of macaroni and cheese makes a great vegetarian main dish. This version is especially appealing because of the colorful mix of vegetables that's stirred in. For other macaroni dishes, see pages 226 and 227.

1½ cups small pasta shells	1 cup cottage cheese
1 cup chopped onion	½ teaspoon mustard powder
1 clove garlic, minced	¼ teaspoon ground black pepper
1 package (10 ounces) frozen mixed peas and carrots	⅛ teaspoon salt
2 cups small broccoli or cauliflower florets	1½ cups shredded sharp Cheddar cheese
2 tablespoons milk	

1. Bring a large pot of water to a boil. Add the pasta, onion, and garlic. Cook for 3 minutes. Add the peas and carrots and broccoli. Cook for 5 to 7 minutes, or until the pasta is just tender. Drain and return the pasta and vegetables to the pot and set aside.

2. In a medium bowl, combine the milk, cottage cheese, mustard, pepper, and salt. Add to the pasta mixture. Stir in the Cheddar.

3. Return the pot to the heat and cook over low heat, stirring constantly, for 2 minutes, or until the cheese melts and the mixture is hot. Let stand for 5 minutes before serving.

Makes 4 servings

Leftovers

Macaroni and Cheese with Vegetables is not just for kids! It's a great take-along snack for times when you know you'll be working late and want to avoid the candy machines. Pack a 1-cup microwaveable container with leftover pasta, sauce, and vegetables. Microwave on high power for 4 minutes, stirring once, then let stand for 1 minute.

Broccoli and Pepper Strata

Hands-On Time: 45 Minutes ■ Total Time: 1 hour 30 minutes

This easy layered pasta and vegetable casserole has flavors reminiscent of rich Stroganoff dishes.

9 lasagna noodles	2 tablespoons minced fresh parsley
3 tablespoons cornstarch	1 clove garlic, minced
1½ cups vegetable broth	1 teaspoon dried thyme
15 ounces ricotta cheese	½ teaspoon dried rosemary
2 egg whites, lightly beaten	½ teaspoon dried sage
2 jars (7 ounces each) roasted red peppers, drained well	1 package (10 ounces) frozen chopped spinach, thawed and squeezed dry
1 teaspoon olive oil	2 cups steamed chopped broccoli
1 pound mushrooms, thinly sliced	2 to 3 tablespoons grated Parmesan cheese

1. Bring a large pot of water to a boil. Cook the lasagna noodles according to the package directions. Drain, rinse with cold water, and set aside in a single layer on trays lined with paper towels.

2. Meanwhile, in a small bowl, whisk together the cornstarch and about ¼ cup of the broth until the cornstarch is dissolved. Stir in the remaining broth. Set aside.

3. In another small bowl, stir together the ricotta and egg whites. Set aside.

4. Pat the peppers dry with paper towels and cut them into thin strips. Set aside.

5. In a large skillet, heat the oil over medium heat. Add the mushrooms and cook, stirring, for about 5 minutes, or until they release their moisture. Add the parsley, garlic, thyme, rosemary, and sage. Cook, stirring, for about 5 minutes, or until the mushrooms have shrunk and are thoroughly dry.

6. Give the cornstarch mixture a quick stir, then add it to the skillet. Cook, stirring constantly, until the liquid turns clear and thickens. Remove from the heat and stir in the spinach and the ricotta mixture.

7. Preheat the oven to 350°F.

8. Coat a 13" × 9" baking dish with cooking spray. Place 3 of the lasagna noodles in a single layer in the dish. Spread with one-third of the mushroom sauce. Sprinkle with half of the peppers and half of the broccoli.

9. Repeat with another layer of noodles and mushroom sauce. Top with the remaining peppers and broccoli. Finish with a layer of noodles and sauce. Sprinkle with the Parmesan.

10. Bake for 25 minutes, or until bubbly and heated through. Let stand for 15 minutes before cutting.

Makes 6 servings

Spaghetti Squash Casserole

Hands-On Time: 25 minutes ■ Total Time: 1 hour 15 minutes

If you've never cooked a spaghetti squash, you're in for a treat. This creamy yellow winter squash is so named because of its flesh, which, when cooked, separates into yellow-gold spaghetti-like strands. It's a nice alternative to pasta in casseroles.

1 spaghetti squash, halved lengthwise and seeded

1 tablespoon olive oil

1 small onion, chopped

2 cloves garlic, chopped

1 teaspoon dried basil

2 plum tomatoes, diced

8 ounces 1% cottage cheese

½ cup shredded mozzarella cheese

¼ cup chopped fresh parsley

¼ teaspoon salt

¼ cup grated Parmesan cheese

3 tablespoons seasoned dried bread crumbs

1. Preheat the oven to 400°F. Coat a 13" × 9" baking dish and a baking sheet with cooking spray.

2. Place the squash, cut side down, on the prepared baking sheet. Bake for 30 minutes, or until softened. With a fork, scrape the squash strands into a large bowl.

3. Meanwhile, in a medium skillet, heat the oil over medium heat. Add the onion, garlic, and basil. Cook for 4 minutes, or until softened. Add the tomatoes and cook for 3 minutes, or until the mixture is dry.

4. Add the cottage cheese, mozzarella, parsley, salt, and the tomato mixture to the bowl with the squash. Toss to coat. Transfer to the prepared baking dish. Sprinkle with the Parmesan and bread crumbs.

5. Bake for 30 minutes, or until hot and bubbly.

Makes 6 servings

Kitchen Tip

Spaghetti squash can also be prepared in the microwave oven. Pierce the squash in several places with a knife. Place on a microwaveable plate and cover loosely with a piece of plastic wrap. Cook on high power, turning twice, for 20 minutes, or until soft when pierced. Remove and let stand until cool enough to handle.

Roasted Garlic Three Ways

Roasted garlic has an unforgettable sweetness that enhances a wide variety of meatless dishes, from pastas to vegetable stews. Simply mash it and toss the garlic into whatever dish you're making. It's also delicious in sauces, soups, vegetable purées, rice and grain dishes, dressings, dips, and spreads. And for a real treat, serve roasted garlic heads whole with sliced crusty bread. Just squeeze the cloves onto the bread, spreading with a knife. Here are three ways to roast garlic.

To roast a head of garlic: Don't worry about owning one of those clay garlic roasters. Any baking dish or even foil will do. Cut ½" from the top of 1 or several heads of garlic, trimming just enough to expose the tips of the garlic cloves. Remove any loose papery skin. Place the whole head in a small baking dish and drizzle generously with olive oil (alternatively, add water or chicken broth to come about ½" up the sides of the garlic). Cover tightly with foil and bake at 325°F for about 1 hour, or until tender when pierced.

To quick roast a head of garlic: Trim the head of garlic as described above. Pour ⅛" of milk in a microwaveable dish. Place the garlic, cut side down, in the milk, and cover. Microwave on medium power for about 7 minutes, or until the garlic just begins to tenderize. Uncover. Turn the garlic upright, drizzle with ½ teaspoon olive oil, and roast in a 375°F oven for about 20 minutes, or until completely tender.

To roast individual cloves of garlic: Toast the unpeeled cloves in a dry skillet over medium heat, shaking the pan occasionally, for 12 to 15 minutes, or until browned all over. Or wrap the cloves in a single layer in aluminum foil, crimping well to seal. Place in a small, baking dish with ½" of water. Bake at 325°F for about 1 hour, or until tender.

French Vegetable Gratin

Hands-On Time: 15 minutes ■ Total Time: 35 minutes

With the availability of prepackaged sliced fresh vegetables (even onions come prechopped), preparing sophisticated meatless main dishes has never been easier. Choose an ovenproof high-sided skillet—old-fashioned cast iron works beautifully—to brown the peppers, mushrooms, and onions, and you won't have to dirty a baking dish.

2 tablespoons olive oil

2 containers (7 ounces each) chopped tricolor bell peppers

1 package (8 ounces) sliced cremini mushrooms

1½ cups chopped onions

1½ teaspoons herbes de Provence

½ teaspoon salt

2 tablespoons cornmeal

8 ounces goat cheese

1 cup part-skim ricotta cheese

2 eggs

½ teaspoon ground black pepper

1. Preheat the oven to 350°F.

2. In a large ovenproof skillet, heat the oil over medium-high heat. Add the bell peppers, mushrooms, onions, herbes de Provence, and salt. Toss well.

3. Cover and cook over medium-high heat, stirring occasionally, for about 3 minutes, or until the vegetables give off their liquid. Uncover and cook, stirring occasionally, for about 6 minutes, or until the vegetables are browned (reduce the heat if the onions are browning too quickly). Stir in the cornmeal.

4. Meanwhile, in a medium bowl, mash the goat cheese with a fork. Add the ricotta, eggs, and black pepper. Beat until smooth. Dollop over the vegetables, spreading to cover.

5. Bake for about 20 minutes, or until the topping is set.

Makes 4 to 6 servings

Make-Ahead

You can assemble the dish through step 4, then cover tightly with plastic wrap. Refrigerate for up to 3 days. Bake according to the recipe directions.

Veggie Cassoulet

Hands-On Time: 40 minutes ■ Total Time: 2 hours 40 minutes (plus overnight soaking)

This dish takes time, but much of that time is hands-off. Using dried beans is key to the authenticity of this meatless variation on a French classic. Here vegetable-and-grain breakfast links replace pork sausages.

⅔ cup dried great Northern or navy beans

2 large onions, chopped

3 cloves garlic, minced

1½ cups water

½ cup dry-packed sun-dried tomatoes

4 frozen vegetable-and-grain breakfast links, thawed and sliced

2 leeks, white part only, thinly sliced

1 jar (7 ounces) roasted red peppers, drained and chopped

2 large carrots, thinly sliced

1 teaspoon salt

½ teaspoon ground black pepper

½ teaspoon dried rosemary

½ cup fresh whole wheat bread crumbs

1. Rinse the beans and discard any stones or shriveled beans. In a medium saucepan, combine the beans and water to cover by 2". Let soak overnight.

2. Drain the beans and return to the pan. Add the onions, garlic, and water. Bring to a boil over high heat. Reduce the heat to low, cover, and simmer for 1 hour, adding a little water, as necessary, to keep the beans from sticking.

3. Meanwhile, in a small bowl, combine the sun-dried tomatoes with boiling water to cover. Soak for 5 minutes. When softened, drain (reserving the soaking water) and chop coarsely. Set aside.

4. Preheat the oven to 325°F. Coat a 2-quart baking dish with cooking spray.

5. Remove the beans from the heat. Stir in the breakfast links, leeks, roasted peppers, carrots, salt, and black pepper. Add the tomatoes and soaking water and stir to combine. Spoon the mixture into the prepared baking dish. Sprinkle with the rosemary and top with the bread crumbs.

6. Bake for 1 hour, or until the carrots are softened and the bread crumbs are golden brown.

Makes 4 servings

Accompaniments

Serve the casserole with a light salad of mixed greens and a dressing of your choice (see pages 62 to 63). For dessert, offer Light Chocolate Cake (page 314).

Vegetable Lo Mein

Hands-On Time: 30 minutes ■ Total Time: 1 hour 15 minutes

This easy Chinese stir-fry is made with pasta rather than traditional cellophane (or bean thread) noodles. If you prefer to use cellophane noodles, see Variation, below, for how to cook them.

4 ounces vermicelli or thin spaghetti	4 teaspoons peanut oil
¼ cup vegetable broth	1 large red onion, cut into thin wedges
2 tablespoons oyster sauce	2 carrots, julienned
1 tablespoon mirin or other vinegar	1 red bell pepper, julienned
1 tablespoon cornstarch	1 cup broccoli florets
1 clove garlic, minced	¼ teaspoon sesame oil

1. Bring a large pot of water to a boil. Cook the pasta according to package directions just until al dente. Do not overcook. Pour into a colander, rinse with cold water, and drain well. Coat a large platter with cooking spray. Transfer the pasta to the platter and spread it out in a thin layer to cool. Refrigerate for at least 20 minutes.

2. Meanwhile, in a small bowl, whisk together the broth, oyster sauce, mirin, cornstarch, and garlic. Set aside.

3. Heat a wok or large skillet over medium-high heat. Add 1 teaspoon of the peanut oil. Add the pasta and cook, stirring frequently, for several minutes to lightly brown. Remove from the pan and set aside.

4. Add the remaining 1 tablespoon peanut oil to the pan and heat for 1 minute. Add the onion and cook, stirring constantly, for 2 minutes, or until it's slightly softened and just beginning to brown.

5. Add the carrots, pepper, and broccoli. Cook, stirring constantly, for about 2 minutes, or until it's crisp-tender. Pour the reserved broth mixture over the vegetables and cook, stirring, for about 4 minutes, or until it's thickened and shiny.

6. Add the sesame oil and pasta. Toss to combine. Serve immediately.

Makes 4 servings

Variation

To substitute cellophane noodles for the pasta, cook them in boiling water for 2 minutes. Pour into a sieve, rinse with cold water, and drain well. Transfer the noodles to a platter in a very thin layer to minimize clumping. Use scissors to cut them into 2" lengths for easier handling when cooking in the wok or skillet. Let cool.

Spicy Fried Rice and Vegetables

Hands-On Time: 40 minutes ■ Total Time: 40 minutes

A vegetable medley like this is just brimming with dietary fiber—and that pays you double health benefits. The insoluble portion of the fiber is essential for digestive health, and the accompanying soluble fiber helps control cholesterol levels. Using good-for-you olive oil and cholesterol-free egg substitute keeps this stir-fry ultrahealthy.

1 large bunch broccoli	2 cups sliced mushrooms
1½ tablespoons olive oil	1 cup snow peas
1 tablespoon plus 1 teaspoon minced garlic	2 tablespoons reduced-sodium soy sauce
1 teaspoon minced fresh ginger	3 cups cooked white rice
1 red bell pepper, cut into thin strips	1½ teaspoons hot chili oil
1 onion, thinly sliced	Pinch of red pepper flakes
½ cup vegetable broth	½ cup fat-free egg substitute
3 cups cut Napa cabbage (1" pieces)	2 to 3 tablespoons chopped fresh cilantro or Italian parsley

1. Cut off the top portion of the broccoli and separate it into small florets. Halve the stalk portion lengthwise and thinly slice.

2. In a wok or large, heavy saucepan, heat the oil over high heat. Add the garlic and ginger and cook, stirring constantly, for 30 seconds, or just until fragrant.

3. Add the bell pepper, onion, and broccoli. Cook, stirring constantly, for 1 minute, or until well coated with oil. Pour in the broth, cover, and simmer for 3 minutes, or until the vegetables are nearly softened.

4. Add the cabbage, mushrooms, snow peas, and 1 tablespoon of the soy sauce. Cook, stirring constantly, for 1 minute, or until the cabbage cooks down. Cover and simmer for 2 minutes, or until the vegetables are softened. Using a slotted spoon, transfer the vegetables to a large bowl.

5. To the liquid remaining in the wok, add the rice, chili oil, red pepper flakes, and the remaining 1 tablespoon soy sauce. Cook, stirring, for 1 to 2 minutes, or until the rice is heated through.

6. Reduce the heat to medium-low. Pour in the egg substitute and cook for 3 to 4 minutes, turning the mixture occasionally with a spatula, or until set. (Don't stir vigorously.)

7. Spoon the rice mixture onto a large serving platter. Top with the vegetables and sprinkle with the cilantro.

Makes 4 servings

Best-Ever Rice,
Beans & Grains

"I was determined to know beans."

—Henry David Thoreau

Spiced Brown Rice with Cashews

Hands-On Time: 20 minutes ■ Total Time: 1 hour 15 minutes

Aromatic basmati rice, favored by Indian cooks, has more fiber and a stronger flavor than white basmati, and is well worth the extra time it takes to cook. Once you've tasted basmati, you'll never want to go back to regular rice.

½ tablespoon olive oil

1 medium onion, chopped

1 cup brown basmati or long-grain brown rice

3 to 4 whole cardamom pods or ½ teaspoon ground cardamom

1 stick cinnamon (4" long), broken in half, or ¼ teaspoon ground cinnamon

2 cups chicken broth

⅓ cup unsalted cashews, toasted

1. In a large saucepan, heat the oil over medium heat. Add the onion and cook, stirring frequently, for 4 minutes, or until softened.

2. Add the rice, cardamom, and cinnamon. Cook, stirring constantly, for 2 minutes, or until the rice just starts to brown lightly. Add the broth and bring to a boil over high heat. Reduce the heat to low, cover, and simmer for 50 minutes, or until the liquid is absorbed and the rice is very tender.

3. Stir in the cashews. Remove from the heat and let stand for 5 minutes. Remove and discard the cardamom pods and cinnamon stick.

Makes 6 servings

Creole Red Beans and Rice

Hands-On Time: 35 minutes ■ Total Time: 50 minutes

This homey dish, which practically cooks itself, is a Monday supper tradition in the city of New Orleans. The flavor actually improves if it's prepared a few days in advance of serving (see Make-Ahead, below). Pass extra hot pepper sauce at the table.

2 tablespoons olive oil

1 cup chopped celery

1 cup chopped onion

1 cup chopped red, green, and/or yellow bell peppers

1 tablespoon minced garlic

2 teaspoons herbes de Provence

½ teaspoon salt

3 cans (15 ounces each) red kidney beans, rinsed and drained

2 cans (15 ounces each) chicken broth

½ pound ham steak, cut into 1" chunks

½ pound smoked, fully cooked kielbasa sausage, halved lengthwise, cut into 1" chunks

2 teaspoons hot pepper sauce

1 cup instant brown rice

1. In a large saucepan, heat the oil over medium-high heat. Add the celery, onion, peppers, garlic, herbes de Provence, and salt. Stir well. Cook, stirring occasionally, for 5 minutes, or until the onion is golden.

2. Add the beans, broth, ham, sausage, and hot pepper sauce. Reduce the heat to medium-low. Cover and simmer, stirring occasionally, for 10 minutes. Stir in the rice. Cover and simmer for 10 minutes, or until the rice is tender. Remove the pan from the heat. Let stand for 5 minutes.

Makes 4 to 6 servings

Make-Ahead

Refrigerate the red beans and rice in an airtight container for up to 1 week or freeze for up to 3 months. If frozen, thaw in the refrigerator for 24 hours before reheating. To reheat, place in a large pot with ½ cup water. Cover and reheat over medium-low heat for 15 minutes, or until heated through.

Mexican Red Rice and Beans

Hands-On Time: 20 minutes ■ Total Time: 40 minutes

Here's a soul-satisfying side dish that proves you can enjoy Mexican-style cooking with little fat and even less effort. It's easy on the budget, too.

2 teaspoons olive oil

1 cup chopped onion

1 clove garlic, minced

2 tablespoons plus 1½ cups water

1 cup long-grain white rice

1 can (8 ounces) tomato sauce

1 small green bell pepper, chopped

½ teaspoon chili powder

½ teaspoon ground cumin

½ teaspoon dried oregano leaves

¼ teaspoon salt (optional)

2 or 3 drops hot pepper sauce

1 can (15 ounces) kidney beans, rinsed and drained

3 plum tomatoes, diced

1. In a large saucepan, heat the oil over medium heat. Add the onion, garlic, and 2 tablespoons of the water. Cook, stirring frequently, for 6 to 7 minutes, or until the onion is softened.

2. Add the rice, tomato sauce, bell pepper, chili powder, cumin, oregano, salt (if using), hot pepper sauce, and the remaining 1½ cups water. Stir well. Increase the heat and bring to a boil. Reduce the heat to low and simmer for 20 minutes, or until the rice is tender and the liquid is absorbed.

3. Stir in the beans and tomatoes. Cook over low heat for 2 minutes, or until heated through.

Makes 4 servings

Leftovers

Make Red River Burritos: Wrap 4 flour tortillas in a damp paper towel and microwave on high power for 1 minute to soften. Reheat 2 cups of leftover Mexican Red Rice and Beans and divide among the tortillas. Roll tightly. Arrange the burritos, seam side down, in a baking dish, top with ⅓ cup shredded low-fat Cheddar cheese, and broil for 2 minutes to melt the cheese. Top each burrito with a spoonful of salsa, a dollop of yogurt, and some chopped cilantro for color.

Rice Riches

Today's supermarkets stock dozens of different rices, each with its own taste and texture. Rice can be defined by color, the length of the grain, processing method, variety, and other characteristics. Here are some terms associated with rice, as well as some common varieties.

- **Long-grain:** Available in white and brown varieties, the grains are four to five times longer than they are wide. They cook up fluffy and well-separated. This is the most common rice used in America. Carolina, basmati, and jasmine are long-grain rices.

- **Medium-grain:** Consisting of shorter, plumper grains that cling together, medium-grain rice is used for rice pudding, croquettes, and molded dishes. Arborio, Valencia, and "sushi" rice are medium-grain varieties.

- **Short-grain:** Soft and sticky when cooked, this type of rice is often used in Asian dishes because it's easy to eat with chopsticks. Sticky, or sweet, rice is a short-grain type.

- **Parboiled:** Soaked, steamed, and dried before milling, parboiled rice retains many of the nutrients that otherwise are lost during processing. Also called converted rice, it's available in white and brown.

- **Instant:** This is rice that has been previously cooked and dried. At home, it requires rehydrating rather than cooking, so it can be made quickly. It's available in white and brown.

- **Brown:** Higher in fiber and vitamin E than white rice, brown rice requires longer cooking because the outer shell (the bran) is left intact.

- **Arborio:** A medium-grain rice, Arborio is prized for making risotto and other dishes requiring a firm-textured yet creamy grain.

- **Aromatic:** This is an umbrella term for a variety of rices that give off a nutty aroma while being cooked. Basmati, jasmine, pecan, and popcorn rice are among the most popular.

- **Basmati:** An aromatic, long-grain rice much prized in India and Pakistan, basmati has a nutty taste and rich, aromatic smell. It's available in white and brown.

- **Black Forbidden:** This short-grain rice becomes dark purple when cooked. It has a deep nutty taste and will turn the cooking water purple.

- **Bomba:** This short-grain rice from Spain is typically used in paella. It can absorb up to one-third more liquid than other rices.

- **Jasmine:** This long-grain rice has a slight floral bouquet and is good for making fried rice.

- **Sweet:** Also called sticky rice or glutinous rice, this is a short, stubby grain that sticks together when cooked.

Tomato and Mozzarella Rice

Hands-On Time: 10 minutes ■ Total Time: 30 minutes

This zesty rice may remind you of your favorite cheese-topped pizza. It contains many of the same ingredients—tomatoes, mozzarella, garlic, and herbs—but the fat content is minimal. Spoon the rice alongside turkey burgers or baked chicken breasts and even "junk food junkies" will clean their plates.

2 large plum tomatoes, diced

6 scallions, sliced

2 cloves garlic, minced

¼ teaspoon salt

4 tablespoons plus 1 cup chicken broth

1 cup long-grain white rice

1 cup water

½ teaspoon dried basil

½ teaspoon ground black pepper

½ teaspoon dried thyme

2 tablespoons plus 4 teaspoons shredded part-skim mozzarella cheese

1. In a medium saucepan, combine the tomatoes, scallions, garlic, salt, and 2 tablespoons of the broth. Cook, stirring, over high heat for 3 to 4 minutes, or until the scallions are wilted, the tomatoes are very soft, and the broth has nearly evaporated.

2. Stir in the rice, then add the water, basil, pepper, thyme, and the remaining 1 cup broth. Bring to a boil. Reduce the heat to low, cover, and simmer for 25 to 30 minutes, or until the rice is tender and the liquid has been absorbed.

3. Remove the pan from the heat and transfer the rice to a serving bowl. Sprinkle with the mozzarella and serve.

Makes 4 servings

Kitchen Tip

Packaged preshredded cheese saves time in the kitchen, but it tends to be a bit more expensive than a whole piece of cheese. If you shred the mozzarella yourself, spray the grater lightly with cooking spray and the cheese will slide off easily. Cheese shreds more cleanly when it is well-chilled.

Basic Risotto

Hands-On Time: 25 minutes ■ Total Time: 55 minutes

Risotto requires constant stirring but is well worth the effort. It's a fun dish to make when guests are willing to join you in the kitchen (let them help stir). As a variation, add mushrooms or chopped fresh herbs, such as parsley or thyme.

2 teaspoons butter
1 teaspoon olive oil
1 cup chopped onion
1 cup Arborio rice
1 clove garlic, minced

4 to 5 cups chicken broth
Salt
Ground black pepper
2 tablespoons grated Parmesan cheese

1. In a large saucepan, heat the butter and oil over medium-high heat. Add the onion and cook, stirring occasionally, for about 7 minutes, or until the onion is softened and starting to brown. Stir in the rice and garlic. Cook, stirring constantly, for 1 minute.

2. While the onions are cooking, bring the broth to a simmer in a medium saucepan over medium heat. Reduce the heat to low and maintain the simmer.

3. Slowly add ½ cup of the broth to the rice mixture, stirring constantly. Continue stirring until the broth is absorbed. Repeat with the remaining broth, adding ½ cup at a time, and stirring constantly, until each addition of broth is absorbed and the risotto is creamy but still firm to the bite. (You may not need to use all of the broth.)

4. Add salt and pepper to taste. Stir in the Parmesan.

Makes 4 servings

Kitchen Tips

For great risotto every time, follow these tips.

Use a heavy saucepan of medium depth with a wide bottom. This type of pan will distribute the heat over a larger area and help speed cooking.

Cook over medium-high heat.

Always use hot, simmering broth so that the rice will cook properly. Keep a pot of simmering broth on the stove while you stir the risotto.

Add no more than ½ cup of broth at a time. After each addition, stir the rice constantly until all of the liquid is absorbed. Constant stirring encourages the grains to release their starch, creating the creamy texture that is unique to risotto.

Molasses "Baked" Beans

Hands-On Time: 15 minutes ■ Total Time: 30 minutes

Baked beans are an all-American dish. To enhance the flavor, we added turkey sausage rather than traditional bacon. Although the recipe uses canned beans, and they're cooked on top of the stove to save time, these beans have a baked-all-day flavor.

⅓ cup turkey sausage, casings removed

¾ cup chopped onion

1 can (15 ounces) pinto beans, rinsed and drained

¼ cup molasses

3 tablespoons chili sauce

2 teaspoons Worcestershire sauce

1. Crumble the sausage into a 2-quart saucepan. Cook over medium heat for 3 minutes, breaking up the sausage with a wooden spoon. Add the onion and cook for 3 to 4 minutes, or until the onion is translucent.

2. Stir in the beans, molasses, chili sauce, and Worcestershire. Bring to a boil, reduce the heat to medium-low, and cook for 10 to 15 minutes, or until the sauce has thickened.

Makes 4 servings

Accompaniments

Serve with Great Turkey Burgers (page 126) and Calico Slaw
with Poppy Seed Dressing (page 69).

John's Famous Beans 'n' Beef

Hands-On Time: 20 minutes ■ Total Time: 3 hours (plus overnight soaking)

We don't know who John is, but this recipe was passed on from friends. Here we add ground beef to make this bean dish a filling main course.

2½ cups dried pinto beans, soaked overnight and drained

10 cups water

1½ pounds lean ground beef

1 can (14.5 ounces) diced tomatoes, with juice

1 large onion, chopped

4 cloves garlic, minced

3 tablespoons reduced-sodium Worcestershire sauce

2 tablespoons chopped fresh cilantro

2 tablespoons picante sauce

1½ teaspoons chili powder

1 teaspoon ground cumin

Shredded Cheddar cheese (optional)

1. In a Dutch oven, combine the beans and water. Bring to a boil over high heat. Reduce the heat to medium, cover, and simmer for 1½ hours, or until the beans are almost tender. Drain, reserving 1 cup of the liquid.

2. When the beans are nearly cooked, coat a large skillet with cooking spray. Add the beef and cook over medium-high heat, stirring occasionally and breaking up the meat with the back of a wooden spoon, until browned and no longer pink.

3. Add the reserved liquid back to the beans. Stir in the cooked beef, tomatoes (with juice), onion, garlic, Worcestershire, cilantro, picante sauce, chili powder, and cumin. Bring to a boil over high heat. Reduce the heat to medium, cover, and simmer for 45 to 60 minutes, or until the beans are tender and the mixture is of the desired consistency.

4. Transfer to individual bowls and serve with Cheddar for sprinkling, if desired.

Makes 8 servings

Kitchen Tip

If you don't want to soak the beans overnight, use this quicker method. In a Dutch oven, combine the pinto beans and 10 cups cold water. Bring to a boil and boil for 2 minutes. Remove from the heat and let stand for 1 hour. Drain and rinse the beans. Continue as above.

The Power of Beans

Beans contain a healthy dose of fiber—approximately 7 grams per ½ cup—and they have been shown in studies to help lower cholesterol, stabilize blood sugar, reduce the risk of breast and prostate cancer, and prevent heart disease in people with diabetes.

Although dried beans have negligible amounts of sodium, the easy-to-use canned varieties are packed in a salt brine. If you're sodium-sensitive, look for reduced-sodium canned beans, and always rinse the beans to reduce their sodium content.

To prevent the gas that often follows a bean dish, toss the beans with summer savory, ginger, or cumin. These spices have been shown to reduce the gas-producing effects of beans.

Here are some delicious ways to get more beans into your diet.

- Toss beans into soups to help thicken them.

- Add beans to stir-fry dishes.

- Add beans to salads instead of using turkey or chicken.

- Add beans to vegetable dishes during the last 3 minutes of cooking.

- Make guacamole with half mashed beans and half avocado.

- Stir beans into stews.

- Combine beans with jalapeño peppers and fresh chopped cilantro, and fill tortillas with the mixture.

- Add beans to salsa for a hearty dip.

- Mash beans with rice and veggies, and form into bean burgers.

- Mash beans with minced vegetables and slather on bread topped with lettuce, tomato, and another bread slice.

Triple-Bean Bake

Hands-On Time: 25 minutes ■ Total Time: 3 hours 25 minutes (plus overnight soaking)

This tempting bean-and-tomato medley gets its irresistible flavor from ketchup, molasses, and brown sugar. Be sure to use dried beans, not canned. For quick soaking, see page 264.

1 cup dried black beans, soaked overnight and drained

1 cup dried great Northern beans, soaked overnight and drained

1 cup dried red kidney beans, soaked overnight and drained

3 bay leaves

8 cups water

1 can (14.5 ounces) diced tomatoes, with juice

1 medium onion, chopped

1 green bell pepper, chopped

1 cup brewed coffee or water

⅔ cup ketchup

½ cup dark molasses

⅓ cup packed brown sugar

1 tablespoon Worcestershire sauce

2 teaspoons mustard seeds

½ teaspoon salt

1. In a Dutch oven, combine the black beans, great Northern beans, kidney beans, bay leaves, and water. Bring to a boil over high heat. Reduce the heat to medium, cover, and simmer for 1 hour, or until the beans are almost tender. Drain and return the beans to the pan.

2. Preheat the oven to 350°F.

3. Add the tomatoes (with juice), onion, pepper, coffee, ketchup, molasses, brown sugar, Worcestershire, mustard seeds, and salt to the beans. Bake, covered, stirring occasionally, for 2 hours, or until the beans are tender and the mixture thickens. Remove and discard the bay leaves.

Makes 12 servings

Bean and Grain Patties

Hands-On Time: 30 minutes ■ Total Time: 30 minutes

These make a nice side-dish alternative to just plain beans and rice. Or eat them just as you would a hamburger.

1 can (15 ounces) chickpeas, rinsed and drained

2 eggs

⅓ cup shredded Cheddar cheese

¼ cup cooked rice

¾ cup dried bread crumbs

3 cloves garlic, minced

2 tablespoons chopped fresh parsley

2 scallions, chopped

4 pitas (6" in diameter)

1 tomato, thinly sliced

4 large leaves lettuce

½ cup prepared hummus

1. In a medium bowl, mash the chickpeas with a fork. Stir in the eggs, Cheddar, rice, bread crumbs, garlic, parsley, and scallions.

2. Coat a large nonstick skillet with cooking spray. Using a large spoon, divide the chickpea mixture into four patties, each about 4" in diameter. (The mixture will be wet.) Transfer the patties to the skillet. Cook over medium-high heat for 5 minutes, then turn and flatten with a spatula. Cook for 3 to 5 minutes, or until firm and lightly browned.

3. Trim one edge off each pita. Open the pitas along the rim and tuck in the patties, tomato, and lettuce. Top each with the hummus.

Makes 4 servings

Barley-Mushroom Bake

Hands-On Time: 15 minutes ■ Total Time: 40 minutes

Barley comes in many forms, pearled barley being the most familiar. Although the husk and bran are removed during the milling process, pearled barley is still considered a whole grain and is an excellent source of soluble fiber, which helps to lower blood cholesterol. Quick-cooking barley is pearled barley that has been precooked by steaming, and it retains virtually all of its nutritional value.

¼ ounce dried mushrooms (¼ cup)

¾ cup boiling water

1 cup quartered small fresh mushrooms

1 small onion, thinly sliced

1 cup chicken broth

½ cup quick-cooking pearled barley

Ground black pepper

1. Preheat the oven to 375°F.

2. In a medium bowl, combine the dried mushrooms and boiling water. Let stand for 4 minutes, or until the mushrooms are softened. Meanwhile, line a small strainer with cheesecloth and suspend it over a cup.

3. Using a slotted spoon, remove the soaked mushrooms from the liquid. Chop the mushrooms if the pieces are large. Pour the soaking liquid through the cheesecloth-lined strainer and discard any grit.

4. In a heavy, medium ovenproof saucepan or Dutch oven, combine the fresh mushrooms and onion. Drizzle 1 tablespoon of the broth over them, then cook, stirring occasionally, over medium-high heat for 3 to 4 minutes, or until the mushrooms are slightly softened. Drizzle in another 1 tablespoon of the broth as the mushrooms and onions cook.

5. Add the dried mushrooms, the strained soaking liquid, barley, pepper to taste, and the remaining broth. Bring to a boil over high heat. Cover the pan (if it doesn't have a lid, cover it tightly with foil) and bake for 25 minutes, or until the barley is tender and the liquid has been absorbed.

Makes 4 servings

Accompaniments

This savory side dish is wonderful with roast chicken or turkey breast, taking the place of stuffing (with much less fuss). Make a low-fat gravy by using chicken broth rather than the fatty drippings from the roasting pan. The barley is delicious with gravy.

Couscous with Vegetable Sauce

Hands-On Time: 20 minutes ■ Total Time: 35 minutes

This side dish pairs quick-cooking couscous with chickpeas and summer-fresh zucchini. Herbs and scallions help dress it up.

Vegetable Sauce

1 can (15 ounces) chickpeas, rinsed and drained

2 cans (8 ounces each) tomato sauce

1 cup diced zucchini

1 teaspoon dried thyme

½ teaspoon dried basil

¼ teaspoon salt (optional)

⅛ teaspoon ground black pepper

Couscous

1½ cups water

¼ cup thinly sliced scallions

1 large clove garlic, minced

1 teaspoon dried basil

½ teaspoon dried thyme

½ teaspoon salt

¾ cup uncooked couscous

1. *To make the vegetable sauce:* In a medium saucepan, combine the chickpeas, tomato sauce, zucchini, thyme, basil, salt (if using), and pepper. Stir well and bring to a boil over high heat. Reduce the heat to low, cover, and simmer for 15 minutes, or until the zucchini is tender.

2. *To make the couscous:* Meanwhile, in a medium saucepan, combine the water, scallions, garlic, basil, thyme, and salt. Cover and bring to a boil. Stir in the couscous. Remove from the heat, cover, and let stand for 5 minutes. Fluff with a fork.

3. Serve the couscous topped with the vegetable sauce.

Makes 4 servings

Variations

For a heartier offering, you can add bits of ground lamb to this dish. Either way, be sure to serve it with spicy harissa, a fiery chile sauce available in Middle Eastern and gourmet markets.

Tabbouleh

Bulgur is an extremely fast-cooking grain that's the mainstay of many Middle Eastern salads, including tabbouleh. If you have red or yellow cherry tomatoes, use them in place of the diced tomatoes for a prettier presentation.

1 cup chicken broth

1 cup bulgur

2 medium tomatoes, diced

½ cup chopped fresh parsley

¼ cup chopped chives

2 tablespoons chopped fresh mint

3 tablespoons fresh lemon juice

1½ tablespoons extra-virgin olive oil

1 clove garlic, minced

1. In a 1-quart saucepan, bring the broth to a boil over high heat. Stir in the bulgur. Cover, remove from the heat, and let stand for 15 minutes, or until the bulgur is tender and the liquid has been absorbed. Fluff with a fork and transfer to a large bowl.

2. Add the tomatoes, parsley, chives, and mint. Toss lightly.

3. In a cup, whisk together the lemon juice, oil and garlic. Pour over the bulgur mixture and toss to mix well.

Makes 4 servings

Accompaniments

You can use tabbouleh instead of rice for Greek Lamb Kebabs with Confetti Rice (page 164).
The tabbouleh would also be delicious with Lamb Curry (page 170).

Tabbouleh with Fruit

Hands-On Time: 25 minutes ■ Total Time: 1 hour 10 minutes

This is a nice variation on traditional Tabbouleh (page 271). The addition of all the high-antioxidant fruits makes this dish especially healthy.

1 cup orange juice

½ cup bulgur

1 large tomato, seeded and finely diced

½ small cantaloupe, finely chopped

1 cup finely chopped hulled fresh strawberries

½ pint fresh blueberries

½ pint fresh raspberries

¼ cup chopped parsley

½ small red onion, finely chopped

2 tablespoons fresh lemon juice

1 tablespoon chopped fresh mint plus leaves for garnish (optional)

1 tablespoon extra-virgin olive oil

¾ teaspoon ground cumin

½ teaspoon ground cinnamon

¼ teaspoon salt

¼ teaspoon ground black pepper

Lettuce leaves (optional)

1. In a medium bowl, combine the orange juice and bulgur. Let stand for 30 minutes, or until tender and softened.

2. Drain the bulgur in a strainer, pressing out any excess liquid, and place in a large bowl.

3. Add the tomato, cantaloupe, strawberries, blueberries, raspberries, parsley, onion, lemon juice, mint, oil, cumin, cinnamon, salt, and pepper. Toss gently to combine. Let stand at room temperature for at least 15 minutes, to allow the flavors to blend.

4. To serve, line salad bowls with lettuce leaves, if desired; spoon the tabbouleh into the bowls; and garnish with the mint leaves, if using.

Makes 4 servings

Millet Pilaf

Hands-On Time: 20 minutes ■ Total Time: 55 minutes

This protein-rich grain, which can be found in health food stores, is often forgotten. Prepare it instead of rice or bulgur as a delicious side dish with fish, chicken, or beef.

1 cup millet

1½ cups water

1 cup chicken broth

¼ teaspoon salt

½ cup golden raisins

2 tablespoons dry sherry

1 tablespoon extra-virgin olive oil

⅓ cup unsalted raw almonds, coarsely chopped

1½ teaspoons chopped fresh rosemary

2 tablespoons chopped flat-leaf parsley

1. In a medium saucepan over medium-low heat, cook the millet, stirring frequently, for 4 minutes, or until the grains are fragrant, browned in spots, and just beginning to crackle.

2. Add the water, broth, and salt. Bring to a boil over high heat. Reduce the heat to low, cover, and simmer for 25 minutes, or until the millet is tender, some grains have burst, and the water has evaporated. Remove from the heat and let stand, covered, for 10 minutes.

3. Meanwhile, in a small bowl, soak the raisins in the sherry for 10 minutes.

4. In a small skillet, heat the oil over medium heat. Add the almonds and cook, stirring frequently, for 4 minutes, or until lightly toasted. Stir in the rosemary and raisins and cook, stirring, for 30 seconds. Remove from the heat.

5. Fluff the millet with a fork. Stir in the almond mixture and sprinkle with the parsley.

Makes 4 servings

Quinoa with Peperonata

Hands-On Time: 35 minutes ■ Total Time: 50 minutes

A peperonata is an Italian condiment, typically featuring bell peppers, tomatoes, onions, and garlic cooked in olive oil. In Italy, it's served hot with meats or cold as an antipasto. Here we use it as a topping for nutty-tasting quinoa, which contains more protein than any other grain. The addition of orange zest and capers gives this dish extra zip.

1 cup quinoa

2 cups water

¼ teaspoon salt

2 tablespoons extra-virgin olive oil

3 large red bell peppers, cut into ½" squares

1 medium red onion, chopped

2 inner stalks celery with leaves, thinly sliced

3 cloves garlic, minced

¼ teaspoon salt

¼ teaspoon ground black pepper

1 can (14.5 ounces) diced tomatoes, drained, with 2 tablespoons of the liquid reserved

2 strips orange zest (each 2" long), removed with a vegetable peeler

1 tablespoon rinsed and drained capers, chopped

1. Place the quinoa in a fine-mesh strainer and rinse under cold running water until the water runs clear.

2. In a medium saucepan, bring the water to a boil over high heat. Add the quinoa and salt and return to a boil. Reduce the heat to low, cover, and simmer for 20 minutes, or until the quinoa is tender and the water is absorbed.

3. Meanwhile, in a large skillet, heat the oil over medium heat. Add the bell peppers, onion, celery, garlic, salt, and black pepper. Cook, stirring frequently, for 8 minutes, or until the peppers are crisp-tender.

4. Stir in the tomatoes and the reserved 2 tablespoons liquid, the orange zest, and the capers. Bring to a boil over high heat. Reduce the heat to low, cover, and simmer, stirring occasionally, for 12 minutes, or until the vegetables are very soft. Remove and discard the orange zest.

5. Fluff the quinoa with a fork, and spoon it into a shallow serving dish. Top with the bell pepper mixture.

Makes 4 servings

Kitchen Tip

You must thoroughly rinse the quinoa to remove the saponin,
a naturally occurring coating on the grain that has a bitter flavor.

Quinoa Pilaf with Toasted Pistachios

Hands-On Time: 20 minutes ■ Total Time: 50 minutes

Toasted pistachios add crunch and a touch of elegance to this pretty dish.

½ cup quinoa

¾ teaspoon peanut oil

⅓ cup shelled unsalted pistachios

1 bunch scallions, white and light green parts, chopped (½ cup)

⅓ cup chopped dried apricots plus apricot slices for garnish (optional)

2 teaspoons minced fresh ginger

1 clove garlic, minced

1 cup chicken broth or vegetable broth

Hot pepper sauce

2 tablespoons chopped fresh cilantro

1. Place the quinoa in a fine mesh strainer and rinse under cold running water until the water runs clear. Set it aside.

2. In a medium saucepan, heat the oil over medium heat. Add the pistachios and cook, stirring frequently, for 2 to 3 minutes, or until the nuts are fragrant and golden. With a slotted spoon, remove them to a small bowl.

3. Add the scallions, chopped apricots, ginger, and garlic to the pan, and cook, stirring constantly, for 2 minutes. Stir in the broth and hot pepper sauce to taste. Bring to a boil.

4. Stir in the quinoa and cilantro. Reduce the heat to low, cover, and simmer for 20 to 25 minutes, or until the liquid is absorbed. Remove from the heat and let stand for 5 minutes. Fluff with a fork and stir in the pistachios. Garnish with the apricot slices, if desired.

Makes 4 servings

Accompaniments

Serve the pilaf with Greek-Style Lemon-Garlic Chicken
(page 97) or Apple-Orchard Pork Chops (page 152).

Great Grains

Grains are not only nutritious and delicious, they're wonderfully easy to prepare. Here are cooking instructions and uses for some of the most common grains—and a few that aren't so common.

GRAIN	COOKING TIPS	USE
Amaranth	Simmer 1 part amaranth in 3 parts water for 20 to 25 minutes.	Cereal
Barley, pearl	Simmer 1 part barley in 4 parts water for 30 to 40 minutes.	Side dishes, pilafs
Buckwheat groats (kasha)	Simmer 1 part groats in 2 parts water for 15 minutes.	Pilafs
Bulgur	Pour 1½ cups boiling water over 1 cup bulgur and let stand for 30 minutes.	Side dishes, cold salads
Cornmeal	Simmer 1 part cornmeal in 4 parts water for 30 minutes.	Cereal, polenta
Couscous	Pour 1½ cups boiling water over 1⅓ cups couscous and let stand for 5 minutes.	Side dishes
Hominy	Soak overnight, then simmer 1 part hominy in 3 parts water for 2½ to 3 hours.	Cereal, side dishes
Millet	Simmer 1 part millet in 2 parts water for 25 to 30 minutes.	Soups, stews, side dishes
Oats, old-fashioned rolled	Simmer 1 part oats in 2 parts water for 10 minutes and let stand for 2 minutes.	Cereal, baking
Oats, steel-cut	Simmer 1 part oats in 4 parts water for 30 to 40 minutes.	Cereal
Quinoa	Rinse before using. Simmer 1 part quinoa in 2 parts water for 15 to 20 minutes.	Side dishes
Rice, brown	Simmer 1 part rice in 2 parts water for 30 to 40 minutes.	Side dishes, casseroles, pilafs, soups
Rice, white	Simmer 1 part rice in 2 parts water for 15 to 20 minutes.	Side dishes, casseroles, pilafs, soups
Triticale	Simmer 1 part triticale in 4 parts water for 1 hour.	Cereal, casseroles, pilaf
Wheat berries	Soak overnight, then simmer 1 part wheat berries in 3 parts water for 2 hours.	Stuffings, casseroles, side dishes, cereals
Wheat, cracked	Simmer 1 part cracked wheat in 2 parts water for 25 minutes.	Cereal, side dishes, salads, casseroles
Wild rice	Simmer 1 part rice in 3 parts water for 45 to 60 minutes.	Stuffings, casseroles, side dishes

Mixed Grain Pilaf with Almonds

Hands-On Time: 15 minutes ■ Total Time: 40 minutes

Before the advent of parcooked whole grains, a pilaf could take nearly an hour to prepare. By combining a multirice mix with quick-cooking barley, this grain medley is ready sooner.

1 box (6 ounces) long-grain and wild-rice mix

2 tablespoons butter

¼ cup sliced almonds

¼ cup shredded carrot

¼ cup minced onion

½ teaspoon ground black pepper

3 cups vegetable broth

½ cup quick-cooking barley

1. Remove the seasoning packet from the rice mix. Measure 2 tablespoons of the seasoning and discard the remainder. Set aside.

2. In a medium saucepan, heat the butter over medium heat. Add the almonds and cook, stirring with a fork, for 2 minutes, or until the almonds are golden. Use the fork to transfer the almonds to a plate, leaving the butter in the pan.

3. Add the long-grain and wild rice, carrot, onion, and pepper to the pan. Cook, stirring, for 2 minutes, or until the rice is glazed with the butter.

4. Add the broth and the reserved seasoning. Bring almost to a boil. Reduce the heat to medium-low. Cover and simmer for 15 minutes.

5. Stir in the barley. Cover and cook for 10 minutes, or until all the broth is absorbed. Sprinkle the almonds over each serving.

Makes 4 to 6 servings

Polenta with Caramelized Onions and Mushrooms

Hands-On Time: 35 minutes ▪ Total Time: 45 minutes

Polenta, made of coarsely ground cornmeal, can be served soft or firmed up. Here it's soft, topped with a sweet ragout of caramelized onions and mushrooms. To make it firm, pour it into a shallow pan and let it stand until set. Unmold and cut with a knife.

2 teaspoons olive oil	¼ cup balsamic vinegar
2 large onions, thinly sliced	5 cups water
¼ cup vegetable broth or water	1¼ cups quick-cooking polenta
3 cups sliced mushrooms	½ cup shredded reduced-fat Cheddar cheese
2 cloves garlic, minced	
½ cup chopped fresh parsley	2 tablespoons grated Parmesan cheese

1. In a Dutch oven, heat the oil over medium-high heat. Add the onions and broth. Reduce the heat to medium-low. Cover the pan and cook, stirring frequently, for 15 minutes, or until the onions are very soft.

2. Add the mushrooms and garlic. Increase the heat to medium. Cook, stirring frequently, for 10 minutes, or until the onions are golden and the mushrooms are lightly browned.

3. Add the parsley and vinegar. Cook for 1 minute, or until the liquid is reduced by half. Remove from the heat and keep warm.

4. In a medium saucepan, bring the water to a boil. Gradually whisk in the polenta. Cook, stirring, for 5 minutes, or until the water is absorbed. Add the Cheddar and Parmesan and stir well.

5. Serve the polenta topped with the onion and mushroom mixture.

Makes 4 servings

Ingredients Note

For a richer dish, use cremini or chanterelle mushrooms. If you use chanterelles, be sure to remove the tough stems.

Accompaniments

This polenta makes a fine accompaniment to Grilled Italian Sausage–Stuffed Zucchini (page 160). Offer a tossed green salad, as well.

Vegetables
on the Side

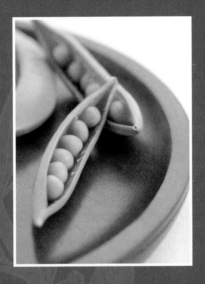

*"There's someone at every party
who eats all the celery."*

—KIN HUBBARD

Artichoke Gratin

Hands-On Time: 10 minutes ■ Total Time: 25 minutes

This easy vegetable side dish goes from freezer to plate in a flash. It's a perfect accompaniment to simple broiled chicken or steak.

2 packages (9 ounces each) frozen artichoke hearts

1 tablespoon fresh lemon juice

3 tablespoons plain dried bread crumbs

1 tablespoon grated Parmesan cheese

1 teaspoon dried Italian herb seasoning

1 clove garlic, minced

1 teaspoon olive oil

1. Preheat the oven to 375°F. Coat a 9" glass pie plate with cooking spray.

2. Place the artichokes in a colander and rinse well with cold water to separate. Drain well, then pat dry with paper towels. Place in the prepared pie plate and sprinkle with the lemon juice.

3. In a small bowl, combine the bread crumbs, Parmesan, Italian seasoning, garlic, and oil. Sprinkle the mixture evenly over the artichokes.

4. Bake for 15 minutes, or until the topping is golden.

Makes 4 servings

Ingredients Note

Using Parmigiano-Reggiano instead of prepackaged Parmesan would take this dish over the top, flavorwise. You could also use Pecorino Romano.

Asparagus with Roasted Peppers and Olives

Hands-On Time: 15 minutes ■ Total Time: 15 minutes

This is a lively dish that's wonderful alongside grilled or broiled pork or chicken. Tossed with pasta, it becomes a light meal. It is equally good hot or at room temperature.

2 teaspoons olive oil

1 pound asparagus, trimmed and cut into 1" pieces

2 cloves garlic, minced

2 tablespoons fresh lemon juice

1 jar (3.5 ounces) chopped roasted red bell peppers, drained

2 tablespoons chopped pitted black olives

1 tablespoon chopped fresh parsley

Dash of hot pepper sauce

Salt

Ground black pepper

2 tablespoons shredded provolone cheese

1. In a large nonstick skillet, heat the oil over medium heat. Increase the heat to medium-high and add the asparagus and garlic. Cook, stirring, for 1 minute. Add the lemon juice. Cover and cook for 2 minutes, or until the asparagus is bright green and crisp-tender.

2. Stir in the bell peppers, olives, parsley, and hot pepper sauce. Add salt and black pepper to taste. Sprinkle with the provolone and serve.

Makes 4 servings

Ingredients Note

Provolone is cow's milk cheese from southern Italy and is available in most supermarkets. Its firm texture makes this cheese excellent for shredding or grating. You could also shred or shave ricotta salata or Manchego cheese and use that, if you prefer.

Freezer-Fresh Vegetables

Who says the early bird always catches the worm? You can get great bargains on vegetables at the farmers' market if you shop near the end of the day, when sellers are eager to pack up and go home. Sometimes a bushel of green beans, broccoli, or carrots can be yours for less than $5. If your freezer is small, split the bounty with friends.

At home, wash and trim the vegetables. Most vegetables need to be blanched before freezing. Blanching is an easy technique that inactivates vegetables' enzymes so they don't lose quality in the freezer.

To blanch, bring a large pot of water to a boil, then immerse the vegetables for the required time (see below). Drain and rinse under cold water. Drain again and pat dry. Pack into servings of whatever size you need in freezer-quality containers or zip-top plastic bags.

Keep optimum flavor, color, and nutrients in your frozen vegetables by removing as much air as possible from the package before freezing. When too much air remains in the freezer package, it can cause freezer burn—an undesirable drying and discoloration of the food's surface. This happens because the air holds moisture, which freezes into ice crystals that leach vegetables' vitality. So press out as much excess air as possible before sealing the bag, and fill a rigid container nearly to the top. Label and date, then freeze for up to 6 months.

Smart summer shopping and an hour in your kitchen will yield plenty of good eating from the freezer throughout the winter months.

Asparagus: Leave the asparagus whole or cut into thirds, then blanch in boiling water for 30 seconds. Cool, then pack into freezer-quality zip-top plastic bags.

Beans, green: Leave the beans whole or cut into thirds, then blanch in boiling water for 3 minutes. Cool, then pack into freezer-quality zip-top plastic bags.

Beets: Steam whole baby beets or sliced beets for 10 minutes, or until tender. Slip off the peels and discard. Cool, then pack into freezer containers.

Broccoli: Break the broccoli into florets, then blanch in boiling water for 3 minutes. Cool, then pack into freezer-quality zip-top plastic bags.

Brussels sprouts: Leave the brussels sprouts whole, then blanch in boiling water for 3 minutes. Cool, then pack into freezer-quality zip-top plastic bags.

Cabbage: Slice or coarsely chop the cabbage, then blanch in boiling water for 3 minutes. Cool, then pack into freezer-quality zip-top plastic bags.

Carrots: Slice the carrots, then blanch in boiling water for 2 minutes. Cool, then pack into freezer-quality zip-top plastic bags.

Cauliflower: Break the cauliflower into florets. Blanch in boiling water for 4 minutes. Cool, then pack into freezer-quality zip-top plastic bags.

Corn: Blanch whole ears in boiling water for 3 minutes. Cool, then cut kernels off the cobs. Pack into freezer-quality zip-top plastic bags.

Eggplant: Peel, then slice or cube the eggplant. Blanch in boiling water, with 1 tablespoon of lemon juice to 1 quart of water, for 4 minutes. Cool, then pack into freezer-quality zip-top plastic bags.

Peas (green): Shell, then blanch the peas in boiling water for 2 minutes. Cool, then pack into freezer-quality zip-top plastic bags.

Peas (snow or sugar snap): Blanch the peas in boiling water for 2 minutes. Cool, then pack into freezer-quality zip-top plastic bags.

Peppers, bell (sweet): Halve the peppers, then blanch in boiling water for 1 minute. Cool, then pack into freezer-quality zip-top plastic bags.

Tomatoes: Plunge the tomatoes into boiling water for 30 seconds, then remove with a slotted spoon into a sinkful of cold water. Peel, then pack whole in freezer containers.

Zucchini: Shred, slice, or cube the zucchini, then blanch in boiling water for 2 to 3 minutes. Cool, then pack into freezer-quality zip-top plastic bags.

Garlicky Green Beans

Hands-On Time: 35 minutes ■ Total Time: 35 minutes

Don't be concerned about the amount of garlic used here. Boiling mellows and sweetens its sharp flavor.

6 whole cloves garlic, peeled

1 pound green beans, trimmed

2 tablespoons fresh lemon juice

1 teaspoon extra-virgin olive oil

⅛ teaspoon ground black pepper

1. Bring a large pot of water to a boil over medium-high heat. Add the garlic and cook for 10 minutes, or until softened when pierced with the tip of a knife. Remove with a slotted spoon and place in a small bowl.

2. Add the beans to the water. Cook for 5 minutes, or until the beans are crisp-tender. Drain and return the beans to the pot.

3. Mash the garlic with a fork. Stir in the lemon juice, oil, and pepper. Pour over the beans and toss to coat.

Makes 4 servings

Kitchen Tip

To easily remove the skin from a clove of garlic, cut the root end off and firmly press (or carefully smash) the flat side of a wide knife blade down on the clove. The skin will loosen and the clove will easily slip out.

Stir-Fried Broccoli and Mushrooms with Tofu

Hands-On Time: 30 minutes ■ Total Time: 30 minutes

This pretty side dish is quite filling, thanks to the addition of tofu. It could easily make a meal for two served over brown basmati rice.

⅓ cup chicken or vegetable broth

1 tablespoon apricot all-fruit spread

1 tablespoon dry sherry

1 tablespoon reduced-sodium soy sauce

2 teaspoons cornstarch

1 tablespoon olive oil

1 large bunch broccoli, cut into small florets

4 cloves garlic, minced

1 tablespoon finely chopped fresh ginger

4 ounces mushrooms, sliced

1 cup halved cherry and/or yellow pear tomatoes

8 ounces firm tofu, drained and cut into ½" cubes

1. In a cup, whisk together the broth, all-fruit spread, sherry, soy sauce, and cornstarch. Set aside.

2. In a large nonstick skillet, heat the oil over medium-high heat. Add the broccoli, garlic, and ginger. Cook, stirring constantly, for 1 minute. Add the mushrooms and cook, stirring frequently, for 3 minutes, or until lightly browned.

3. Add the tomatoes and tofu. Cook, stirring frequently, for 2 minutes, or until the tomatoes begin to collapse.

4. Add the cornstarch mixture to the skillet and stir. Cook, stirring, for 2 minutes, or until the mixture boils and thickens.

Makes 4 servings

Kitchen Tip

Place the tofu on paper towels, cover with more paper towels, and let drain well before cutting. It will cut more evenly.

Balsamic Broccoli Rabe

Hands-On Time: 15 minutes ■ Total Time: 15 minutes

Broccoli rabe (also called rapini) is a green vegetable that has long stalks and scattered clusters of buds that resemble broccoli flowers. Its pungent flavor, here heightened by balsamic vinegar, makes it an ideal complement to pasta. Look for it next to the regular broccoli in most supermarkets.

1 pound broccoli rabe

1 tablespoon balsamic vinegar

1 tablespoon grated Parmesan cheese

2 teaspoons extra-virgin olive oil

1 teaspoon minced fresh thyme

1. Rinse the broccoli rabe in cold water and shake off the excess water. Cut the thick stems into 1" pieces. Cut the leafy tops into 3" pieces. Place the stems and tops in a large, heavy saucepan or Dutch oven with just the water left clinging to the pieces.

2. Cover the pan and cook the broccoli rabe over medium heat for 5 minutes, or until softened. Drain and transfer to a serving platter.

3. Sprinkle with the vinegar, Parmesan, oil, and thyme. Toss to coat.

Makes 4 servings

Curried Brussels Sprouts

Hands-On Time: 15 minutes ■ Total Time: 30 minutes

Brussels sprouts and curry powder have a natural affinity. If you like, you can use reduced-fat milk and light mayonnaise instead of the full-fat versions in this recipe.

2   cups trimmed brussels sprouts

1   cup sliced mushrooms

½   cup diced red, yellow, and/or green bell pepper

¼   cup milk

1   tablespoon mayonnaise

2   teaspoons cornstarch

1   tablespoon minced fresh parsley

1   teaspoon curry powder

¼   teaspoon ground black pepper

1. In a steamer basket over simmering water, cook the brussels sprouts, partially covered, for 5 to 8 minutes, or until just softened.

2. Add the mushrooms and bell pepper and steam for 2 minutes longer. Remove the vegetables from the steamer. Drain the pan, reserving ¼ cup of the steaming liquid in the pan.

3. In a cup, combine the milk, mayonnaise, and cornstarch. Stir until the cornstarch is dissolved. Add it to the liquid in the pan. Cook over medium heat, whisking constantly, until the mixture thickens and bubbles.

4. Stir in the parsley, curry powder, and black pepper. Return the steamed vegetables to the pan, toss with the sauce, and heat through.

Makes 4 servings

Kitchen Tip

The vegetables can be cooked in the microwave. Place the brussels sprouts in a 1-quart casserole with 2 tablespoons water. Cover and microwave for 3 to 4 minutes, stirring once. Let stand for about 3 minutes. Place the mushrooms and peppers in another bowl, cover, and microwave for 1 minute.

Roasted Carrots and Parsnips

Hands-On Time: 15 minutes ■ Total Time: 55 minutes

Roasting carrots and parsnips brings out their natural sweetness. This combo is perfect with roast chicken or turkey.

1 pound carrots, cut into 1" chunks

1 pound parsnips, cut into 1" chunks

4 small red onions, cut into wedges

6 cloves garlic

½ tablespoon extra-virgin olive oil

½ teaspoon salt

½ teaspoon grated lemon zest

1. Preheat the oven to 375°F. Coat a medium baking pan with cooking spray.

2. Add the carrots, parsnips, onions, garlic, oil, salt, and lemon zest to the baking pan. Toss to coat well.

3. Bake, stirring occasionally, for 40 minutes, or until the vegetables are golden and softened.

Makes 6 servings

Ingredients Note

Fresh parsnips are available year-round but are best during fall and winter. Look for firm, small to medium roots that are not spotted.

Variation

You can add turnips and white or sweet potatoes to this recipe and mash, if you like. See page 312 for another root vegetable recipe.

Cheesy Baked Cauliflower

Hands-On Time: 20 minutes ■ Total Time: 40 minutes

This recipe calls for frozen cauliflower and carrots to save time, but you can adapt the recipe to use fresh, if you like (see Kitchen Tip, below). You could use reduced-fat milk and cheese, if calories are a concern.

2 teaspoons olive oil	1½ cups milk
1 small onion, chopped	½ cup shredded Monterey Jack cheese
2 cloves garlic, minced	¼ cup grated Parmesan cheese
2 tablespoons all-purpose flour	1 pound frozen cauliflower pieces, thawed
¼ teaspoon salt	1 pound frozen sliced carrots, thawed
⅛ teaspoon ground nutmeg	⅓ cup crushed Ritz crackers

1. Preheat the oven to 350°F. Coat a medium baking dish with cooking spray.

2. In a medium saucepan, heat the oil over medium heat. Add the onion and garlic. Cook, stirring often, for 5 minutes, or until softened. Sprinkle with the flour, salt, and nutmeg. Cook, stirring constantly, for 1 minute. Stir in the milk. Cook, stirring often, for 5 minutes, or until thickened.

3. Remove the pan from the heat. Stir in the Monterey Jack and Parmesan until melted. Add the cauliflower and carrots. Stir to coat. Spoon into the prepared baking dish. Sprinkle with the crackers.

4. Bake for 15 to 20 minutes, or until heated through and bubbly.

Makes 6 servings

Variation

Try cooked fresh cauliflower (the florets from 1 head)
and cooked sliced fresh carrots (1 pound) in this dish.

Leftovers

Make Creamy Cheesy Cauliflower Soup: In a food processor, combine 3 cups of the leftover Cheesy Baked Cauliflower, 1 cup milk, and 1 cup reduced-sodium chicken broth. Pulse to purée. Pour into a medium saucepan. Cook over medium heat until hot. Season to taste with salt and ground black pepper. Garnish with chopped fresh parsley, if desired. Makes 4 servings.

Cauliflower with Bell Pepper and Garlic

Hands-On Time: 15 minutes ▪ Total Time: 25 minutes

This recipe is a nice change of pace from typical buttered cauliflower. Bell pepper adds color, and the garlic, thyme, and paprika add complementary flavors.

1 large head cauliflower, cut into small florets

1 large red bell pepper, cut into 1" squares

2 tablespoons extra-virgin olive oil

4 cloves garlic, minced

1 tablespoon red wine vinegar

2 teaspoons chopped fresh thyme or ¼ teaspoon dried

¾ teaspoon paprika

½ teaspoon salt

1. Place a steamer basket in a large saucepan with ½" of water. Place the cauliflower and pepper in the steamer. Bring to a boil over high heat. Reduce the heat to medium, cover, and cook for 4 minutes, or until crisp-tender. Place in a serving bowl.

2. In a small skillet, heat the oil over medium heat. Remove the pan from the heat and stir in the garlic.

3. When the sizzling stops, stir in the vinegar, thyme, paprika, and salt. Add to the vegetables and toss to coat well.

Makes 4 servings

Ingredients Note

Paprika can range from mild to hot. Look for Hungarian paprika,
considered by many to be superior, in the spice sections of better supermarkets.
Replace paprika every 6 months for the freshest flavor.

Corn Casserole Soufflé

Hands-On Time: 15 minutes ■ Total Time: 55 minutes

This savory side dish is reminiscent of a Tex-Mex version of spoon bread. It's a delicious accompaniment to Charred Flank Steak with Picadillo Relish (page 134).

1 teaspoon olive oil

½ cup finely chopped onion

1 can (16.5 ounces) cream-style corn

½ cup milk

2 egg whites, lightly beaten

1 can (4 ounces) diced green chile peppers, drained

½ cup yellow cornmeal

½ teaspoon garlic powder

¼ teaspoon baking soda

1. Preheat the oven to 350°F. Coat an 8" x 8" baking pan with cooking spray.

2. In a small nonstick skillet, heat the oil over medium-high heat. Add the onion and cook, stirring, for about 5 minutes, or until softened.

3. Transfer the onion to a large bowl. Add the corn, milk, egg whites, and chile peppers.

4. In a small bowl, combine the cornmeal, garlic powder, and baking soda. Add to the corn mixture and stir well. Spoon the mixture into the prepared baking pan.

5. Bake for 35 minutes, or until a knife inserted in the center comes out clean. Let stand for 5 minutes before serving.

Makes 4 servings

Ingredients Note

You can use fresh jalapeño or serrano chile peppers for more heat. Be sure to wear plasic gloves when handling them.

Sesame Edamame with Scallions

Hands-On Time: 10 minutes ■ Total Time: 25 minutes

Edamame is the Japanese name for green soybeans, which are sold frozen in most super-markets. These tasty soybeans are a rich source of protein as well as the mineral calcium.

1 bag (12 ounces) frozen shelled edamame

½ cup water

1 tablespoon soy sauce

1½ teaspoons sesame oil

2 tablespoons minced scallions

⅛ teaspoon ground black pepper

Dash of hot pepper sauce (optional)

1. In a medium saucepan, combine the edamame, water, and soy sauce. Bring to a boil over high heat, stirring occasionally. Reduce the heat to low and simmer for 12 minutes, or until the beans are tender. If any liquid remains, increase the heat to medium-high and continue to cook, stirring occasionally, until the liquid has evaporated.

2. Remove the pan from the heat. Stir in the oil, scallions, black pepper, and hot pepper sauce, if using.

Makes 4 servings

Variation

Edamame are delicious steamed and served at room temperature,
or chilled and topped with a sprinkling of sea salt.

Baked Fennel with Cheese

Hands-On Time: 15 minutes ■ Total Time: 55 minutes

Fennel is easy to grow in the garden and is often a bargain at farm stands during the summer months. Its delicious licorice flavor sweetens as it bakes.

2 medium fennel bulbs, trimmed, peeled, and julienned

3 cloves garlic, thinly sliced

½ teaspoon dried thyme

1 cup chicken broth

2 teaspoons Dijon mustard

½ teaspoon ground nutmeg

1 cup dried bread crumbs

2 tablespoons grated Parmesan cheese

1. Preheat the oven to 400°F.

2. Coat a 1½-quart shallow casserole dish with cooking spray. Spread the fennel and garlic in the dish. Sprinkle with the thyme.

3. In a small bowl, combine the broth, mustard, and nutmeg. Stir well and pour over the fennel. Top the fennel with the bread crumbs and Parmesan.

4. Cover and bake for 20 minutes. Uncover and bake for 20 minutes longer, or until golden brown.

Makes 4 servings

Kitchen Tip

Trim the fennel bulb by peeling away any tough outer layer and cutting off the feathery tips. Save them to add to soup stock or chop them up for salads.

Portobello Caps Stuffed with Chile Polenta and Cheese

Hands-On Time: 10 minutes ■ Total Time: 20 minutes

Even meat lovers will respond to the toothsome texture and rich flavor of this savory mushroom dish, which can be served as a side or a main. You can easily shred your own mozzarella and provolone rather than buying the packaged mix.

1 tube (16 ounces) refrigerated green chile–cilantro polenta, cut into ½"-thick slices

8 large portobello mushroom caps, stems removed

Olive oil

2 teaspoons minced garlic

1½ cups shredded mozzarella and provolone cheese blend

Ground black pepper

Parsley sprigs, for garnish (optional)

1. Coat a broiler-pan rack with cooking spray. Preheat the grill or broiler.

2. Place the polenta in a single layer on a microwaveable plate. Cover with plastic wrap. Microwave on high power for 3 minutes, or until heated through. Set aside.

3. Coat a sheet of heavy-duty foil with cooking spray. Place the mushrooms, gill side down, on the foil. Brush with olive oil to coat. Flip the mushrooms. Spread about ¼ teaspoon of the garlic over each mushroom.

4. Pat the polenta slices into rounds that are as wide as the mushrooms. Place the polenta on the mushrooms. Sprinkle with the cheese. Drizzle each with a little more olive oil.

5. Leaving the mushrooms on the foil, broil the mushrooms for about 8 minutes, or until the cheese is bubbling. Season to taste with the pepper and garnish with parsley, if desired.

Makes 8 servings

Ingredients Note

Some people prefer to remove the gills from portobellos before grilling. To do so, simply scrape the gills out with the tip of a teaspoon, being careful not to penetrate or break the cap.

Minted Sugar Snap Peas

Hands-On Time: 15 minutes ■ Total Time: 15 minutes

Sugar snap peas—which can be eaten uncooked, pod and all—have a short season at the beginning of summer. Look for them at farmers' markets, and taste one first to make sure it's still sweet. If the peas are left in the sun too long, they can turn starchy quickly.

3 cups trimmed sugar snap peas

⅓ cup apple juice

2 teaspoons chopped fresh mint

¼ teaspoon grated lemon zest

1 teaspoon butter

1. In a large nonstick skillet, combine the peas and apple juice. Bring to a boil over medium-high heat. Cover and cook for 2 minutes, or until the peas are crisp-tender. Using a slotted spoon, transfer the peas to a colander, rinse with cold water to stop the cooking, and drain again.

2. Add the mint and lemon zest to the juice remaining in the skillet. Bring to a boil. Cook, stirring, for 1 minute, or until the liquid has been reduced by half.

3. Add the butter and the peas. Toss well.

Makes 4 servings

Kitchen Tip

Be sure to remove the stems and "zip off" the tough strings from
both sides of the peas before cooking.

Braised Italian Peppers with Onions and Thyme

Hands-On Time: 20 minutes ▪ Total Time: 30 minutes

Sweet Italian frying peppers, which are long and thin, come in red and green. At farmers' markets, they are sometimes labeled cubanelle peppers. Anaheim peppers or banana peppers would also be fine for this recipe.

1 tablespoon extra-virgin olive oil	⅛ teaspoon ground black pepper
8 Italian frying peppers, cut into 2" chunks	⅛ teaspoon salt
1 large red onion, cut into wedges	2 plum tomatoes, cut into ½" chunks
1 tablespoon balsamic vinegar	3 tablespoons chicken or vegetable broth
2 teaspoons coarsely chopped fresh thyme or ¼ teaspoon dried	

1. In a large skillet, heat the oil over medium heat. Add the frying peppers and onion and cook, stirring occasionally, for 5 minutes, or until the onion starts to soften.

2. Add the vinegar, thyme, black pepper, and salt. Cook for 1 minute.

3. Add the tomatoes and broth. Reduce the heat to low, cover, and simmer, stirring occasionally, for 8 minutes, or until the vegetables are very soft.

Makes 4 servings

Variation

Serve this pepper-and-onion medley over pasta or with grilled sausages on Italian heroes. It makes a delicious sauce.

Roasted Peppers

One of the best convenience foods out there, roasted bell peppers have plenty of uses. Put them in bruschetta. Layer them into lasagna or sandwiches. Or mix them into a sauce. Here are some grilling and roasting tips and six ideas for ways to use roasted peppers. If you don't feel like grilling or roasting them yourself, buy the best-quality roasted peppers you can find. Peppers with plenty of blackened bits are usually better-tasting than small, limp pieces of perfectly clean peppers with no signs of charring.

How to Broil or Grill Peppers

Some people like to broil or grill bell peppers whole, but a quicker way is to slice each pepper lengthwise into four or five flattish panels. Throw away the stem, ribs, and seeds. Place the pieces on the grill, skin-side down, or on a broiler-pan rack, skin-side up. Cook about 4 inches from the heat for about 6 minutes, or until the skin is totally blackened. (Don't worry, the peppers will be fine.) Place the peppers in a closed paper bag or a covered bowl and let them sit for about 15 minutes to loosen the skin. Then simply peel off the skin with your fingers (using a paper towel helps) or a paring knife.

Fire-Roasting Peppers

Another way to roast just a few peppers is to fire-roast them whole. Cut a slit near the stem of each, then put the pepper on a long-handled cooking fork. Hold it over the flame of a gas stove or grill, turning to char the skin evenly (you may want to wear a mitt). Once charred, follow the procedure above for removing the skin.

6 Uses for Roasted Peppers

1. **Marinated Roasted Bell Peppers.** In a large, shallow dish, combine ⅓ cup olive oil, 1 tablespoon balsamic vinegar, 1 tablespoon red wine vinegar, ½ teaspoon ground black pepper, and ½ teaspoon salt. Toss with 3 cups roasted bell pepper strips (use various colors, if possible). Cover and refrigerate for at least 2 hours or up to 2 days. Makes 8 appetizer servings.

2. Roasted Bell Peppers with Olives. Toss together 2 chopped roasted bell peppers, 2 cups green olives with their brine, 1 tablespoon minced garlic, 1 tablespoon white wine vinegar, and $\frac{1}{8}$ teaspoon ground red pepper. Makes 8 appetizer servings.

3. Roasted Bell Peppers with Anchovies. Toss 3 cups roasted bell pepper strips with 6 julienned oil-packed anchovies, 1 tablespoon of the oil in which the anchovies were packed, 1 teaspoon white wine vinegar, $\frac{1}{2}$ teaspoon minced garlic, and a pinch of red pepper flakes. Makes 8 appetizer servings.

4. Creamy Roasted Bell Pepper Sauce. In a mini food processor, combine 1 cup roasted red or green bell peppers, 2 tablespoons softened cream cheese, 1 teaspoon white wine vinegar, $\frac{1}{2}$ teaspoon sugar, $\frac{1}{4}$ teaspoon salt, and $\frac{1}{8}$ teaspoon ground red pepper. Blend until smooth, scraping down the sides once or twice. Refrigerate for up to 3 days. Makes 1 cup.

5. Cream of Roasted Red Pepper and Tomato Soup. In a food processor or blender, purée 3 cans (10.75 ounces each) ready-to-serve creamy tomato soup (not condensed), $\frac{3}{4}$ cup roasted red bell peppers, and $\frac{1}{2}$ cup chicken broth. Pour into a saucepan and bring to a boil. Add $\frac{1}{4}$ teaspoon dried basil, reduce the heat to medium-low, and simmer for 5 minutes. Makes about 4 servings.

6. Roasted Bell Pepper Pesto Pizza. Preheat the oven to 400°F. Unroll one can (10 ounces) refrigerated pizza dough and cut in half. Coat one large or two smaller baking sheets with cooking spray. On the prepared baking sheets, pat and shape each half into two pizza crusts, each about 10 inches in diameter. Spread each pizza crust with 3 tablespoons prepared pesto. Then top each with $\frac{3}{4}$ cup roasted red bell pepper strips, $\frac{1}{4}$ cup diced drained canned tomatoes, and $\frac{1}{2}$ cup crumbled gorgonzola cheese. Bake for about 10 minutes, or until the cheese melts and the crust bottoms are nicely browned. Makes about 4 servings.

Mashed Sweet Potatoes with Honey

Hands-On Time: 15 minutes ■ Total Time: 40 minutes

It seems a pity to serve sweet potatoes only during the holidays—and it's practically a crime to bury their velvety texture and wonderful natural sweetness under a layer of marshmallows and brown sugar. This notably nutritious vegetable, available year-round in most supermarkets, can be boiled, steamed, baked, roasted, or even grilled. Bring out the sweet potato's savory side with the same toppings you'd use for white potatoes—such as yogurt and chives—or enhance its sweetness with a touch of honey and some apricot nectar, as here.

1 pound sweet potatoes, peeled and cut into 1" chunks

¼ cup apricot nectar

1 tablespoon honey

⅛ teaspoon ground cinnamon

Large pinch of ground black pepper

1. In a medium saucepan, combine the sweet potatoes and enough cold water to cover them. Cover the pan and bring to a boil over high heat. Reduce the heat to medium-low and simmer for 12 to 15 minutes, or until the potatoes are fork-tender.

2. Meanwhile, in a small saucepan, warm the apricot nectar over medium-low heat.

3. Drain the potatoes in a colander and return them to the medium saucepan. Add the apricot nectar, honey, cinnamon, and pepper. Mash until smooth.

Makes 4 servings

Ingredients Note

Although sweet potatoes look quite sturdy, they are highly susceptible to decay. Buy potatoes that are smooth, firm, and free of shriveled or dark areas. Store them in a cool, dry place (about 55°F is best), not in the refrigerator, where their natural sugars will turn to starch, robbing the potatoes of their unique flavor.

Buttermilk Mashed Potatoes

Hands-On Time: 15 minutes ■ Total Time: 30 minutes

Mashed potatoes give meals the comforting taste of home. Traditionally, the potatoes would be finished with butter and cream, but there are other ways to add richness. For this recipe, the potatoes are cooked in broth with garlic cloves, then mashed with buttermilk and sliced scallions. Mash the potatoes smooth, or leave them truly "homestyle"—a bit lumpy.

1 pound baking potatoes, such as russets, peeled and cut into 1" chunks

1 cup water

½ cup chicken broth

2 cloves garlic, unpeeled

¼ cup buttermilk

2 tablespoons thinly sliced scallions

⅛ teaspoon ground white pepper

Large pinch of salt

1. In a medium saucepan, combine the potatoes, water, broth, and garlic. Cover and bring to a boil over high heat. Reduce the heat to medium-low and simmer for 12 to 15 minutes, or until the potatoes are fork-tender.

2. Just before the potatoes are done, place the buttermilk in a small, heavy saucepan and warm over low heat.

3. Drain the potatoes well. Discard the garlic.

4. Return the potatoes to the pan and mash them with a potato masher. Stir in the warmed buttermilk, scallions, pepper, and salt.

Makes 4 servings

Kitchen Tip

Using a traditional potato masher requires a fair amount of pressure.
The more open wire masher is a little easier to use because there's less
resistance, but an electric mixer on low speed is the easiest way to mash potatoes.

Variation

If you like garlicky potatoes, simply peel the garlic after it has been
cooked with the potatoes and mash it right in, rather than discarding it.

Herbed Oven Fries

Hands-On Time: 10 minutes ▪ Total Time: 35 minutes

The next time you're tempted by fast-food french fries, consider baking a batch of these herbed potatoes instead. A medium portion of fast-food fries may be laden with as much as 20 grams of fat. These have a little over 2 grams.

1 pound russet potatoes	1/2 teaspoon dried thyme
1 tablespoon chopped fresh parsley	1/4 teaspoon ground black pepper
1 1/2 teaspoons extra-virgin olive oil	1/8 teaspoon salt

1. Preheat the oven to 450°F. Coat a rimmed baking sheet with cooking spray.

2. Scrub the potatoes and cut them into 1/2"-thick matchsticks. Pile the potato sticks in the center of the prepared baking sheet and sprinkle with the parsley, oil, thyme, pepper, and salt. Toss to coat well, then spread the potatoes out in an even layer.

3. Bake the potatoes, turning them several times, for 20 to 25 minutes, or until they're crisp and browned.

Makes 4 servings

Variation

You can use fresh parsley plus any dried herb or combination of herbs you like on the potatoes. Basil, marjoram, dill, and oregano are all good.

Stuffed Baked Potatoes

Hands-On Time: 15 minutes ■ Total Time: 1 hour 20 minutes

Make extra stuffed potatoes for lunch later in the week. They are convenient and delicious reheated. They keep for about 4 days in the refrigerator.

6 large baking potatoes

1 cup plain yogurt

¼ cup crumbled blue cheese

4 scallions, white and light green parts, finely chopped

⅛ teaspoon paprika

1. Preheat the oven to 425°F.

2. Pierce the potatoes with a fork and place them on the oven rack. Bake for 1 hour, or until they're very soft. Check by inserting the tip of a sharp knife into a potato.

3. Preheat the broiler and broiler-pan rack.

4. Slice off the top third of each potato and reserve for another use (see Kitchen Tip, below). Remove enough of the potato pulp to leave ½" shells.

5. In a medium bowl, combine the potato pulp, yogurt, blue cheese, and scallions. Mash well. Spoon the filling into the potato shells. Sprinkle with the paprika.

6. Broil for 5 minutes, or until the tops are lightly browned.

Makes 6 servings

Ingredients Note

The leftover potato tops can be coated with cooking spray, sprinkled with ground black pepper, and baked at 375°F until crisp for a fast, low-fat snack.

Spinach with Mushrooms

Hands-On Time: 25 minutes ■ Total Time: 25 minutes

We've come a long way since the time when cookbooks directed that spinach and other tender greens be "stewed" for half an hour, turning them into a gray mush with little nutritional value. When spinach is cooked just long enough to wilt, the leaves stay a vibrant green and little of the vitamin C is lost.

2 large shallots or 1 small onion, chopped

¼ cup chicken broth or water

¾ teaspoon olive oil

4 ounces small mushrooms, quartered

1 pound spinach, tough stems removed

⅛ teaspoon ground black pepper

⅛ teaspoon salt

1. In a large nonstick skillet, combine the shallots, 2 tablespoons of the broth, and the oil. Cook over medium-high heat, stirring constantly, for 3 to 4 minutes, or until the shallots are softened.

2. Add the mushrooms and the remaining 2 tablespoons broth. Cook, stirring frequently, for 4 to 6 minutes, or until the mushrooms are softened.

3. Increase the heat to high. Add the spinach by handfuls and stir constantly until the spinach wilts. Cook for 1 minute longer, and season with the salt and pepper.

Makes 4 servings

Corn and Zucchini Cakes

Hands-On Time: 35 minutes ■ Total Time: 35 minutes

This dish is best made at the height of summer, when corn and zucchini are fresh from the garden or farm stand. The recipe can easily be doubled or tripled for more people.

¼ cup all-purpose flour

¼ cup cornmeal

½ teaspoon baking powder

½ teaspoon salt

2 cups fresh or frozen and thawed corn kernels

⅓ cup water

2 teaspoons olive oil

1 small zucchini, cut into ¼" pieces

1 small onion, chopped

2 tablespoons chopped fresh basil

¼ cup milk

2 eggs

1. In a large bowl, combine the flour, cornmeal, baking powder, and salt. Stir to mix. Set aside.

2. In a medium skillet, combine the corn and water. Cook over medium-high heat for 2 to 3 minutes, or until the corn is softened and the water has evaporated. Transfer about 1 cup of the corn to a food processor or blender. Add the remaining corn to the flour mixture.

3. In the same skillet, heat the oil over medium heat. Add the zucchini, onion, and basil. Cook for 3 to 4 minutes, or until the vegetables are softened. Transfer to the flour mixture.

4. Meanwhile, add the milk and eggs to the corn in the food processor or blender. Process to make a coarse purée. Add to the flour mixture. Stir to make a batter.

5. Coat a large skillet with cooking spray and heat over medium heat. Spoon about 2 tablespoons of the batter into the pan to form 3"-wide cakes. Cook for 3 minutes, or until golden brown and crisp on the bottom. Flip the cakes and cook for 3 minutes longer, or until golden brown and heated through. Transfer to a platter and keep warm.

6. Repeat with the remaining batter, carefully removing the skillet from the heat to add more cooking spray as necessary, to make a total of 12 cakes.

Makes 4 servings

Variation

Serve the cakes with Chunky Tomato Sauce. This light tomato sauce is best when made with garden tomatoes. In a medium skillet, warm 1 tablespoon extra-virgin olive oil over medium heat. Add 1 pound peeled, seeded, and diced tomatoes and 1 minced clove garlic. Cook, stirring occasionally, for 5 to 7 minutes, or until heated through. Stir in ¼ cup chopped fresh basil leaves. Season with salt and ground black pepper to taste. Stir to mix. Makes 4 servings.

The Zucchini Are Coming!

If you've ever grown zucchini or lived near someone who does, you've probably been overwhelmed by nature's (or your neighbor's) bounty. Zucchini are one of the easiest vegetables to grow, and they provide one of the most abundant harvests. The trick to handling such largesse with the coolness of a cucumber is to create a simple zucchini base that can be used in a variety of recipes. Use a food processor with the shredding blade to make quick work of the zucchini (large zucchini grate best), or use a hand grater.

All-Purpose Zucchini Base. In a large saucepan, heat 2 tablespoons olive oil over medium heat. Add 1 finely chopped onion and 1 minced garlic clove. Cook, stirring occasionally, until softened, about 5 minutes. Add 5 pounds zucchini, shredded. Cook, stirring occasionally, until the zucchini is softened, 4 to 5 minutes. Cool and drain. Squeeze the cooked zucchini in a clean dish towel or press in a colander to remove most of the moisture. Use to make the recipes below. Refrigerate up to 3 days or freeze indefinitely in zip-top plastic bags. Makes 8 cups.

Zucchini Soup. In a large saucepan, heat 2 tablespoons butter over medium heat. Add 1 finely chopped onion and 1 minced garlic clove. Cook, stirring occasionally, until the onion is softened, 4 to 5 minutes. Add 3½ cups All-Purpose Zucchini Base (see above), 3 cups chicken or vegetable broth, 1 teaspoon curry powder, and ⅛ teaspoon ground red pepper. Simmer for 10 minutes. Add 1 cup light cream and heat through. Makes 4 to 6 servings.

Chilled Zucchini Soup. Follow the recipe for Zucchini Soup (see above), but use 3½ cups chicken broth, 2 teaspoons curry powder, 1 teaspoon ground coriander, and ¼ teaspoon ground red pepper. Replace the light cream with plain yogurt. Chill and garnish with ¼ cup chopped walnuts just before serving. Makes 4 to 6 servings.

Zucchini Pasta Primavera. In a large pot of salted boiling water, cook ¾ pound shaped pasta (such as rotelle) according to package directions until al dente. Meanwhile, in a large saucepan, heat 2 tablespoons olive oil over medium heat. Add 1 halved and thinly sliced onion and 1 minced garlic clove and cook, stirring occasionally, for about 4 minutes, or until the onion is softened. Add 3 cups All-Purpose Zucchini Base (see above), 2 diced medium tomatoes, and 1 tablespoon finely chopped fresh basil. Cook for 2 minutes. Drain the pasta and toss with the sauce. Top with ¼ cup grated Parmesan cheese. Makes 4 modest servings.

Stuffed Zucchini Primavera. Follow the recipe for Zucchini Pasta Primavera (see above), but omit the pasta. Preheat the oven to 350°F. Split 2 large zucchini lengthwise and hollow out the centers. Fill with the sauce and top with the cheese. Place on a baking sheet and bake for about 20 minutes, or until tender and heated through. Makes 4 servings.

Root Vegetable Mash

Hands-On Time: 25 minutes ■ Total Time: 50 minutes

This recipe combines sweet potatoes and celeriac (celery root), a knobby brown vegetable with a white interior that looks nothing like celery. Celeriac tastes like a cross between strong celery and parsley.

3 pounds sweet potatoes, peeled and cut into small chunks

1 pound celeriac, peeled and cut into small chunks

2 cloves garlic

1 small onion, peeled and chopped

⅓ cup milk

1½ tablespoons olive oil

½ teaspoon salt

1. Place a steamer basket in a large saucepan with ½" of water. Place the sweet potatoes, celeriac, and garlic in the steamer. Bring to a boil over high heat. Reduce the heat to medium, cover, and cook for 10 minutes.

2. Add the onion. Cover and cook for 10 minutes longer, or until the onion and celeriac are very soft.

3. Transfer the vegetables to a large bowl and mash with a potato masher. Add the milk, oil, and salt. Mash to blend.

Makes 8 servings

Kitchen Tip

If you're not using celeriac immediately after chopping, place it in a bowl of lemon water to keep it from discoloring.

Nutri-Note

Both sweet potatoes and celeriac provide fiber, vitamin B, and iron. Steaming them retains the nutrients.

Sweet Endings

"Sweets stay long in the stomach."

—JAPANESE PROVERB

Light Chocolate Cake

Hands-On Time: 15 minutes ■ Total Time: 45 minutes (plus cooling)

This rich-tasting snack cake has old-fashioned chocolate flavor, yet it's very light, thanks to the buttermilk. Extra pieces make great lunchbox treats.

1 cup all-purpose flour	¼ cup canola oil
½ cup unsweetened cocoa powder	1 tablespoon vanilla extract
1 teaspoon ground cinnamon	1 egg
½ teaspoon ground nutmeg	½ cup buttermilk
½ teaspoon baking powder	2 egg whites
½ teaspoon baking soda	Confectioners' sugar
1 cup packed brown sugar	

1. Preheat the oven to 350°F. Lightly coat an 8" × 8" baking dish with cooking spray.

2. In a medium bowl, whisk together the flour, cocoa, cinnamon, nutmeg, baking powder, and baking soda.

3. In a large bowl, whisk together the brown sugar, oil, vanilla extract, and egg. Alternately beat in a little of the flour mixture and a little of the buttermilk, beginning and ending with the flour mixture.

4. In the bowl of an electric mixer, beat the egg whites at high speed until soft peaks form. Fold the egg whites into the batter. Pour the batter into the prepared baking dish.

5. Bake for 25 to 30 minutes, or until a wooden pick inserted in the center comes out clean. Cool the cake in the pan on a wire rack. Dust with confectioners' sugar before slicing.

Makes 12 servings

Carrot Cake with Cream Cheese Icing

Hands-On Time: 20 minutes ■ Total Time: 1 hour 5 minutes (plus cooling)

Each bite of this traditional homey carrot cake is rich, moist, and spicy.

2¾ cups all-purpose flour

2 teaspoons baking powder

2 teaspoons baking soda

2 teaspoons ground cinnamon

1 teaspoon ground nutmeg

¾ teaspoon ground allspice

¼ teaspoon salt

4 eggs

1 cup packed brown sugar

1 cup sour cream

½ cup unsalted butter, softened

2 cups grated carrots

1 cup drained canned crushed pineapple

⅔ cup currants or raisins

8 ounces cream cheese, softened

1 box (16 ounces) confectioners' sugar

2 teaspoons vanilla extract

1. Preheat the oven to 325°F. Coat a 13" × 9" baking dish with cooking spray.

2. In a medium bowl, whisk together the flour, baking powder, baking soda, cinnamon, nutmeg, allspice, and salt.

3. In the bowl of an electric mixer, beat the eggs on medium speed until foamy. Add the brown sugar. Beat for 3 minutes. Add the sour cream and butter. Beat until creamy. With the mixer on low speed, beat in the flour mixture. Gently stir in the carrots, pineapple, and currants. Spread in the baking dish.

4. Bake for 40 to 45 minutes, or until a wooden pick inserted in the center comes out clean. Cool in the pan on a wire rack.

5. In a large bowl, beat the cream cheese, confectioners' sugar, and vanilla extract until smooth. Spread the icing over the cooled cake.

Makes 16 servings

Variation

Add ¾ to 1 cup chopped pecans, if desired.

Southern Sour Cream–Coconut Layer Cake

Hands-On Time: 25 minutes ■ **Total Time: 1 hour 10 minutes (plus cooling)**

Majestic is the word that best describes this dreamy, old-fashioned layer cake. Offer it for a special occasion or serve it simply to make the occasion special.

1 box (18 ounces) white cake mix	1⅓ cups sour cream
¾ cup milk	⅓ cup plus 3¾ cups confectioners' sugar
3 egg whites	¾ cup solid vegetable shortening
1½ tablespoons coconut extract	1 cup flaked sweetened coconut

1. Preheat the oven to 350°F. Coat two 9" round cake pans with cooking spray. Dust with flour, shaking out any excess.

2. In the bowl of an electric mixer, combine the cake mix, milk, egg whites, coconut extract, 1 cup of the sour cream, and ⅓ cup of the sugar. Blend for about 30 seconds on low speed, or until the dry ingredients are moistened. Beat at high speed for 3 minutes, or until the batter is smooth and fluffy.

3. Pour the batter into the prepared pans. Bake for 30 to 35 minutes, or until the cake springs back when lightly touched and a wooden pick inserted in the center comes out clean. Cool in the pans on a wire rack for 10 minutes. To remove the cake from the pans, run a thin knife around the outside edges. Turn the layers onto a wire rack to cool completely.

4. Meanwhile, in the bowl of an electric mixer, combine the shortening, the remaining 3¾ cups sugar, and the remaining ⅓ cup sour cream. Blend on low speed for about 1 minute, or until the sugar is moistened. Beat at high speed for 3 minutes, or until smooth and fluffy.

5. Place one cake layer on a serving plate. Frost the top. Sprinkle with ¼ cup of the coconut. Top with the second layer. Frost the sides and top. Using the palm of one hand, press about 1 tablespoon of coconut at a time onto the side of the cake. Continue while rotating the cake until the sides are coated. Sprinkle the remaining coconut over the top.

Makes 8 to 10 servings

Heavenly Orange Cake

Hands-On Time: 30 minutes ■ Total Time: 2 hours 20 minutes

You'll need a 9" or 10" tube pan for this really heavenly cake. If you like, you can flavor the cake with another extract—such as almond, cherry, maple, peppermint, or black walnut—and serve it with other fruit, such as raspberries, blueberries, peaches, or strawberries.

Orange Cream

1 cup cottage cheese	⅓ cup orange juice concentrate
1 cup vanilla yogurt	

Cake

¾ cup sifted all-purpose flour	1½ teaspoons orange extract
¼ cup sifted whole wheat pastry flour	½ cup honey
12 egg whites, at room temperature	2 cups orange sections
1 teaspoon cream of tartar	1 cup sweet cherries, pitted

1. *To make the orange cream:* In a food processor, purée the cottage cheese for about 4 minutes, or until completely smooth. Stop frequently to scrape down the sides of the container. Transfer the cottage cheese to a small bowl. Lightly whisk in the yogurt and orange juice concentrate. Chill until ready to use.

2. *To make the cake:* Preheat the oven to 325°F.

3. Sift the all-purpose flour and pastry flour together into a large bowl.

4. In the bowl of an electric mixer, beat the egg whites on medium speed until bubbly. Add the cream of tartar and orange extract. Beat on high speed until soft peaks form. Gradually beat in the honey until the whites are stiff.

5. Sift about ¼ cup of the flour over the whites. Carefully fold it in with a large spatula. Repeat until all the flour has been incorporated.

6. Spoon the batter into an uncoated 9" or 10" tube pan with a removable bottom. Level the top with a spatula.

7. Bake for 40 to 50 minutes, or until the top is golden and springs back when lightly touched. Invert the pan onto a wire rack and let the cake cool for 1 hour.

8. To remove the cake from the pan, run a thin knife around the outside edges. Remove the outer portion of the pan. Run a thin knife around the center tube and also around the bottom of the cake. Slice the cake and serve with the orange cream, oranges, and cherries.

Makes 10 servings

Peach Upside-Down Cake

Hands-On Time: 20 minutes ■ Total Time: 1 hour

Fresh peaches are a refreshing change from canned pineapple in this tempting cake. Half the butter in the cake is used where it has the greatest flavor impact: It is melted with sugar to form a caramel-like glaze on the peaches.

2½ pounds large, ripe freestone peaches (5 or 6 peaches)

⅔ cup sugar

4 tablespoons unsalted butter

1 cup all-purpose flour

1 teaspoon baking powder

½ teaspoon baking soda

½ teaspoon ground cinnamon

¼ teaspoon salt

1 large egg

1 teaspoon vanilla extract

1 teaspoon almond extract

½ cup low-fat buttermilk

1. Preheat the oven to 375°F. Bring a large saucepan of water to a boil.

2. Score the stem end of each peach and place the peaches in the boiling water. Boil for about 1 minute, or until the skins soften. Transfer to a bowl of cold water to cool. When they're cool enough to handle, peel, halve, and pit the peaches.

3. In a 9" cast-iron skillet, combine ⅓ cup of the sugar with 2 tablespoons of the butter. Cook over medium heat for 3 to 5 minutes, or until the sugar begins to melt. Add the peaches to the skillet, cut side up, in one layer. (The fruit should fit tightly.) Remove the pan from the heat and set aside.

4. In a medium bowl, combine the flour, baking powder, baking soda, cinnamon, and salt. Set aside.

5. In the large bowl of an electric mixer, beat the remaining ⅓ cup sugar and 2 tablespoons butter at medium speed until combined. Add the egg, beating until smooth. Then beat in the vanilla extract and almond extract. With the mixer on low speed, add the buttermilk and the flour mixture, beating until just incorporated.

6. Spoon the batter evenly over the peaches in the skillet. Bake, uncovered, for 20 to 25 minutes, or until a wooden pick inserted in the center of the cake comes out clean.

7. Transfer the skillet to a wire rack to cool for 3 to 4 minutes. Loosen the edges of the cake with a knife. Invert the skillet over a serving plate. If any of the peaches stick to the skillet, remove them with a knife and replace them on the cake.

Makes 8 servings

Tiramisu Cheesecake

Hands-On Time: 10 minutes ■ Total Time: 10 minutes

The cream, coffee, and chocolate flavors of traditional tiramisu really pop in this oh-so-easy cake. If you can plan ahead, allow the cheesecake to thaw slowly in the refrigerator to produce a creamier texture.

1   New York–style frozen cheesecake (1 pound 14 ounces), thawed

1   container (8 ounces) coffee-flavored mascarpone cheese

¼   cup (2 ounces) semisweet mini chocolate morsels

1   tablespoon unsweetended cocoa powder

1   tablespoon confectioners' sugar

1. Remove the paper collar from the cheesecake. Place the cake on a serving dish.

2. In a medium bowl, stir the mascarpone until smooth. Add 2 tablespoons of the chocolate morsels. Spread the mixture over the cheesecake. Sprinkle the remaining 2 tablespoons morsels over the top.

3. Cut the cake into wedges and place on plates.

4. Combine the cocoa and sugar in a small fine sieve, and sprinkle it over the cake and the surrounding plate.

Makes 6 servings

Chocolate-Orange Swirl Cheesecake

Hands-On Time: 10 minutes ■ Total Time: 40 minutes (plus chilling)

Cheesecake is always a family favorite. The marbleized effect makes each serving particularly pretty.

1½ cups chocolate cookie crumbs

8 ounces cream cheese, softened

1 cup ricotta cheese

2 eggs

3 tablespoons cornstarch

1 tablespoon grated orange zest

¾ cup plus 2 tablespoons sugar

¼ cup unsweetened cocoa powder

1. Preheat the oven to 400°F. Coat a 9" pie plate with cooking spray.

2. Press the cookie crumbs evenly over the bottom and up the sides of the pie plate.

3. In a large bowl, beat together the cream cheese and ricotta until smooth. Stir in the eggs, cornstarch, orange zest, and ¾ cup of the sugar.

4. Pour half of the mixture into another bowl and set aside. Stir the cocoa and the remaining 2 tablespoons sugar into the first bowl. Pour the cocoa mixture into the pie plate.

5. Spoon the reserved cheese mixture over the top and swirl with a knife to achieve a marbleized effect. Bake for 30 minutes, or until a knife inserted in the center comes out clean. Chill for at least 8 hours or overnight.

Makes 12 servings

Variation

You may substitute graham cracker crumbs for the chocolate cookie crumbs.

Easy Pumpkin Pie

Hands-On Time: 5 minutes ■ Total Time: 50 minutes (plus cooling)

The superquick prep on this pumpkin pie makes it an easy option any night of the week. Offer whipped topping on the side.

1 cup canned pumpkin purée	$\frac{1}{2}$ teaspoon ground ginger
3 eggs	$\frac{1}{8}$ teaspoon ground nutmeg
1 cup evaporated milk	$\frac{1}{8}$ teaspoon ground allspice
$\frac{3}{4}$ cup packed brown sugar	1 prepared unbaked piecrust
$\frac{1}{2}$ teaspoon ground cinnamon	

1. Preheat the oven to 375°F.

2. In a large bowl, whisk together the pumpkin, eggs, milk, sugar, cinnamon, ginger, nutmeg, and allspice. Pour into the unbaked crust.

3. Bake for 40 to 45 minutes, or until the center of the filling is set. Cool before serving.

Makes 8 servings

Variation

You can turn Easy Pumpkin Pie into Praline Pumpkin Pie. Before baking the pie crust, add a layer of praline. To make the praline, cut 2 teaspoons butter into $\frac{1}{4}$ cup packed brown sugar. Stir in 1 tablespoon maple syrup and $\frac{1}{3}$ cup chopped toasted pecans. Press the praline mixture evenly into the bottom of the unbaked pie crust. Bake at 425°F for 10 minutes. Remove from the oven, allow to cool, then fill with the pumpkin mixture. Bake as directed. Makes 8 servings.

How to Make a Tender, Flaky Piecrust

The key to tenderness and flakiness is keeping everything cold, particularly the butter, shortening, or other fats. Cold fat makes steam in the oven, which puffs the layers apart and makes a flaky pastry.

- Chill all your equipment in the refrigerator for 30 minutes before using: mixing bowl or food processor bowl and blade, pastry cutter, rolling pin, and pastry board. Avoid working in a hot room or near a hot oven.

- Use cold butter and minimize handling. Use a sharp knife to quickly cut a stick of butter into ¼" cubes. After chopping the butter, chill it for 20 minutes before cutting it into the flour.

- Mix the dough quickly in a food processor instead of by hand. You're less likely to overwork the dough, warm it, or add water, all of which can make a tough, chewy crust.

- If you don't have a food processor, use a pastry cutter. This inexpensive kitchen tool works much more efficiently than the last-resort option of using the tines of a fork or 2 table knives. If you prefer to use your fingertips, you'll need to keep them cold and work quickly.

- While cutting the butter into the flour, constantly keep the butter covered with flour to help avoid mashing the butter. The goal is a coarse mixture in which the flour-coated butter pieces are about the size of small peas. Avoid cutting in the butter too finely.

- As you add water or other liquid to gather the dough into a ball, work quickly and with a gentle hand. Handle the dough as little as possible—just enough for it to come together. Little gobs of butter in the formed dough are a good sign.

- Overhandling dough develops excess gluten, a network of protein strands that makes pie dough tough. To help prevent gluten development, add a bit of lemon juice as you gather the dough into a ball.

- Press the ball of pastry into a flattened disk and chill for 20 minutes. Then let it soften until it can be gently squeezed (10 minutes or so at room temperature) before rolling it out.

- Avoid overworking the dough when rolling it out. Flour the work surface just enough to prevent sticking.

- Roll the dough from the center outward rather than back and forth. Turn the dough (or pastry board) clockwise a little each time you roll. Ease up slightly on the rolling pin as you near the edge of the dough to prevent flattening the edges.

- If the dough feels difficult to roll out, let it rest in the refrigerator for 20 minutes.

- After placing the pastry in the pie pan, chill it for 20 minutes before filling and baking.

Four-Berry Pie

Hands-On Time: 35 minutes ■ Total Time: 1 hour 45 minutes

Here's ample incentive for a trip to a "pick-your-own" berry farm. If the berries are tart, add another ¼ cup sugar.

Crust

2 cups all-purpose flour

2 teaspoons sugar

½ teaspoon salt

8 tablespoons chilled unsalted butter, cut into small pieces

6 tablespoons sour cream

1 tablespoon cold water plus 1 additional teaspoon, if necessary

¼ teaspoon almond extract

Filling

2 cups halved fresh strawberries

2 cups fresh raspberries

1 cup fresh blackberries

1 cup fresh blueberries

3 tablespoons fresh lemon juice

¾ cup sugar

3 tablespoons cornstarch

3 tablespoons instant tapioca

1. *To make the crust:* In a food processor, combine the flour, sugar, and salt. Pulse briefly to mix. Add the butter and pulse until the mixture resembles coarse meal. Add the sour cream, 1 tablespoon of the cold water, and the almond extract, and process until the mixture just comes together. (If the dough seems too dry, add a few more drops of cold water.) Gather the dough and shape it into two disks. Wrap each disk in plastic wrap and refrigerate for at least 15 minutes, or until ready to use.

2. *To make the filling:* Meanwhile, in a large bowl, combine all the berries and the lemon juice. In a small bowl, combine the sugar, cornstarch, and tapioca. Stir into the fruit. Let stand for 15 minutes.

3. Move the oven rack to the bottom setting. Preheat the oven to 400°F. Line a baking sheet with foil.

4. On a floured surface, roll out the dough into two 10" rounds. Keeping one round covered with a towel, fit the other round into a 9" pie plate, leaving the overhang. Spoon the filling into the shell.

5. Cut the remaining round into ¾"-wide strips. Place half the strips over the filling, spacing them evenly. Place the remaining strips at a 45-degree angle to the first strips, to form a lattice pattern. Trim the ends of the lattice strips and the bottom crust to a ½" overhang, fold the bottom crust over the lattice ends, and crimp or pinch the edges to seal.

6. Place the pie on the baking sheet and bake for 45 to 50 minutes, or until the crust is golden brown and the juices begin to bubble. Transfer the pie to a wire rack to cool for 15 minutes before serving.

Makes 8 servings

Shoofly Pie

Hands-On Time: 10 minutes ■ Total Time: 1 hour 5 minutes (plus cooling)

A favorite in Pennsylvania's Amish Country, shoofly pie is said to have gotten its name because the sweet ingredients attract flies when the pie is cooling—and the cook has to shoo the flies away.

Crumb Topping

1½ cups all-purpose flour

2 tablespoons butter

½ cup packed brown sugar

1 teaspoon ground cinnamon

Filling

1 cup boiling water

1 teaspoon baking soda

1 cup unsulfured molasses

¼ teaspoon ground ginger

1 prepared unbaked piecrust

1. *To make the crumb topping:* In a medium bowl, combine the flour and butter. Use a pastry blender or two knives to cut in the butter until the mixture resembles coarse crumbs. Stir in the sugar and cinnamon until well-blended. Set aside.

2. Preheat the oven to 450°F.

3. *To make the filling:* In another medium bowl, whisk the water and baking soda until the baking soda dissolves. Stir in the molasses and ginger. Mix well. Allow the mixture to cool slightly, then pour it into the unbaked pie crust. Sprinkle the top evenly with the crumb mixture.

4. Bake for 10 minutes. Reduce the heat to 350°F and bake for 30 to 40 minutes longer, or until the center of the filling is set and the crumbs are golden brown. Place the pie on a wire rack to cool completely before serving.

Makes 8 servings

Ingredients Note

If you can find it, use Barbados molasses, also known as unsulfured or West Indies molasses, in this recipe. It is made from the first press of sugarcane, amber in color, and more delicate in flavor than blackstrap molasses.

Accompaniment

For a tasty topping, spoon a dollop of vanilla frozen yogurt over each slice of pie.

Apple-Oatmeal Crumble

Hands-On Time: 20 minutes ■ Total Time: 50 minutes

Firm, tasty apples that hold their shape when heated—and don't turn to applesauce—are best for baking. The versatile Granny Smith and Golden Delicious (both popular for eating raw, as well) are excellent in baked desserts. You can use just about any type of apple in this crumble, but be prepared to adjust the seasonings according to the flavor of the apples. Very tart varieties, such as Rhode Island Greenings, may call for a bit more sugar, while bland McIntoshes could probably use a touch more lemon juice and spice—or even a few drops of vanilla extract.

½ cup old-fashioned rolled oats

¼ cup packed dark brown sugar

½ cup all-purpose flour

Pinch of salt

1 teaspoon ground cinnamon

4 tablespoons cold unsalted butter, cut into small pieces

3 large Granny Smith apples, cored and quartered

¼ cup frozen apple juice concentrate, thawed

3 tablespoons dried currants

1 tablespoon honey

1 teaspoon fresh lemon juice

1. Preheat the oven to 450°F.

2. In a medium bowl, stir together the oats, sugar, flour, salt, and ½ teaspoon of the cinnamon. Using your fingers or a pastry blender, lightly mix in the butter until coarse crumbs form. Set aside.

3. In a food processor fitted with the slicing blade (or by hand), thinly slice the apples.

4. Place the apples in another medium bowl. Add the apple juice concentrate, currants, honey, lemon juice, and the remaining ½ teaspoon cinnamon. Toss until well mixed. Transfer to a 9" deep-dish pie plate. Top with the crumb mixture.

5. Bake for 10 minutes, or until the topping begins to brown in patches. Reduce the oven temperature to 400°F, cover loosely with foil, and bake for 15 to 20 minutes longer, or until the apples are tender and the filling is bubbly. Place the pie plate on a wire rack to cool slightly. Serve the crumble warm.

Makes 6 servings

Mix-and-Match Fruit Desserts

Crumble, crunch, cobbler, crisp, brown Betty, grunt—these are the names of some of America's simplest and best-loved desserts. All are essentially sweetened baked fruit with a crumbly or biscuitlike topping. Here are four easy steps to creating 36 possible flavor combinations. Just pick a fruit filling, match it with any of the toppings, and bake as directed. Each recipe makes 4 to 6 servings.

1. Pick a fruit or fruit combo.

   Apple-Pear. 3 cups each peeled, cored, and sliced Granny Smith apples and Bosc pears (1 pound whole apples and 1½ pounds whole pears)

   Apricot-Raspberry. 4 cups thickly sliced pitted apricots (about 1½ pounds whole apricots) and 1 pint fresh raspberries

   Mango-Raspberry. 4 cups pitted, peeled, and cubed mangoes (about 3 medium mangoes) and 1 pint fresh raspberries

   Mixed Berry. 1 pint each fresh raspberries, blueberries, and blackberries

   Plum. 6 cups thickly sliced pitted fresh plums (about 2½ pounds whole plums)

   Strawberry-Rhubarb. 1 pint hulled and quartered fresh strawberries and 4 cups ½"-long rhubarb pieces (about 1¼ pounds)

2. Toss the fruit with ½ cup sugar, 1 tablespoon fresh lemon juice, and 2 tablespoons flour. Spread in a greased 2-quart baking dish.

3. Choose a topping (see below and opposite).

4. Bake at 400°F for 30 to 40 minutes, or until the top is golden brown and bubbly. Serve warm with ice cream or heavy cream.

CRUMBLE

1¼ cups all-purpose flour

½ cup rolled oats

⅓ cup packed brown sugar

¾ teaspoon ground cinnamon

¼ teaspoon salt

6 tablespoons cold, unsalted butter, cut into small pieces

In a food processor, combine the flour, oats, sugar, cinnamon, and salt. Add the butter and pulse just until the mixture is the texture of coarse crumbs. Sprinkle the topping over the fruit in the baking dish.

CRISP

¾ cup brown sugar

½ cup all-purpose flour

½ cup rolled oats

1½ teaspoons ground cinnamon

½ teaspoon salt

1 stick (½ cup) cold unsalted butter, cut into pieces

In a food processor, combine the sugar, flour, oats, cinnamon, and salt. Add the butter and pulse until the mixture resembles coarse crumbs. Sprinkle the topping over the fruit in the baking dish.

COBBLER

1 cup all-purpose flour

1 teaspoon baking powder

½ teaspoon baking soda

¼ teaspoon salt

4 tablespoons sugar

½ stick (¼ cup) cold unsalted butter, cut into small pieces

⅔ cup buttermilk

In a food processor, combine the flour, baking powder, baking soda, salt, and 3 tablespoons of the sugar. Add the butter and pulse just until the mixture resembles coarse crumbs. Add the buttermilk and pulse just until the mixture comes together. Spoon the dough over the fruit in the baking dish and sprinkle the top with the remaining 1 tablespoon sugar.

CRUNCH

1 stick (½ cup) unsalted butter, cut into pieces

1 cup brown sugar

¾ cup flour

⅓ cup chopped pecans or walnuts

½ teaspoon ground cinnamon

¼ teaspoon freshly grated nutmeg

¼ teaspoon salt

Melt the butter in a large saucepan over low heat or in a microwaveable bowl on medium power for 2 minutes. Stir in the sugar, flour, pecans, cinnamon, nutmeg, and salt. Sprinkle the topping over the fruit in the baking dish.

BROWN BETTY

3 tablespoons unsalted butter

¾ cup graham cracker crumbs

¾ cup brown sugar

½ teaspoon ground cinnamon

½ teaspoon ground nutmeg

¼ teaspoon salt

Melt the butter in a large saucepan over low heat or in a microwaveable bowl on medium power for 2 minutes. Stir in the graham cracker crumbs, sugar, cinnamon, nutmeg, and salt. Sprinkle the topping over the fruit in the baking dish.

GRUNT

5 tablespoons unsalted butter, cut into pieces

2 cups flour

3 tablespoons sugar

2 teaspoons baking powder

¾ teaspoon salt

¾ cup milk

Melt the butter in a large saucepan over low heat or in a microwaveable bowl on medium power for 2 minutes. In another bowl, combine the flour, sugar, baking powder, and salt. Stir in the melted butter and the milk until all the ingredients are moistened. Spoon the batter over the fruit in the baking dish.

Honey-Baked Pears

Hands-On Time: 10 minutes ■ Total Time: 40 minutes (plus cooling)

Baked pears are a deliciously light alternative to pie at holiday dinners. Here the pears poach as they bake in apple-cinnamon herbal tea, a flavorful alternative to water. You can use any fruit-flavored herbal tea you prefer.

2 bags apple-cinnamon tea or other herbal tea

1¼ cups boiling water

4 small firm-ripe pears

3 tablespoons golden or dark raisins

2 tablespoons honey

1½ teaspoons fresh lemon juice

1½ teaspoons vanilla extract

1. Preheat the oven to 425°F.

2. Place the tea bags in a small heatproof bowl and add the boiling water. Cover and steep for 5 minutes.

3. Meanwhile, peel and core the pears. Cut them into ¼"-thick wedges. Arrange the pears in an 11" × 7" baking dish and sprinkle with the raisins.

4. Remove the tea bags and stir the honey, lemon juice, and vanilla extract into the tea. Pour the tea mixture over the pears and cover the dish with foil. Bake for 20 to 25 minutes, or until the pears are tender.

5. Remove the baking dish from the oven, uncover, and let the pears cool until just warm. Serve the pears with the raisins and juices.

Makes 4 servings

Ingredients Note

Pears are usually picked slightly underripe, so they often need some time to ripen after you buy them. Choose unblemished pears, and leave them at room temperature for a few days. When ripe, the pears will be fragrant and will give to gentle pressure at the stem end. Some varieties, such as Bartletts and Clapps, develop a rosy "blush" as they ripen.

Variations

Try flavoring the pears with dark rum rather than vanilla extract.
Substitute chopped dried figs for the raisins.

Crispy Mocha-Almond Cookies

Hands-On Time: 20 minutes ■ Total Time: 45 minutes

Mild chocolate and light almond flavor come together nicely in this crunchy cookie, which has a texture similar to biscotti. They're great for dunking into coffee or espresso.

1¼ cups all-purpose flour

½ cup sugar

½ teaspoon baking powder

¼ teaspoon baking soda

¼ teaspoon salt

1 egg

1 egg white

1 teaspoon vanilla extract

½ teaspoon almond extract

1 tablespoon instant coffee powder

1 tablespoon warm water

1 square (1 ounce) unsweetened chocolate, melted

⅓ cup slivered almonds, toasted

1. Preheat the oven to 350°F. Coat an 11" × 7" baking dish with cooking spray.

2. In a large bowl, whisk together the flour, sugar, baking powder, baking soda, and salt.

3. In a medium bowl, whisk together the egg, egg white, vanilla extract, and almond extract.

4. In a cup, dissolve the coffee in the water. Stir into the egg mixture. Stir in the chocolate. Pour the chocolate mixture over the flour mixture and stir well. Stir in the almonds.

5. Press the dough into the prepared baking dish. Bake for 25 minutes, or until firm. Transfer to a wire rack and cut into 30 fingers. Cool before serving.

Makes 30 cookies

Apricot Squares

Hands-On Time: 15 minutes ■ Total Time: 55 minutes (plus cooling)

Apricot preserves spread over a buttery, rich crust balance the sweet topping of these tender bars. Not quite a cookie, not quite a cake—enjoy them whenever you yearn for a treat.

½ teaspoon baking powder

½ teaspoon salt

2½ cups all-purpose flour

¾ cup butter

1½ cups packed brown sugar

1 jar (12 ounces) apricot preserves

2 eggs

1 teaspoon vanilla extract

1 tablespoon confectioners' sugar

1. Preheat the oven to 325°F. Coat a 13" × 9" baking pan with cooking spray.

2. In a small bowl, combine, the baking powder, salt, and ½ cup of the flour. Set aside.

3. In the bowl of an electric mixer, beat the butter and ½ cup of the brown sugar on medium speed until light and creamy. Gradually add the remaining 2 cups flour, beating on low speed, just until the mixture resembles coarse crumbs. Press into the prepared pan. Top with the preserves.

4. Clean the bowl of the mixer, then add the eggs and the remaining 1 cup brown sugar. Beat on high speed until thick. Beat in the vanilla extract. With the mixer on low speed, gradually add the flour mixture, beating just until combined. Spread over the preserves.

5. Bake for 40 minutes, or until lightly browned. Place the pan on a rack to cool completely. Dust with the confectioners' sugar before cutting into 24 squares.

Makes 24 squares

Variations

You could make these cookies with any type of
fruit preserves, such as lemon or orange marmalade.

Cranberry Macaroons

Hands-On Time: 20 minutes ■ Total Time: 40 minutes (plus cooling)

Traditional macaroons feature almonds or coconut. These scrumptious goodies have both, plus cranberries and chocolate-covered raisins, for added visual and flavor appeal.

1 package (14 ounces) shredded coconut

1 can (14 ounces) sweetened condensed milk

1 cup dried cranberries

¾ cup all-purpose flour

¾ cup blanched slivered almonds, toasted

¾ cup chocolate-covered raisins

1 teaspoon almond extract

1. Preheat the oven to 350°F. Coat 2 large baking sheets with cooking spray.

2. In a large bowl, combine the coconut, milk, cranberries, flour, almonds, raisins, and almond extract. Stir well. Drop by tablespoonfuls, about 1" apart, onto the prepared baking sheets.

3. Bake for 14 minutes, or until the macaroons are lightly golden. Cool on the baking sheets for 2 minutes, then transfer them to a rack to cool completely.

Makes 40 macaroons

Chocolate Chunk Cookies

Hands-On Time: 25 minutes ■ Total Time: 40 minutes (plus cooling)

Be sure to scoop up and mix in all the crumbs that accumulate from chopping the chocolate. These tiny bits increase the chocolate density of the cookies.

1½ cups all-purpose flour

½ teaspoon baking soda

¼ teaspoon salt

6 ounces bittersweet chocolate

4 tablespoons butter, at room temperature

⅓ cup packed brown sugar

⅓ cup granulated sugar

1 egg

2 teaspoons vanilla extract

1. Preheat the oven to 375°F.

2. In a medium bowl, combine the flour, baking soda, and salt.

3. Coarsely chop the chocolate, reserving all the chunks and chocolate crumbs.

4. In the bowl of an electric mixer, beat the butter, brown sugar, and granulated sugar on medium speed for 3 minutes, or until light and fluffy. Beat in the egg and vanilla extract. Beat in the flour mixture, a little at a time, until well-blended. Stir in the chopped chocolate.

5. Drop by tablespoonfuls about 2" apart onto 2 large ungreased baking sheets. Bake for 10 minutes, or until the cookies are golden brown. Cool the cookies on the baking sheets for 2 minutes, then transfer to a rack to cool completely.

Makes 36 cookies

Double Chocolate–Peanut Cookies

Hands-On Time: 35 minutes ■ Total Time: 1 hour (plus cooling)

These yummy chocolate treats are studded with peanut butter chips and white chocolate chips. If white chocolate isn't your passion, milk chocolate would be just as delicious.

2¼ cups all-purpose flour	2 eggs
⅔ cup unsweetened cocoa powder	1 teaspoon vanilla extract
1 teaspoon baking soda	1 teaspoon warm water
1¼ cups butter, at room temperature	1 cup white chocolate chips
⅔ cup packed brown sugar	1 cup peanut butter chips
⅔ cup granulated sugar	

1. Preheat the oven to 350°F.

2. In a medium bowl, combine the flour, cocoa, and baking soda.

3. In the bowl of an electric mixer, beat the butter, brown sugar, and granulated sugar at medium speed for 3 minutes, or until light and fluffy. Beat in the eggs, vanilla extract, and water. Beat in the flour mixture, a little at a time, until well-blended. Stir in the chocolate chips and peanut butter chips.

4. Drop by tablespoonfuls about 2" apart onto 2 large uncoated baking sheets. Bake for 10 minutes, or until the cookies are golden brown. Cool the cookies on the baking sheets for 2 minutes, then transfer them to a rack to cool completely. Repeat with the remaining dough.

Makes 60 cookies

Blondies

Hands-On Time: 15 minutes ▪ Total Time: 35 minutes (plus cooling)

Blondies are un-chocolate brownies—in fact, they were originally called blond brownies.
They're rich, chewy bar cookies made with brown sugar, giving them a butterscotch flavor.

1 cup packed dark brown sugar	1¾ cups all-purpose flour
4 tablespoons butter, melted	2 teaspoons baking powder
2 large eggs	½ teaspoon salt
1½ teaspoons vanilla extract	½ cup chopped walnuts

1. Preheat the oven to 350°F. Coat a 13" × 9" baking pan with cooking spray.

2. In the bowl of an electric mixer, beat the sugar, butter, eggs, and vanilla extract at medium speed until well combined.

3. With the mixer on low speed, beat in the flour, baking powder, and salt. Stir in the walnuts.

4. Spread the mixture evenly in the prepared pan. Bake for 15 to 20 minutes, or until a wooden pick inserted in the center comes out clean. Remove the pan to a wire rack to cool completely. Cut into 24 bars.

Makes 24 blondies

Kitchen Tip

Brown sugar stored in the box often turns lumpy and hard. To avoid this,
transfer the sugar to a jar or zip-top bag and add a slice of fresh bread.
Wait 24 hours before using the sugar. When the bread gets hard, replace it.

Variations

Leave out the walnuts and add ½ cup sweetened flaked coconut to the batter. If you do this,
you can also substitute ½ teaspoon almond extract for the ½ teaspoon vanilla extract. Or
try ½ cup semisweet, milk chocolate, or butterscotch chips instead of the walnuts.

Marbled Brownies

A cream cheese mixture is swirled through these brownies, creating a rich flavor and a sophisticated marbled appearance.

5 squares (1 ounce each) unsweetened chocolate

6 tablespoons butter

1¾ cups sugar

3 eggs plus 1 egg yolk

1 tablespoon vanilla extract

1 cup plus 1 tablespoon all-purpose flour

8 ounces cream cheese, at room temperature

1. Preheat the oven to 375°F. Coat an 8" × 8" baking pan with cooking spray.

2. In a medium, heavy saucepan, melt the chocolate and butter over low heat.

3. Stir in 1½ cups of the sugar until well-blended. Add the 3 eggs, one at a time, stirring after each addition, until well-blended. Stir in the vanilla extract and 1 cup of the flour.

4. Spread the mixture into the prepared pan.

5. In the bowl of an electric mixer, beat the cream cheese, egg yolk, the remaining ¼ cup sugar, and the remaining 1 tablespoon flour on low speed for about 3 minutes, or until creamy. Pour the cream cheese mixture over the chocolate mixture and, using a knife, swirl to marble.

6. Bake for 40 minutes, or until a wooden pick inserted in the center comes out clean. Remove the pan to a wire rack to cool completely. Cut into 16 squares.

Makes 16 brownies

Spicy Molasses Cookies

Hands-On Time: 15 minutes ■ Total Time: 35 minutes (plus cooling)

You'll hear the "clink" of the cookie-jar lid often when these richly spiced, chewy cookies are around. When trying this recipe for the first time, check the oven after about 8 minutes to see whether the cookies are done. Baked goods with molasses have a tendency to overbrown, and the baking time may be shorter than what's suggested.

2 cups all-purpose flour	½ teaspoon ground black pepper
2 teaspoons ground cinnamon	½ cup unsalted butter
2 teaspoons ground ginger	1 cup sugar
1 teaspoon baking soda	¼ cup molasses
½ teaspoon ground cloves	2 large egg whites
½ teaspoon salt	

1. Preheat the oven to 350°F. Coat 2 large baking sheets with cooking spray.

2. In a large bowl, combine the flour, cinnamon, ginger, baking soda, cloves, salt, and pepper. Stir well and set aside.

3. In the bowl of an electric mixer, beat the butter, sugar, molasses, and egg whites at medium speed for 1 minute, or until well-combined.

4. With the mixer on low speed, gradually beat in the flour mixture until well-combined.

5. Drop the dough by level tablespoons 1" apart onto the prepared baking sheets. Bake for 10 minutes (switching the position of the sheets halfway through baking), or until the cookies are lightly browned. Transfer the cookies to wire racks to cool. Repeat with the remaining dough, spraying the baking sheets again, if necessary.

Makes 3½ dozen cookies

Ingredients Note

You can use any type of molasses you want for this recipe. Blackstrap, which is the least refined, has the most nutrients.

Warm Blueberry Biscuit Shortcakes

Hands-On Time: 15 minutes ■ Total Time: 25 minutes

You can savor a taste of summer anytime with these oh-so-easy berry delights. Packaged tube biscuits, frozen berries, and prepared topping save time.

1 tube (16 ounces) large refrigerated biscuits (8 biscuits)

2 tablespoons brown sugar

¼ teaspoon ground cinnamon

¼ cup granulated sugar

2 tablespoons frozen limeade concentrate

2 teaspoons cornstarch

1 bag (12 ounces) frozen loose-pack blueberries, thawed, with juice

1½ cups whipped topping

1. Preheat the oven to 350°F.

2. Place the biscuits on a baking sheet. On a small sheet of wax paper, combine the brown sugar and cinnamon. Sprinkle half of the mixture over the biscuits. Bake for 18 minutes, or until browned. Transfer to a rack.

3. Meanwhile, in a large saucepan, combine the granulated sugar, limeade concentrate, and cornstarch. Whisk until smooth. Add the berries (with juice). Cook, stirring constantly, over medium-high heat for about 5 minutes, or until the mixture is thickened. Remove from the heat and allow to cool for 10 minutes.

4. Split the biscuits in half. Place the bottoms, cut side up, on individual plates or a platter. Sprinkle with the remaining cinnamon sugar. Spoon the berry mixture over the bottoms. Cover generously with whipped topping. Cover with the biscuit tops. Dollop with additional whipped topping.

Makes 8 servings

Old-Fashioned Strawberry Shortcake

Hands-On Time: 20 minutes ■ Total Time: 50 minutes

This old-fashioned favorite is a Pennsylvania Dutch heirloom recipe. The real key to success is using the ripest local berries you can find.

1¼ cups milk

2 teaspoons vinegar

2¼ cups all-purpose flour

2 teaspoons baking powder

½ cup plus ⅓ cup sugar

Pinch of salt

2 tablespoons solid shortening

2 egg whites, lightly beaten

½ teaspoon baking soda

4 cups sliced strawberries

1 cup whipped topping

1. Preheat the oven to 325°F. Lightly coat a 9" round cake pan with cooking spray.

2. In a small bowl, combine the milk and vinegar. Stir well.

3. In a large bowl, combine the flour, baking powder, ½ cup of the sugar, and the salt. Using a pastry blender or two knives, cut in the shortening. Stir in the milk mixture, egg whites, and baking soda until well-mixed but still slightly lumpy.

4. Pour into the prepared pan. Bake for 30 minutes, or until the top is golden and firm to the touch.

5. Meanwhile, in a small bowl, stir together the strawberries and the remaining ⅓ cup sugar. Let sit at room temperature while the shortcake bakes.

6. To serve, cut the shortcake into 6 wedges. Slice the wedges in half horizontally, making 2 layers. Place both layers of each wedge on individual dessert plates, turning the top layers upside down. Spoon some of the strawberries and juice over the bottom layers, cover with the top layers, and spoon the remaining strawberries over the tops of each. Dollop each serving with some of the whipped topping.

Makes 6 servings

Variations

This shortcake is also delicious topped with slightly sweetened raspberries, blackberries, peaches, or nectarines. Vanilla yogurt is a tasty substitute for the whipped topping.

Cherry Clafouti

Hands-On Time: 10 minutes ■ Total Time: 40 minutes

A clafouti is a thick, sweet pancake, studded with fruit and baked. This summer treat is traditionally made with fresh black cherries, but you can substitute frozen unsweetened Bing cherries in other seasons.

1 teaspoon unsalted butter, at room temperature

½ cup granulated sugar

1 cup milk

⅔ cup all-purpose flour

2 large eggs

2 large egg whites

1 teaspoon vanilla extract

⅛ teaspoon almond extract

2 cups pitted sweet cherries

1½ teaspoons confectioners' sugar

1. Preheat the oven to 375°F. Coat an 8" × 8" baking dish or a 9" pie plate with the butter and dust with 1 tablespoon of the granulated sugar.

2. In a blender, combine the milk, flour, eggs, egg whites, vanilla extract, almond extract, and the remaining granulated sugar. Blend until smooth.

3. Pour half of the batter into the prepared baking dish or pie plate. Add the cherries and pour in the remaining batter.

4. Bake for 20 to 30 minutes, or until the clafouti is puffed, browned, and firm. Transfer to a rack to cool slightly.

5. To serve, place the confectioners' sugar in a small strainer and dust over the top of the clafouti. Cut the clafouti into 6 pieces.

Makes 6 servings

Kitchen Tip

Use a cherry pitter to pit the cherries. Simply place one cherry at a time in the pitter and squeeze the handles to pit. Or, if you don't have a cherry pitter, unfold one end of a large paper clip and use the "hook" to remove the pits.

Creamy Banana Pudding

Hands-On Time: 15 minutes ■ Total Time: 15 minutes (plus chilling)

One of the South's most beloved desserts, this family-pleaser depends on sweet, ripe bananas for its flavor. You can add a touch of dark rum, if you like.

¾ cup sweetened condensed milk

1 tablespoon plus 1 teaspoon fresh lemon juice

2 cups heavy cream

½ cup sour cream

1 teaspoon vanilla extract

⅓ cup cold water

1 envelope unflavored gelatin

4 large bananas

20 vanilla wafers

1. In a medium bowl, whisk the condensed milk with 1 tablespoon of the lemon juice until slightly thickened. Whisk in the heavy cream, sour cream, and vanilla extract until smooth.

2. Pour the cold water into a small saucepan. Sprinkle the gelatin over the water and let soften for 2 minutes. Cook the gelatin mixture over medium heat, stirring constantly, for 1 to 2 minutes, or until the gelatin is completely dissolved and the mixture is heated through. Stir the dissolved gelatin into the cream mixture.

3. Slice 3 of the bananas into ¼"-thick rounds and place in a small bowl. Drizzle with the remaining 1 teaspoon lemon juice. Fold the bananas into the pudding. Pour the pudding into 8 dessert glasses or a serving bowl, cover, and chill for at least 2 hours, or until the pudding is set but still has a soft texture.

4. Just before serving, slice the remaining banana into ¼"-thick slices. Arrange the banana slices and the vanilla wafers on top of the pudding. To soften the cookies, let the pudding stand before serving.

Makes 8 servings

Cinnamon-Raisin Bread Pudding with Whiskey Sauce

Hands-On Time: 20 minutes ▪ Total Time: 1 hour

A taste of old New Orleans cooking is yours in a jiffy when you start with packaged cinnamon-raisin bread. If kids are at the table, serve them plain caramel sauce without the whiskey.

6 eggs

3 cups half-and-half

½ cup brown sugar

2 teaspoons vanilla extract

1 loaf (1 pound) cinnamon-raisin bread, toasted (12 slices)

1 jar (12 ounces) caramel sauce

¼ cup whiskey

1. Preheat the oven to 325°F. Coat a 13" × 9" ceramic or glass baking dish with cooking spray.

2. Break the eggs into the baking dish. Tipping the dish slightly, beat the eggs with a fork. Add the half-and-half, sugar, and vanilla extract. Stir well.

3. Place a solid layer of toast into the dish, tearing slices to fit. Press with a fork to saturate. Cover with a layer of the remaining toast. Press with a fork. Let stand for 5 minutes, pressing frequently, until the second layer of toast is thoroughly saturated.

4. Bake for about 30 minutes, or until the top puffs up and the custard is set. Let stand for 10 minutes.

5. Meanwhile, in a small saucepan, combine the caramel sauce and whiskey. Stir until smooth. Heat over low heat for about 5 minutes, or until hot. Serve the pudding drizzled with the sauce.

Makes 8 servings

Make-Ahead

Toast the bread earlier in the day, if you like.

Coffee Cup Soufflés

Hands-On Time: 25 minutes ■ Total Time: 40 minutes

What more appropriate servers for a mocha soufflé than coffee cups? Use heavy porcelain cups—don't put your fine bone china in the oven. This is a dessert you'll need to make and bake right before serving.

1 tablespoon unsalted butter, at room temperature	¼ teaspoon ground cinnamon
¼ cup plus 1 tablespoon granulated sugar	1¼ cups half-and-half
¼ cup cornstarch	6 large egg whites
3 tablespoons light brown sugar	⅛ teaspoon salt
3 tablespoons unsweetened cocoa powder	2 teaspoons vanilla extract
1½ teaspoons instant espresso powder	Espresso beans (optional)

1. Preheat the oven to 400°F. Coat six 7-ounce ovenproof coffee cups, soufflé dishes, or custard cups with the butter. Dust evenly with 2 tablespoons of the granulated sugar, turning the cups or dishes to coat the sides completely. Place the cups on a baking sheet.

2. In a medium, heavy saucepan, whisk together the cornstarch, brown sugar, cocoa, espresso powder, cinnamon, and 2 tablespoons of the remaining granulated sugar. Gradually whisk in the half-and-half until the mixture is smooth.

3. Cook over medium heat, whisking frequently and then constantly as the mixture gets hotter, until it comes to a boil and thickens. Remove the pan from the heat. Place a sheet of plastic wrap directly onto the surface of the mixture to prevent a skin from forming. Set aside.

4. In the bowl of an electric mixer, beat the egg whites and salt at high speed until foamy. Gradually beat in the remaining 1 tablespoon granulated sugar and continue beating until stiff peaks form.

5. Whisk the vanilla extract into the half-and-half mixture. Stir in a big spoonful of the beaten whites to lighten it. Then pour the half-and-half mixture into the beaten whites. With a large rubber spatula, fold it into the whites until no white streaks remain. Divide the mixture evenly among the prepared cups or dishes.

6. Bake the soufflés for 13 to 15 minutes, or until they're puffed and firm to the touch. Remove from the oven and serve immediately, garnished with espresso beans, if desired.

Makes 6 servings

Pumpkin Panna Cotta

Hands-On Time: 5 minutes ■ Total Time: 5 minutes (plus chilling)

Pumpkin pie mix can be used for a whole lot more than Thanksgiving. This sophisticated Italian restaurant dessert is deceptively simple. Your guests will never guess that you prepared it in 5 minutes with just 5 ingredients. If you don't have a microwave, you can do this in a saucepan.

1 cup milk

1 box (3 ounces) orange gelatin mix

1 pint half-and-half

1 cup canned pumpkin pie mix

Whipped topping

1. Set ten 4-ounce custard cups or small bowls on a tray.

2. Place the milk in a large bowl. Microwave on high power for 2 minutes, or until steaming hot. Whisk in the gelatin until dissolved.

3. Whisk in the half-and-half and the pie mix.

4. Ladle the mixture into the prepared cups. Cover with wax paper and refrigerate for at least 2 hours, or as long as overnight, to set. Dollop each with some whipped topping.

Makes 10 servings

Variation

You can shave some bittersweet chocolate over the whipped topping for an elegant presentation. Make sure the chocolate is cold, and use a vegetable peeler to shave it.

Fresh Berry Sorbet

Hands-On Time: 15 minutes ■ Total Time: 4 hours 35 minutes

You don't need a fancy sorbet maker for this frozen dessert—just a shallow pan. Be sure to use perfectly ripe strawberries in season.

6 cups sliced strawberries	½ cup sugar
½ cup raspberries	¼ cup fresh lemon juice

1. In a blender or food processor, combine the strawberries, raspberries, sugar, and lemon juice. Process until puréed. Pour the mixture into a large, shallow pan. Freeze for 4 hours, or until solid.

2. Cut the fruit mixture into chunks and return it to the blender or food processor. Process again until puréed. Spoon the sorbet into 8 serving bowls.

3. Freeze for 20 minutes, or until the mixture is solid but still soft enough to eat with a spoon.

Makes 8 servings

Chocolate Syrup 6 Ways

Generally, chocolate syrup is drizzled onto ice cream, but it can be an extremely versatile condiment. You can use store-bought or make your own chocolate syrup (see Homemade Chocolate syrup, below). Here are a few ideas for ways to use it.

1. **Chocolate-Cinnamon Pears.** Drizzle chocolate syrup over cinnamon-poached pears.

2. **Chocolate Trifle.** Make a chocolate trifle with layers of ladyfingers, vanilla pudding, and chocolate syrup.

3. **Hot Mocha.** Mix ¾ cup milk, ¼ cup brewed coffee, 2 tablespoons chocolate syrup, and ¼ teaspoon vanilla extract in a microwaveable mug. Microwave for 1 to 2 minutes, stirring once or twice, until hot. Top with whipped cream and a dash of cinnamon. Makes 1 serving.

4. **Chocolate Fruit Dip.** In a food processor, purée 1 package (8 ounces) cream cheese with ¼ to ⅓ cup chocolate syrup (just enough to make a thin, puddinglike consistency). Use for dipping fruit and store-bought pound cake. Makes about 1¼ cups.

5. **Easy Chocolate Glaze.** In a medium bowl, combine ⅔ cup confectioners' sugar and 3 tablespoons chocolate syrup. Stir until smooth. Use to glaze the top of a store-bought angel-food cake. Makes about ½ cup.

6. **Effortless Chocolate Sorbet.** Combine 2 cups water, 1 cup chocolate syrup, 1 cup brown sugar, and 2 tablespoons corn syrup. Stir until smooth. Freeze in a metal cake pan until crystals form. Break up and stir the crystals, then refreeze for 4 to 6 hours, or until solid. Scrape off into serving dishes with a spoon. Makes 4 to 6 servings.

Homemade Chocolate Syrup

In a medium saucepan, combine 1½ cups water, 1½ cups sugar, 1 cup unsweetened cocoa powder, and a pinch of salt. Stir well. Bring to a boil over medium heat, stirring constantly, and continue to cook for 2 to 5 minutes, or until the mixture thickens. Allow the syrup to cool, then stir in 1 teaspoon vanilla extract. Use immediately or store in a covered container in the refrigerator for a few days.

Banana-Glazed Pecan Ice-Cream Sundaes

Hands-On Time: 10 minutes ■ Total Time: 10 minutes

When your family is in the mood for something special, suggest these simple sundaes. You can buy glazed pecans or make your own (see Kitchen Tip, below).

½ cup brown sugar

2 tablespoons butter

2 bananas, cut diagonally into thick slices

1½ pints vanilla ice cream

½ cup packaged glazed pecans

1. In a skillet, combine the sugar and butter. Cook, stirring, over medium-high heat, for 2 minutes, or until bubbling. Add the bananas. Stir gently to coat with the sugar mixture. Set aside.

2. Scoop the ice cream into 6 dessert bowls. Top with the banana sauce and the pecans.

Makes 6 servings

Kitchen Tip

You can buy glazed pecans in many supermarkets, or it's easy to make your own. In a saucepan, combine 1 cup sugar, ¼ cup evaporated milk, and 2 tablespoons water. Cook, stirring constantly, over medium heat, until the mixture forms a soft ball that doesn't hold its shape. Remove the pan from the heat and add 1 tablespoon butter and ½ teaspoon vanilla extract. Stir in 2 cups pecans and keep stirring until a glaze forms on the nuts. Transfer the pecans to a baking sheet to cool.

Easy Equivalents

ITEM	THIS . . .	EQUALS THIS . . .
Apples	1 pound	3 cups sliced
Bananas	3–4 medium	2 cups mashed
Carrots	1 pound	3 cups shredded
Cocoa	3 tablespoons plus 1 tablespoon oil	1 ounce unsweetened chocolate
Cornmeal	1 pound	3 cups
Cottage cheese	8 ounces	1 cup
Egg	1 large	1/4 cup liquid egg substitute
Elbow macaroni	1 pound	4 cups dry
Elbow macaroni	1 cup uncooked	2 cups cooked
Flour, all-purpose	1 pound	About 4 cups
Garlic	1 small clove	1/8 teaspoon garlic powder
Honey	1 cup	1 1/2 cups granulated sugar plus 1/4 cup liquid
Lemon or lime	1	2–4 tablespoons juice
Lemon or lime	1	2 teaspoons grated zest
Lentils	2 1/4 cups dried	5 cups cooked
Mushrooms	8 ounces	1 cup sliced
Oatmeal	1 pound	5 cups cooked
Orange	1	6–8 tablespoons juice
Orange	1	2–3 tablespoons grated zest
Potatoes	3 medium	1 3/4 cups mashed
Raisins	1 pound	3 1/4 cups
Rhubarb	1 pound fresh	2 cups cooked
Rice, white	2 cups uncooked	6 cups cooked
Yeast, active dry	2 teaspoons	1 package

Emergency Substitutions

IF YOU DON'T HAVE THIS...	USE THIS . . .	ADJUSTMENTS
Alcohol (rum, sherry, or brandy), 1 teaspoon	1 teaspoon vanilla extract	Vanilla is strongly flavored, so if more than 1 teaspoon is needed, make up the difference with fruit juice.
Baking powder	¼ teaspoon baking soda plus ⅝ teaspoon cream of tartar	No change.
Bread crumbs, 1 cup	¾ cup crushed crackers	Adjust seasonings to compensate for salt (if any) in the crackers.
Broth (beef or chicken), 1 cup	1 bouillon cube in 1 cup water	Bouillon is saltier than broth, so you may want to dilute 1 cube in 2 cups water.
Butter, 1 cup	⅞ cup vegetable oil	Oil causes a looser crumb in baked products, so work gently to prevent crumbling.
Buttermilk, 1 cup	1 cup low-fat or nonfat plain yogurt	For baking, no change needed. In casseroles, you may want to use ¾ cup, because the yogurt is denser.
Cornstarch, 1 tablespoon	2 tablespoons all-purpose flour	The flour will cause a somewhat duller appearance, so it's best used for gravies, stews, or other mixed combos.
Herbs, fresh, 1 tablespoon	1 teaspoon dried	Dried herbs are stronger, so add them earlier in the recipe.
Lemon juice	Half as much vinegar	This is not recommended for baked goods.
Milk, fat-free, 1 cup	⅓ cup nonfat dry milk mixed with ¾ cup water	No change for baking.
Mustard, prepared, 1 teaspoon	Equal amount mustard powder	Mustard powder is concentrated, so use it sparingly.
Olive oil	Equal amount of any vegetable oil	The consistency will be the same, but the flavor will change.
Roasted red bell peppers	Equal amount of pimientos	No change.
Sour cream, 1 cup	1 cup evaporated skim milk plus 1 tablespoon lemon juice	To speed curdling, microwave on high power for 30 seconds.
Tomato juice, 1 cup	½ cup tomato sauce plus ½ cup water	Tomato sauce has more added salt, so adjust your seasonings accordingly.
Tomato sauce, 1 cup	⅜ cup tomato paste plus ½ cup water	No change.
Vinegar, 1 teaspoon	2 teaspoons lemon juice	Adjust seasonings for changed flavor.

Estimating Food for a Crowd

It's probably not often that you serve 12 guests, but when you do, you want to get the right amount of food. Amounts below are calculated for 12 guests, allowing 2 modest servings each.

FOOD	TOTAL AMOUNT NEEDED
BEEF	
Barbecued brisket	1 whole brisket, about 10 pounds
Flank steak	3 steaks, 2 pounds each
London broil/shoulder steak	10 pounds
Rib-eye roast, boneless	6 pounds
Rib-eye steak	12 steaks, 10 ounces each, halved
Rib roast, bone-in	16 pounds
Sirloin roast	2 roasts, 3 pounds each
Tenderloin or filet mignon steaks	6 pounds
CHICKEN	
Bone-in parts	20 pounds
Breasts, bone-in	24 medium breasts
Breasts, boneless, for stir-frying	6 pounds
Breasts/cutlets, boneless	20–24 boneless breast halves
Whole	4 roasters, 4 to 4½ pounds each
LAMB	
Leg of lamb, bone-in	2 legs, about 6 pounds each
Leg of lamb, butterflied	2 boned legs, about 4 pounds each
Rack of lamb	6 racks
PORK	
Center-cut loin, bone-in	12 pounds
Center-cut loin, boneless	6 pounds
Chops, bone-in	24 chops
Chops, boneless	6 pounds
Ham, boneless	6 pounds
Spare ribs	24 pounds
Tenderloin	6 pounds

FOOD	TOTAL AMOUNT NEEDED
SEAFOOD	
Clams, mussels, oysters, or shrimp, fresh	144–180 pieces
Fish, fresh cleaned	6–8 pounds
Fish, fresh fillets or steaks	4–6 pounds
Fish, fresh whole	9–12 pounds
Lobsters, live	12 lobsters, 1–2 pounds each
Scallops or cleaned squid, raw	3–5 pounds
Shrimp, crabmeat, or lobster meat, cooked	3–5 pounds
TURKEY	
Whole	18–20 pounds
BEVERAGES	
Coffee	8–12 ounces ground beans
Soft drinks	3 bottles, 2 liters each
Tea, hot or iced	5–6 quarts (20–30 tea bags)
SNACKS AND CRUDITÉS	
Broccoli or cauliflower florets	4 heads, 1 pound each
Carrot sticks	1¼ pounds
Celery sticks	2–3 bunches
Chips or pretzels	1¼ pounds
Olives	3–4 cups
OTHER	
Pizza	6 pizzas, 16" each
Rice	6 cups uncooked
Salad, green	6 quarts
Soup	2½ gallons
DESSERTS	
Cake	2 cakes, 13" × 9" each
Ice cream or frozen yogurt	3 quarts
Pie	3 pies, 9" each

INDEX

Underscored page references indicate boxed text or tips. **Boldfaced** page references indicate photographs.

L

M

Q

R

S